AF505808

CONRAD: EASTERN AND WESTERN PERSPECTIVES
General Editor: Wiesław Krajka

VOLUME V

CONRAD AND POLAND

Edited with an Introduction by
ALEX S. KURCZABA

EAST EUROPEAN MONOGRAPHS, BOULDER
MARIA CURIE-SKŁODOWSKA UNIVERSITY, LUBLIN
DISTRIBUTED BY COLUMBIA UNIVERSITY PRESS, NEW YORK

1996

Copyright 1996 by Maria Curie-Skłodowska University, Lublin
ISBN 0-88033-355-3
Library of Congress Catalog Card Number 96-61648

Printed in the United States of America

TABLE OF CONTENTS

ABBREVIATIONS

I. Conrad's Works

AF	*Almayer's Folly*
AG	*The Arrow of Gold*
Ch	*Chance*
LE	*Last Essays*
LJ	*Lord Jim*
MS	*The Mirror of the Sea*
N	*Nostromo*
NLL	*Notes on Life and Letters*
NN	*The Nigger of the "Narcissus"*
OI	*An Outcast of the Islands*
PR	*A Personal Record*
SA	*The Secret Agent*
SL	*The Shadow-Line*
SS	*A Set of Six*
TH	*Tales of Hearsay*
TLS	*'Twixt Land and Sea*
TS	*Typhoon and Other Stories*
TU	*Tales of Unrest*
UWE	*Under Western Eyes*
V	*Victory*
WT	*Within the Tides*
YS	*Youth: A Narrative, and Two Other Stories*

All references to Conrad's works in the following essays, unless otherwise noted, are to the Dent Collected Edition (1946-55) or Oxford University Press's World's Classics Edition, whose pagination is identical to the Dent.

II. Conrad's Letters

CL *The Collected Letters of Joseph Conrad*
ed. F. R. Karl and L. Davies (Cambridge: Cambridge U.P., 1983-), 4 vols.

ACKNOWLEDGEMENTS

I wish to thank the National Endowment for the Humanities for a Fellowship for Independent Study and Research which provided the first occasion for formulating ideas on Conrad and comparative criticism. I am grateful to the Institute for the Humanities at the University of Illinois at Chicago for a Faculty Fellowship and grants-in-aid which facilitated work on this project.

I am deeply indebted to Ewa M. Thompson for her insights and encouragement. In its various incarnations the manuscript benefited from the sharp eye of my editiorial assistant, Jurate Avizienis. Gene W. Ruoff and Linda Vavra, guardians of the lower depths of Stevenson Hall, helped guide the project on a course straight and narrow. I am gratified by the collegiality of the contributors to this volume and the unfailing support of the Series Editor, Wiesław Krajka. My greatest debt is to my wife Wendy who shares the rigors of the Academy.

A.S.K.

ACKNOWLEDGMENTS

Alex S. Kurczaba,
University of Illinois at Chicago,
Chicago, USA

Introduction

"Wer den Dichter will verstehen | Muss in Dichters Lande gehen."[1] ["He who wishes to understand the poet must visit the poet's country."] Goethe's prescription, which Adam Mickiewicz applied as motto to his *Crimean Sonnets,* normally receives a literal gloss: to understand an artist's work, one must understand the culture that shaped the artist. This charge becomes enormously complicated with a writer like Joseph Conrad shaped as he was by Polish, French,[2] and British cultures. Of these three the author of *The Secret Agent* spent his most impressionable years within the sphere of Polish culture. Hence, an empathetic understanding of Polish culture in its full sweep, that is in its defining pre- as well as post-Partition phases, is a sine qua non for a genuine understanding of Conrad's oeuvre.[3]

Goethe's suggestion carries another implication. It points to the study of reception and influence as avenues of insight into the work of a writer. "Heart of Darkness" generates different responses with Zairian, Belgian, and Polish readers. These differences are rooted in the divergent historical nd cultural experiences which readers bring to bear on the text; since history does not end, readings within the same culture also change over time: survivors of Hitler's camps and Stalin's *gulag* bring to bear to their reading of "Heart of Darkness" and *Under Western Eyes* a burden of experience unimaginable prior to the Nazi and Soviet regimes. To paraphrase Goethe: to understand a writer one might consider the particular readings accorded his works within particular cultures. Thus, a study of Polish readings of Conrad's texts, especially as such readings manifest themselves among Polish writers and artists, carries the potential of shedding new light on the author of *Lord Jim.*[4]

Such are the issues which animate the essays brought together in this volume. G. W. Stephen Brodsky's opening essay surveys Conrad criticism of the past three decades. Brodsky begins by reminding us of the "duplex" nature of Poland's history: eight centuries of sovereignty during which the Polish cultural identity is forged precede Poland's time of troubles in the nineteenth. Western cirtics' neglect of that "further past" in favor of the nineteenth century has often skewed their interpretation of Conrad's life and work; the result for Conrad studies, according to Brodsky: "a critical methodology of guilt, obscuring Conrad's more typically Polish themes of fidelity and inner honor."

Three of the most compelling portraits of women in modern fiction are *The Secret Agent*'s Winnie Verloc and Mrs. Haldin and her daughter Natalia in *Under Western Eyes*; one of the seminal themes of Conrad's fiction concerns the romantic disposition and its pitfalls. These issues come together in Susan Jones's contribution, "Conrad's Women and the Polish Romantic Tradition." Her essay illuminates the role played by female protagonists in Conrad's fiction by considering Conrad's presentations of women in the context of the status and image of women in Polish Romantic literature and culture as well as the female presence during his formative years. Jones makes clear that Conrad's ethics were not, as is commonly accepted, an exclusive product of the moral values of his father and his maternal uncle.

The silences concerning Polishness that characterize Conrad's fiction constitute the point of departure for Addison Bross's essay. Of these silences Bross focuses on the absence in Conrad's writings of references to the January 1863 Rising, the pivotal political event of Conrad's boyhood. The debate spawned by the failure of this struggle against Russian imperialism pitted the Polish Romantic ideology of conspiracy and revolt against the emergent Positivist call for "work on the foundations," that is, the reformation of the economic and social order of partitioned Poland. The argument between the idealism of the romantics and the materialism of the positivists, an argument which defined the Polish intellectual landscape at the time of Conrad's youth is echoed by the antithesis of illusion and reality in Conrad's fiction. This Polish polemic, as Bross shows, holds special relevance for Conrad's treatment of "material interests."

Keith Carabine's essay places Conrad against the background of English novelists of the Victorian and Edwardian periods. With *Under Western Eyes* as his prime example Carabine attributes the markedly new tone Conrad brings to English political fiction to the author's first-hand experience of autocracy and revolution in the Russian Empire and his origins in the multiethnic environment of Ukraine. The multiplicity of perspective deriving from his Polish years, his acute sense of the "irreconcilable antagonisms" at the heart of the human condition, account, in Carabine's view, for the scope and depth of his representations of political conflict and sharply differentiate his fictions from those of Eliot, Trollope, Galsworthy, Bennett, and Wells.

In his contribution to this volume Noel Peacock undertakes an analysis of the metaphors of vision which saturate *Under Western Eyes*. Positing that "the identity of revolution and autocracy...involves not just the shared tyranny of their politics, but the mechanism of exposure and haunting by which autocracy maintains itself," Peacock brings to light the ways in which both the apostles of utopia and the pillars of autocracy employ the instrument of "intrusive vision" as a tool to secure their position and advance their cause. As a Polish critic reminds us: "Conrad's origins in a country where for centuries the East rubbed shoulders with the West...gave the writer both a deeper feeling for Western values and keen insight, free of illusions, into the soul of Russia" (Tarnawski, 160). The implications of Peacock's discussion of surveillance and the repressive effects of "the state's gaze" in *Under Western Eyes* extend in time and space well beyond Tsarist Russia, the classic model for "scopic regimes."

Just as Conrad's Polish roots shaped his perspective on things Russian, they also helped define – as Carola M. Kaplan demonstrates in her essay – his view of England and the West. Neither "an English writer," nor "a Polish author writing in

English," Conrad's work, Kaplan argues, resides "somewhere between these two impossible literary positions." Working within the conceptual framework of postcolonial criticism, Kaplan shows how Conrad's status outside the main stream of English culture, enables him "to subvert the discourse of imperialism." The early Conrad expresses his Polishness, in Kaplan's view, in two ways: "in *Lord Jim* he adopts an ironic mask of approval to expose the fatuousness of English self-regard; in 'Amy Foster' he condemns the xenophobic intolerance that underlies this self-approbation."

One of the enduring riddles of British letters is the masterful control which the Polish-born Conrad wielded over English prose. This achievement, coupled with the exotic style especially evident in early works like *Almayer's Folly* (1895), has prompted a number of stylistic studies. Some perceive the influence of French in Conrad's prose style;[5] others identify Polish as the source of the peculiarities of Conrad's English. In her study, "Polish Influence on Conrad's Style," Mary Morzinski offers ample evidence for the thesis that much of the "foreign flavor" of Conrad's style is rooted in the grammar and syntax of Polish. Attention to matters such as the prominence in Conrad's texts of the reflexive voice, high frequency of intransitive verbs, and atypical handling of word order – features traceable to the structure of his native language – brings to the surface the submerged source of Conrad's impressionistic effects.

With Laurence Davies's essay we turn our attention to one of the most enigmatic personalities of the Enlightenment, the Polish polyglot Jan Potocki. Davies ponders the life and writings of the well-traveled Potocki and their affinities to Conrad's, suggesting the tantalizing possibility that the author of "The Secret Sharer" knew the work of his mercurial compatriot. Aspects of Conrad's poetics such as "delayed decoding" (Ian Watt), "covert plots" (Cedric Watts) and abrupt shifts in perspective bear a remarkable likeness to Potocki's magisterial experiment with the framed narrative, his *Manuscrit trouvé à Saragosse* (*The Saragossa Manuscript*). Parallels at the formal level, Davies argues, extend to thematics: a moral code rooted in honor – affirmed and interrogated – and epistemological doubt reflected in the opposition of illusion and reality pervade Potocki's and Conrad's fictions. Poland, as "the absent center," may well lie at the heart of the affinity linking the culturally variegated worlds imagined by Potocki and Conrad.

Two of the most powerful evocations of isolation and xenophobia in twentieth-century fiction – Conrad's tale "Amy Foster" and Jerzy Kosiński's novel *The Painted Bird* – constitute the focus of Wiesław Krajka's essay. His close comparative reading shows how in both Conrad's and Kosiński's texts an outsider's intrusion into the "sacred realm" of a closed society engenders what may be termed a contamination of the familiar by the alien, a process leading to the repulsion of the alien and culminating in silence. Kosiński, who shared both Conrad's Polish roots and his experience of cultural dislocation, found in Conrad's life and works – as do many other Polish artists and writers of this century – a key to interpreting important aspects of his own experience.

The cinematic quality of Conrad's narrative style has often been noted and many of Conrad's novels and novellas, from "Heart of Darkness" to *The Secret Agent,* have been put to film. Jakob Lothe takes up a comparative examination of one such adaptation: Andrzej Wajda's version of Conrad's late master-piece: *The Shadow-Line.* Wajda's film is itself an interpretation of Conrad's text and Lothe's discussion discloses the ways in which the Polish director departs from Conrad's text in order to translate it into the medium of film. Lothe's analysis offers insights into Conrad's narrative technique and Wajda's cinema-tic style and, in so doing, sensitizes us to the differences between literary art and the art of film.

My own contribution addresses the question of Conrad's influence on the Polish poet Czesław Miłosz. To this end I trace the presence of "Heart of Darkness" in Miłosz's poetry from the 1930s through the postwar period. One of my aims is to suggest the range of Conrad's influence on Polish literature of the twentieth century. Measured today that influence is of a scope and depth substantiating Edward Crankshaw's assertion of 1947:

> Of all the novelists of the youthful century, separated from us by the collapse of Europe and from their immediate predecessors by the break-up of values which heralded the break-up of a society, the one who has most to say to us to-day is Joseph Conrad, the Pole, the voluntary exile, who, remembering always his own origins as a member of an intensely nationalist squirearchy, held down but not silenced by the weight of Tsarist Russia, became a master of English seamanship and prose. (Crankshaw, 643)

The eleven essays of this volume represent a variety of critical methodologies including postcolonial criticism, feminist criticism, comparative literature, literary history, stylistics, sociology of literature and film studies. What unites these diverse approaches to Conrad is the conviction, stated or unstated, that a judicious consideration of Poland as background and as the ground on which Conrad's works have exerted pronounced influence vitally enriches our understanding of Conrad and his works. A product of emerging and established scholars from Canada, England, Norway, Poland, and the United States, *Conrad and Poland* is, in the spirit of the times, very much a joint venture. Like the series within which it appears, this book is an outgrowth of the opening of Central and Eastern Europe spearheaded by *Solidarność*. Two hopes accompany its publication: that it marks a crossing of the shadow line beyond which criticism incorporating Conrad's Polish experience grows to maturity and that it opens the way to further insights into Conrad's life and works, insights emanating not only from Poland and Central Europe but also from Russia, the arena of Ewa and Apollo's agony, and Ukraine, the place of Józef Teodor Konrad Nałęcz Korzeniowski's birth.

NOTES

1. From a quatrain prefixed to J. W. Goethe, "Noten und Abhandlungen zu besserem Verstandnis des *West-östlicher Divans*" [Notes and essays toward a better understanding of the *West-östlicher Divan*], in J. W. Goethe, *West-östlicher Divan,* ed. Ernst Beutler (Bremen: Carl Schünemann Verlag, 1956), 149.

The quatrain reads in full:
Wer das Dichten will verstehen
Muss ins Land der Dichtung gehen;
Wer den Dichter will verstehen
Muss in Dichters Lande gehen.
2. On Conrad's ties to French literature and culture, see Yves Hervouet, *The French Face of Joseph Conrad* (Cambridge: Cambridge U.P., 1990).
3. Gustav Morf, Andrzej Busza, Adam Gillon, and Zdzisław Najder have made definitive contributions to our understanding of the relevance of Conrad's Polish cultural background to his works.
4. Stefan Zabierowski has done pioneering work on Conrad's presence in twentieth-century Polish literature. See his *Dziedzictwo Conrada w litera-turze polskiej XX wieku* [Conrad's legacy in twentieth-century Polish literature] (Kraków: Oficyna Literacka, 1992). Zabierowski's book merits translation into English.
5. See Yves Hervouet, *The French Face of Joseph Conrad,* passim.

WORKS CITED

Crankshaw Edward. "Joseph Conrad and To-Day," *National Review,* 128 (March 1947), 224-30; quoted from *Joseph Conrad: Critical Assessments,* vol. I, ed. Keith Carabine, East Sussex: Helm Information, 1992.
Goethe Johann Wolfgang. *West-östlicher Divan,* ed. Ernst Beutler. Bremen: Carl Schünemann Verlag, 1956.
Tarnawski Wit. *Conrad: Człowiek, Pisarz, Polak.* London: Polish Cultural Foundation, 1972.

Stephen G. W. Brodsky,
Royal Roads Military College (retired),
Victoria, Canada

Conrad's Two Polish Pasts: A History of Thirty Years of Critical Misrule

The centennial year of the publication of Conrad's first novel, *Almayer's Folly* (1895), has been cause for Conrad scholars everywhere to celebrate his art. It seems also an appropriate time to gauge (if not to celebrate) scholarly criticism's achievement since then. During the past thirty years which have been a high water mark for critical biographies of Joseph Conrad (at least in volume), much has been made of his two, three, and even four "lives," each in some way eliding, yet usually treated as discrete. What, precisely, is meant by a "life" in this sense? Obviously Conrad's outward circumstances from Berdichev to Marseilles to Lowestoft to Bishopsbourne were several, as were his employments form *Mont Blanc* to *Loch Etive* to *Otago* to a desk at Oswalds. But these are mere externals. If we mean the inner sense of the artist as it comes to us through his work, then it has the integrity of a single "life," its pasts manifold and one in a single present of a "few simple truths." Conrad said as much repeatedly in various ways, in "Tradition," "Poland Revisited," and throughout the fiction. Yet for years he was not heard by Western critics, their cultural dissonance deafening them to his real voice, which above all is the voice of traditional Polish honor, an oft-repeated word in the canon.

Conrad's one "life" had two "pasts:" Poland's glorious (if idealized) history before the partitions, and its dusty yesterday since Napoleon. Joseph Retinger described Poland's nearer and further pasts that Conrad shared with him in childhood:

> The history of Poland has been at a standstill for over a century. Dust of many sorrowful years covered the multi-coloured traditions of the past; windows were barred with grilles of inept possibilities, doors

9

were closing on themselves, giving way only to those who had the
indignity to abandon the past – and so it seemed to me, and so it must
have looked to Conrad. (Retinger, 17-18)

The latter was the "past" Conrad abandoned without any
sense of guilt, while carrying with him a tradition from "that
more distant past" (*PR,* 31), transmitted to him by his family
and teachers. In this regard, because of the centrality of Conrad's
traditional notion of honor to *Lord Jim,* I shall advert repeatedly
to Jim as his *persona,* and to Jim's death as fidelity *usque ad
finem,* in samplings of flawed interpretations within the western
critical tradition. Jim's dishonoring jump and later fortunes are
not an allegory for Conrad's departure from Poland, but
a symbolizing of his attempted suicide and a celebration of his
spirit's survival to honor its tradition.

By Conrad's own admission the events of 1863 had "coloured
[his] earliest impressions" (*PR,* 56); it could hardly have been
otherwise. Apollo's true legacy to his son was not, however, the
sense of tragic futility of aspiration Conrad experienced with his
dying father in Florian Street among oppressed Cracovian
conspirators; rather, it was the tradition of dutiful nobility and
interior honor symbolized in Wawel Castle (where Conrad took
his own sons to impart a sense of his past). Apollo's lessons of
endurance and fidelity to duty's stern demands were more
important for Conrad than his example of heroic failure.
Claiming membership "in a group...with a Western Roman
culture derived at first from Italy and then from France,"[1]
Conrad called his conscience "[t]hat heirloom of the ages, of the
race, of the group, of the family" (94), a possession of the past
which had nurtured it:

> Colourable and plastic, fashioned by the words, the looks, the acts,
> and even by the silences and abstentions surrounding one's childhood;
> tinged in a complete scheme of delicate shades and crucial colours by
> the inherited traditions, beliefs, or prejudices – unaccountable,
> despotic, persuasive, and often, in its texture, romantic. (94)

In *A Personal Record* also, Conrad wrote of „fidelity to
a special tradition that may last through the events of an

unrelated existence" (35-6). The noble convictions symbolized in the idea of "Poland" were largely impalpable, like the "inexplicable impulse" to which he refers in the same passage, because the national fact itself was a mere abstraction throughout Conrad's youth. The reality of a Polish spirit was rendered the more evanescent by Poland's loss of political existence and by assaults on cultural identity. The Roman Church's support of the Holy Alliance's reactionism and condemnation of Polish messianism through most of the nineteenth century, and the Prussian *Kulturkampf* which was in full swing when Conrad left, threatened even the memory of Poland. During those years when Poland did not exist as a state, the nation ,,could be remembered from the past, or aspired to for the future, but only imagined in the present" (Davies, II, 7). That is precisely why for Conrad fidelity to the memory of a noble tradition's "unrealted existence" loomed so large.

Yet, until recently Conrad's reliance on his cultural past has been misunderstood by both Polish and Anglo-American critics: the former, because of the close relationship between national ideology and literary criticism, and the latter, because of isolation from continental European cultural traditions. In his very useful historical summary, "Conrad and Poland: Under the Eyes of My Generation" Wiesław Krajka has pointed to the deleterious effect of positivism on Conrad scholarship in Poland (Krajka, 48). An ideologically impelled emphasis on "betrayal" (hence the imputed primacy of "guilt" as a recurrent theme) became a *donné*, perpetuating Eliza Orzeszkowa's infamous accusation of linguistic betrayal. Krajka has chided his inward--looking compatriot critics with the critical fiat, "We need no more interpretations under the shadow of the stereotypes of betrayal and the Polish cause." Instead, Krajka has encouraged the Polish "Anglicists," with their "perspectives on English, American and world literature" to bring Poland's "Conradology into the mainstream of world research."

It has only been in the decade of the '90s, since the collapse of the Jaruzelski regime ended the cultural oppressiveness of the Warsaw Pact era, that Conrad studies have entered an exciting

new phase for Polish scholars, who, Wiesław Krajka justly
claims, are "best placed to appreciate and measure [Conrad's]
Polishness, and the relation between his work and Polish
literature and culture." (This has nothing to do with the jealously
parochial concern of some western critics, voiced privately but
unwritten, that Polish literary historians are busy "claiming"
Conrad, as if he were an atrifact in the British Museum filched
from some Polish Parthenon by Anglo-American literary El-
gins.)

A reassessment from the Polish perspective is already overdue
for redress of a critical imbalance resulting in sheer misunder-
standing, which has gone almost unchallenged. Polish Anglicists
should bear that in mind and approach Anglo-American
criticism cautiously, analytically, and even, dare I say, skeptical-
ly. I think Krajka, in his exuberance at Poland's newly reopened
window on the West, risks taking too generous a view. In the
West's vacuum of knowledge about particular cultural background and without a body of accessible Polish scholarship
untainted by political ideology, Zdzisław Najder, Gustav Morf,
and Andrzej Busza have stood out as the only scholars of note to
address Conrad's Polonism at length in major works; and even
Gustav Morf has exaggerated, I believe, Conrad's feelings of
guilt at accusations of desertion.

Early insights into the positive aspects of Conrad's work
grounded in his first "past" have been few, elegant, and largely
unheeded. Without adverting to Conrad's imputed isolation and
guilt, Muriel Bradbrook (*Poland's English Genius,* 1941; reprinted 1966) celebrated Conrad's "power to write of great heroic
themes:" "Fidelity is for Conrad the virtue of virtues: and
betrayal the crime of crimes....Personal honour, in a sense Polish
and perhaps also Latin, dominates *Lord Jim* [*et alia*]" (Bradbrook, 5, 23-4).

Most other critical biographers have acknowledged Conrad's
Polish heritage only *passim,* before retreating hastily to familiar
ground, as if to avoid the embarrassment of nescience. English
criticism too often has been subjectively intuitive, and American
critics have fallen back on archetypes, to plunge (as they have

thought) into Conrad's psyche as if he were a cultural *tabula rasa,* often with weird results. If Polish positivism resulted in a "Conradology" of betrayal, major themes in western criticism have been isolation, guilt, and duality, inferred from the immediate circumstances of Conrad's Polish childhood and English sea life.

These themes have had appeal especially for American scholars bred in a literary tradition molded by Puritan beginnings, revolution, the "frontier experience," and alienation; their tradition has been fertile ground for the New Criticism, and more recently for Deconstructionist and Postmodern critical theory, which have continued a trend of destructive Conrad criticism. Largely restricted in knowledge and sentiment to their own cultural tradition, western critics have found it mirrored in the Conrad canon against the dark background of a Polish cultural *terra incognita.* This neglect of Conrad's centuries-old heritage has resulted in some grotesque interpretations of his work.

The first authoritative biography, *The Sea Dreamer: A Definitive Biography of Joseph Conrad* (1957), graced by its author Georges Jean-Aubry's personal acquaintance with Conrad, etablished a critical mythology of guilt, obscuring Conrad's more typically Polish themes of fidelity and inner honor. While showing admirably Conrad's complexity, Jean-Aubry did not look backward beyond Conrad's paternal grandfather's military service. Focusing on "Conrad's literary obsession with remorse" (Jean-Aubry, 238), he contended that the *point de depart* for Jim's downfall was Conrad's own "dread [of] being found unequal to the task" (239). As with Orzeszkowa in Poland, Jean-Aubry became the bellwether of Conrad critics in the West for over two decades. Most critics since have accepted the novels as, above all, reflections of a tortured age. Jean-Aubry's imitators Albert Guerard (*Conrad, the Novelist,* 1966) and Robert Hodges (*The Dual Heritage of Joseph Conrad,* 1967) perpetuated what Don Avellanos of *Nostromo,* had he been a living guardian of his creator's legacy, might have termed a "tradition of critical misrule."

Criticism assuming Conrad's psychology of failure prevailed, although Conrad himself showed scant shame or remorse and was proud of the past that had shaped him. To a fellow Pole he wrote, "Both at sea and on the land my point of view is English, from which the conclusion should not be drawn that I have become an Englishman. Homo Duplex has in my case more than one meaning." Perhaps inured to being misunderstood by his adopted countrymen, he added pointedly, "You will understand me."[2]

To be sure, critics have hesitated to take Conrad's art at its word, and have emphasized Freud over "fidelity," the first imperative of his stated creed. Thus, they have reflected precisely the bourgeois doubt that Conrad warns against in the opening passages of "Prince Roman." They have inadvertently cast themselves, as it were, in the role of young Lieutenant Byrne ("The Inn of the Two Witches"), who mistakes his cynical sapience for wisdom in disbelieving an aristocratically quixotic Castilian.

Indeed, neglect of Conrad's noble tradition has invited a reading of his tales to infer squalid meaning and invite unworthy suspicion. Adam Gillon, for instance, invoked semantic anachronism to conclude sexual shame. Italicizing *"queer story,"* he characterized Il Conde as "merely a pathetic pederast involved in a rather sordid adventure," as with his inference also of homosexuality in *Victory,* his evidence Heyst's *"gay* gown" (Gillon, *Joseph Conrad,* 138). But Conrad's profundity is never unbecoming obliquity; as a Polish gentleman he expected to be taken at his word. Both tales are laments for Europe's etiolated aristocracies that had become denatured, deracinated, and dishonored. They had traded the will to duty and habit of command for leisure and exquisiteness of taste.

Admitting that Conrad "saw loyalty and service as the central virtues of his world," Thomas Moser (*Joseph Conrad: Achievement and Decline,* 1957) avoided any suggestion that Conrad brought his ideas of honor to his new calling from a cultural past. Indeed, "Prince Roman," "The Duel" (originally published as "The Point of Honour"), "The Warrior's Soul," and "Il Conde," tales making the greatest demands on the reader's understanding of Conrad's tradition, are not discussed; and although *Lord Jim* is all about lost honor, the word itself is absent from Moser's treatment. Moser's cultural perspective is a New World critic's Old Testament sensibility. Referring to Morton D. Zabel's able discussion of the Conradian theme of "test" (Zabel, 1-49), he called the tales a "Pilgrim's Progress" (Moser, 14), an extraordinary parallel for tales of secular knight errantry springing from Conrad's chivalric tradition.

Jerry Allen's fanciful biography, *The Thunder and the Sunshine: A Biography of Joseph Conrad* (1958), began with Poland's time of troubles and the Prussian Frederick II's mid-eighteenth century depredations to show Apollo's heritage. Otherwise, her thesis turned on *The Arrow of Gold*'s alleged fidelity to biographical fact and on Conrad's life as postscripts to the events it portrays (despite historical anomaly). Her only reference to honor was Doña Rita's statement that her devotion to Don Carlos is a *"pun d'onor"* (Allen, *The Thunder and the Sunshine:...*, 124), without any suggestion of its irony in the mouth of a royal drab. Elsewhere, Allen stressed "betrayal," "rejection," "rebellion," "inner weakness," and "tormenting guilt" as the pivots of Conrad's life and work. It would be surprising if he could have functioned as a sailor or written anything at all under such a burden of manic despair.

Allen's *The Sea Years of Joseph Conrad* (1965), building on Conrad's words in *A Personal Record,* "The principal thing was to get away," focused on family disapproval and Conrad's alleged hostility to past associations. Allen dismissed Tadeusz as merely a "disapproving relative" (Allen, *The Sea Years...*, 16), and advanced a perverse theory that Conrad concocted a lie about attempting suicide to avoid his censure for duelling. Throughout, Conrad's Nałęcz pride was not mentioned. Notwithstanding "Prince Roman," "Autocracy and War," and "Poland Revisited," Allen apparently believed that Conrad's competence as sailor and writer was entirely despite his past, a "statelessness of viewpoint...won at great cost" (307).

Adam Gillon's *The Eternal Solitary: A Study of Joseph Conrad* (1960) shared Allen's themes of rejection and disapproval, interpreting Conrad as a Melvillean "isolato." *The Eternal Solitary*:..., "a study in isolation," was laced with the language of existential tragedy: "treachery," "remorse," "crime," "disenchantment," "solitude," "loneliness," "sadness," and of course, "alienation."

Stressing the "atmosphere of defeat and frustration" of Conrad's youth (Gillon, *The Eternal Solitary*:..., 15), Gillon advanced a discouraging interpretation of Poland's moral tradition. By attaining victory over their foes, Poland's epic heroes suffer "personal moral defeat;" thus the romantic ideal sets men apart from their fellows, leading them to ruin instead of glory (93). *The Eternal Solitary*'s distinctions are not clear between legitimate ruse and betrayal, physical destruction and moral death, nor between a sharing of a community's ideals and mere conformity to convention. By that reckoning, Konrad Wallenrod's subversion of the Teutonic Order is morally ambiguous, a view neither his creator Adam Mickiewicz nor Conrad could possibly have shared.

Gillon averred that Jim in Patusan "will seek for a way to come back among people as a trusted and honorable man" (81), thereby implying that Jim's search for honor in obscurity is really a self-defeating effort at reinstatement. Gillon developed his idea of honor's moral paradox on the line that, in Patusan "the force of [Jim's] imagination which creates another reality for him, superior to that of physical reality, has deprived him of contact with other people" (24). Not acknowledged was that, by isolating himself from Jewel and Tamb' Itam to appear alone and unarmed before Doramin, Jim ends his estrangement from his own conscience; in spirit he rejoins the ranks of his craft, class, and race, honoring their ideal by appearing before his judge, this time to face the consequence of his actions without trying to explain them away.

There is no moral ambiguity here, as there need be none in our interpretation by Conrad's lights. The Boethian concept of contingent necessity, expressed in the Polish proverb Conrad embraced but which disgusts his General Santierra ("Gaspar Ruiz"), "Man fires the piece; God guides the bullet," stresses the primacy of individual responsibility as the necessary corollary to Augustinian free will. That precept remained central to Conrad's secular notion of a spectacular cosmos, because it was bred in the bone of a "Pole, Catholic, and Gentleman." Thus, it is not intentionist fallacy to declare that those critics who argue for Jim's "suicide" in delivering himself up to Doramin have not glimpsed what Conrad set about making us see. Lacking insight into Conrad's classical worldview, they have not read the book Conrad wrote.

The primacy of interior honor is the Polish precept upon which the Conrad canon turns. The central ethical conflict is always between the demands of an individual's interior honor, and honor's formal codes of conduct. This is a very Polish problem, for while Poles admired and imitated the Gallic cult of glory that thrived on militarism, the values which had produced the "Golden Freedom" and *"liberum veto"* located ultimate worth in individual conscience.

Conrad's father found a kindred soul in the French former army officer Comte Alfred de Vigny, whose *Chatterton* (1835) he translated. Like *Chatterton,* a play about a good man's moral isolation, de Vigny's *Souvenirs de servitude et grandeur militaires,* published the same year, are tales of silent sacrifice and obscure heroism. The tragically romantic story of Captain Renaud affirms the meaning of true honour: "[L]*es évènements ne sont rien, que l'homme intérieur est tout.*" In thus distinguishing between honor's external form and interior substance, de Vigny echoed the aristocratic ideal of France's *ancien regime* and pre-partition Poland's *szlachta.*

At the start of Conrad criticism's take-off phase in the same year as Gillon's *The Eternal Solitary:...,* Jocelyn Baines's *Joseph Conrad: A Critical Biography* (1960) began to set the record straight: "An increasing awareness among modern students of Conrad of his pessimism, scepticism, and his consciousness of evil had led to a discounting of his proclaimed belief in the simple, practical virtues" (Baines, 450).

Baines's fresh perspective was largely owing to his recognition of the importance of cultural background in the formation of

Conrad's intellect. The influences giving Conrad the outlook of a *szlachcic* are implied in Baines's selection of biographical fact: how Teodor (sic) lost most of the Kortyna estate and the family's money because of his military activities (and mismanagement); how Mikołaj [Nicholas] Bobrowski, Conrad's embittered grand uncle who fought with tragic heroism for Napoleon in Russia, captured Conrad's imagination; how Tadeusz's brother Stanisław (sic) was a "gay and likable Guards officer" (40);[3] and how Stefan was killed in a duel; all these details impart a sense of Conrad's tradition of warrior honor. Similarly, Conrad's familiarity with *Gil Blas* and *Don Quixote* receives respect equal to the fates of Apollo's brothers. (Robert died in the 1863 Rising, and Hilary was exiled to Tomsk.)

Although Baines brought an intellectual awareness of the importance of the Polish tradition to the criticism, his sensibility appears not to have extended to the centrality of Conrad's Polish sense of interior honor. He hinted at honor's importance in "The Warrior's Soul," "The End of the Tether," and "The Secret Sharer;" but while he connected honor with private conscience on the one hand and a public code on the other, its nature remained unstated. In discussing *Lord Jim,* Baines showed Jim from the perspectives of Brierly, Stein, and the French Lieutenant ("[W]hen the honor is gone,..."); yet Baines himself didn't describe Jim in terms of lost honor: Jim's predicament is a matter of blame, a "threat to solidarity" (244). Mentioning honor only once, in reference to Jim's release of Brown as the act of "an honorable, civilized man," Baines apparently meant only something like British fair play.

The importance of Conrad's noble Polish ethos was made clear for the first time in 1964 with Zdzisław Najder's *Conrad's Polish Background: Letters to and from Polish Friends*. Najder deplored western criticism's failure to distinguish between "explaining a work of literature in personal and in generally cultural terms" (Najder, *Conrad's Polish Background:...,* 7), and the consequent distortions of Conrad's worldview:

> [I]n that age of the greatest cultural expansion of the *bourgeoisie* he was anything but a *bourgeois*; he hardly ever wrote about this class

(and if he did, he did so with irony and disdain), and he never represented its attitudes. His was the outlook of an uprooted nobleman, conscious of his chivalric past....The values he wanted to see cherished – honour, duty, fidelity, friendship – were typically romantic and typically chivalrous, and it is only too obvious that we have to look for their origin to Poland, where the life of the whole nation was...dominated by these very values. (30)

For the next dozen years Najder's efforts had little impact. The following year Leo Gurko (*Joseph Conrad: Giant in Exile,* 1965), disregarding Conrad's warrior tradition, perpetuated an uncritical acceptance of Tadeusz's view of Apollo as a failed rebel hothead (Gurko, 18). Conrad himself, Gurko claimed, changed from an idealist with faith in human institutions to a stoic who had learned that society destroys the individual. Gurko found little in the Polish background to infer Conrad's belief in moral values, and seems to have credited his maritime service almost entirely with molding his convictions.

Gurko followed Moser and Gillon in focusing on isolation. In the same way that Moser intimated the individual's helplessness before his own nature, Gurko blamed Jim's failure on his being alone (143). In his discussion of Jim and other characters, the theme of fidelity might have received at least equal weight with shame, the felt need for punishment, exoneration, and expiation (123), if Gurko had found more to respect in Conrad's tradition and Apollo's death.

A year later, Andrzej Busza ("Conrad's Polish Literary Background and Some Illustrations of the Influence of Polish Literature on His Work," 1966)[4] continued Najder's lonely work of establishing Conrad's Polonism by showing instances of Polish literature's likely influence, such as the *gawęda*'s appearing thematically as destructive family honor in "Karain." Meanwhile, however, Norman Sherry (*Conrad's Eastern World,* 1966) continued the critical emphasis on solitariness by asserting Conrad's frustration at life ashore as an outsider (Sherry, 6). While Sherry preeminently, and others, were amassing sources for the sea tales, no major critical biography after Baines's would stress Conrad's cultural beginnings, until Gustav Morf's *The*

Polish Shades and Ghosts of Joseph Conrad (1976); and criticism proceeded independently of things Polish. Admitting his work's resemblance to Moser's, Albert Guerard (*Conrad, the Novelist,* 1966) relied heavily on comparisons with William Faulkner's *Absalom! Absalom!* (1936) for what he termed (ambiguously) *Lord Jim*'s "psycho-moral ambiguities" (Guerard, 131). In that year (1966) the time was right for a reissue of Wilson Follett's *Joseph Conrad* (1915), with the apt admonition, "[T]here has grown a gap between what Mr. Conrad offers himself as being and what he is commonly received for" (Follett, 4).

Follett's reminder of Conrad's "special tradition" (32) had as little influence as Bradbrook's. The following year, Robert Hodges (*The Dual Heritage of Joseph Conrad,* 1967) interpreted *Lord Jim* by finding in *A Personal Record* Conrad's need to erect defenses against "the charge of desertion and infidelity" proceeding initially from his father's indoctrination of him "only as a Pole" (Hodges, 144). Hodges's claim that Conrad's guilt was expiated by his service to Poland during World War I and its aftermath may say something for Hodges's own theory of atonement, but it says nothing of the author whose plots and characters reveal consistently that he regarded every act as final, with thought-denying consolatory action as the means of bearing the crime of being. Conrad, who rejected an ethical universe – and with it, sin and redemption – could not possibly have entertained a notion of "expiation," when his entire canon is about how to endure nobly, having once seen into the abyss.

Advancing the theme of Korzeniowski and Bobrowski temperaments warring within Conrad, Hodges remained self-admittedly unaffected either by Najder's *Conrad's Polish Background:...*or Baines's *Joseph Conrad: A Critical Biography.* Having limited his background concerns mainly to nineteenth-century Polish epic literature and Conrad's life, Hodges concluded that "Prince Roman," the most aristocratic, patriotic, and Polish of all the tales, represents a reconciliation of the idealism and pragmatism inherited by Conrad from his father and uncle (Hodges, 126). This "reconciliation," Hodges claimed, was a sign of Conrad's exhaustion "by poverty and illness" and "subsequent literary decline" (120). The idea that practical idealism was central to the creed of a working gentry (both *possessionati* and *bene nati*) anyway, either had not occurred to the critic, or did not fit a psychological schema grounded primarily on Tadeusz's memoirs.

Hodges interpreted *Lord Jim* the same way, with Marlow and Stein as surrogate "fathers," a theory relying largely on Stein's use of Tadeusz's motto. But while Stein advances the Kierkegaardian idea of immersion in existence, the cautious Marlow remains on the sidelines, counting the cost: the reverse of the identifications Hodges ascribes. These Oedipal excesses led Hodges to identify *The Arrow of Gold*'s Captain Blunt with Conrad the "son" (204), although as a mock-chivalric "*Americain, Catholique, et gentilhomme*" he is a parody of Poland's brooding soldier-of-fortune exiles.

"The Duel" makes clear Conrad's distinction between honor as military fidelity in the person of the aristocratic D'Hubert and the mere bellicosity of the *bourgeois* Feraud. While, like all romantic Polish gentry, Conrad was attracted to the military cult of glory, he understood the difference between a seductive aesthetic and the ethics of honor; despite his self-romanticizing fib to his son John about his scar from attempted suicide being from a duel with a historical J. M. K. Blunt (John Conrad, 81), he had no use for Byronesque characters who lived by their swords.

Bernard C. Meyer's *Joseph Conrad: A Psychoanalytic Biography* (1967) was the nova of psychological criticism. Meyer's Freudian interpretations of images, themes, and personality types is a compendium of derangement. Honor, Polish, British, French, or otherwise, is not mentioned even in connection with "The Return," "Il Conde," and "The Duel." Perhaps it was Meyer's analysis that prompted Douglas Hewitt's exasperation at "the process of relentless symbolization" by which "one novel is replaced by another...brushing aside literal sense" ("Introduction" to the 1969 republication of *Conrad: A Reassessment*, 1952).

In 1974 Zdzisław Najder tried again, with his symposium

offering, "Conrad and the Idea of Honor." For over a decade major criticisms had been appearing at the rate of one a year; and still, none explored Conrad's tradition from before the first partition. Najder observed indignantly that, while Conrad's Polish idea of honor "stands at the very heart of the ethical problems that [Conrad] raised in his books," the fact had been noted "with an ironical shrug." Critics, he complained, "persist in interpreting [Conrad] in terms of...the conventions of middle--class nineteenth-century prose, without knowledge of his tradition in the history or logic of honor," so that "the function and implications of the idea remain largely unanalyzed" (Najder, "Conrad and the Idea of Honor," 103).

That should have been a challenge to Conrad scholars, but no one took up the gauntlet. The focus remained limited largely to Conrad's nineteenth- and twentieth-century contexts: Poland's dissolution, internal strife, and glorious futility, transmuted as tales about English seamen, French military officers, and South American adventurers. At last, two years later in 1976, Gustav Morf reminded critics of the rightful place of Conrad's background in the criticism: *The Polish Shades and Ghosts of Joseph Conrad* evoked the atmosphere and cultural texture of Conrad's beginnings, accounting for both the sailor and writer as later reflections of the young Pole in the bosom of loving families proud of their noble traditions.

If Morf erred, it was in taking Conrad's background into account too uncritically, thus limiting Conrad's attitude to the fatal attraction that *lex talionis* and duelling held for his class:

> Conrad's conception of honour is not only Latin, it is also that of the Polish gentry. It was a precious value which you could lose; and once lost, it could only be restored by bloodshed...."Let pistols speak, swords argue!" (A. Mickiewicz, *Pan Tadeusz*, 55).

Conrad's Napoleonic tales and fiction in an eastern setting, with their representations of vengeance and blood price, reflect his fascination with warrior honor; however, they also show the tragic folly of illusory honor gained or defended by arms, at the expense of the genuine honor of service.

Because Morf himself perhaps believed in objective honor of the sort he described, his treatment of *Lord Jim* and honor was unfortunately one-dimensioned. Calling it a tale "about a man who has lost his honor" (Morf, 154), he echoed inexactly Conrad's own reference to Jim's "acute *consciousness* of lost honor [italics added]" (*LJ,* ix). There is a vast abyss between Morf's (and Jim's) supposition of lost honor and honor's reality. Jim's performance of duty passes for "honor" simply in the sense of his not being "found out," only until his fidelity is put to the test. The interior honor, that is, merited self-approbation, has been lacking all along. It remains, not to be regained in Patusan, but created within, as truth dipped in the lie of Jim's self--fulfilling hero image.

Morf was too confident of his audience's grasp of the *szlachta*'s history in mentioning Prince Roman Sanguszko without comment (Morf, 23); and he accepted too readily Tadeusz's assessment of Apollo and the Nałęcz character (5, 16). However, his inclusion of details such as Apollo's play about Kościuszko goes far in accounting for Conrad's sentiments as a Polish noble steeped in a heroic tradition.

Frederick Karl's encyclopedic *Joseph Conrad: The Three Lives* (1979), another self-admitted "psychological biography," stressed a Natty Bumpo-Captain Ahab theme of the "marginal man." Paying lip service to Conrad's cultural past and the few critics who wrote about it, Karl imputed to Conrad a "shakey ideology based on individual achievement and a chivalric tradition" (Karl, 11). Karl said little about Conrad's first Polish "past," focusing instead on the second, and conditions he believed militated against moral certainties: "Long before Conrad was born,...the stage for his exile and cunning was being prepared" (15). Poland, by Karl's figuring, was "the very country [which] created divisiveness," and made for "constant artifice." He ascribed to Conrad's family "morbidity and self-destructive obsessions as its routine experience" (16). Of Conrad's life in Poland he wrote: "a teetering, near-disastrous experience;" of his life as a writer: "he would...wobble existentially." Other epithets are "hollowness," "emptiness," and "identification with spatiality" (18). Even the heroic name "Konrad" symbolized for Karl only "Poland's role in history as the pawn of larger European powers." Karl acknowledged Conrad's "personal honor" merely as one characteristic among "intense romanticism," "attachment to exotic places," and "frequent flare-ups of violence, temper, and rage" (18).

Not surprisingly, honor received scant notice in Karl's discussion of *Lord Jim,* and then only as Jim's "panic that because of poor reputation he might descend into shabbiness and have to keep running" (461). Karl ascribes Jim's predicament to Conrad's alleged "fear that he might fail as an artist, possibly as a husband," and asserts that "reputation...was everything for him" (461). What Conrad might have thought to be his honor, Karl took as merely an obsessive anxiety to be thought a good writer.

Admittedly, every decent instinct may be taken as dread of isolation and inner emptiness. Laurence Davies, co-editor with Karl of *The Collected Letters of Joseph Conrad,* also mentioned Conrad's "solitude," and opined that Conrad was "pushed...by the apparent hopelessness of the Polish situation" (*CL*, I, xlvii), as if he made an involuntary leap. But Davies wisely tempered his psychological determinism with a telling disclaimer:

> To give priority in a description of the letters to scepticism over belief, nihilism over a sense of moral order, alienation over a sense of destiny shared with the rest of humanity is more an act of preference than one of total comprehension. (xi)

Appearing the same year as Karl's *Joseph Conrad: The Three Lives,* Ian Watt's *Conrad in the Nineteenth Century* (1979) offered relief for the western critical tradition by striking a balance between Conrad's identity as "exile" and his fidelity to his tradition. Watt wrote:

> [Conrad was] the nostalgic celebrant of the civilization of his homeland; and the steady insistence on the patriotic values of courage, tenacity, honor, responsibility and abnegation, gives Conrad's fiction a heroic note. (Watt, 7)

It seems even Gustav Morf had left it for Watt to grasp the important distinction proceeding from Conrad's *szlachcic* idea of honor's doubleness. Watt made a vital distinction in describing Conrad's response to charges of betrayal as "not guilt but shame and anger at what other people think" (9). As adjuncts of what he called Conrad's "nearer" and "farther" visions, Watt distinguished between shame and guilt, in the sense that Conrad may have experienced "shame" as remorse at undeserved censure, but not "guilt" as self-accusation. These are simply obverse terms for external and interior honor, the shadow and substance of Conrad's tradition. Watt's early chapters lay this groundwork for Lord Jim's predicament as a problem of honor, and reveal Conrad's Polish understanding of the term.

While one might wish for more background to Watt's comment that Conrad retained much of the *szlachta*'s "traditional chivalric code," Watt at least recognized its centrality. Yet, even Watt missed the irony of Conrad's proud modesty in dissociating himself from the upper nobility. Conrad was contemptuous of the magnatial class, whose members (such as "Prince Roman"'s Prince John) no longer led, but ingratiated themselves with their oppressors, and stood aside during periods of patriotic unrest. Explaining his nobility, Conrad asked not to be associated with "aristocracy [having] senatorial dignity:" "The Equestrian Order is more the thing."[5] Conrad would have regarded membership in Poland's magnatial class as dishonoring.

Roger Tennant (*Joseph Conrad: A Biography,* 1981) continued the trend away from psychological speculation; but his mentions of Conrad's traditions were tantalizingly brief. The opening chapter, "Pole, Catholic, Gentleman," in its passim reference to the *szlachta* as a "ruling class" is not helpful, nor its observation that "Polish politics in the nineteenth century were of a tragic complexity that almost defies comprehension." *Lord Jim,* he wrote inaccurately, is about a "point of honor" (Tennant, 141); the phrase belongs to the niceties of a life-denying code for which Conrad betrayed a superficial attraction but utterly rejected.

In 1983 Zdzisław Najder published his monumental biography *Joseph Conrad: A Chronicle,* revisiting much of his earlier work. As in the past, he drew attention to the *szlachta*'s "soldierly and chivalric values" (Najder, *Joseph Conrad: A Chronicle,* 3), in devoting the greater part of his "Introduction" to a restatement of Conrad's cultural tradition:

> Leaving his home and country was for Konrad Korzeniowski not tantamount to shedding all habitual attitudes. Polish *szlachta* and Polish intelligentsia were social strata in which reputation, one's evaluation by one's own milieu, was felt to be very important, even essential for one's feeling of self-worth. Men strove continuously to find confirmation of their own self-regard and image in "the eyes of others" rather than basing them on their own conscience. (38)

Najder's statement needs qualification, however. The importance of external honor in Conrad's tradition must not be understood as Frederick Karl's assertion of Conrad's obsessive anxiety for reputation to the exclusion of all else, but in the context of interior honor as an ideal: the central paradox in any honor culture such as the Polish gentry's is that the passport for acceptance is to profess that public esteem weighs light in the balance with self-approbation preceding right conduct. Thus, Jim's honor and death express a vanished gentry class's social ideal which Conrad shared: the individual's transcendence of need for approval.

Najder had begun his *Joseph Conrad: A Chronicle* over a quarter-century earlier, and most of it had already appeared separately, without disturbing many critics' cultural somnolence. Indeed, after Najder's book, biographical criticism reached its nadir with Jeffrey Meyers's superficial work, *Joseph Conrad: A Biography* (1991). Evincing no sense of the Polish psyche and history, Meyers called Conrad's rejection of the epithet "revolutionist" for Apollo "unconvincing," claimed with narrow imprecision that the name "Konrad" symbolized for Poles merely "an anti-Russian fighter," and defined the *szlachta* puzzlingly as a class "below the aristocracy,...combin[ing] the qualities of the gentry and the nobility" (Meyers, 3-4).

For Meyers, so lacking in feeling for the *szlachta* sensibility, the meaning of Jim's death could only be ambiguous. Identifying Stein with Tadeusz Bobrowski, and finding procrustean parallels in drownings elsewhere in the fiction, Meyers appears to have drowned the sense of Stein's gnomic utterance about submission to the destructive element by equating suicide with acceptance of reality.

This moral muddle was not Conrad's doing. Surely the sybil-like Stein is like "The Duel"'s amused surgeon who voices a mortal condition as old as time, and can only patch up the scarring wounds. Stein prescribes a nostrum for ailing humanity in an enigmatic and indifferent universe, spectacular, but not ethical. Like Kierkegaard's Knight of Infinite Possibility, a Conradian gentleman faces existence by immersion in it. As Conrad the sailor-connoisseur of winds knew, active engagement of thought and will with the elements is a condition for vanquishing circumstance; and that in turn demands willed disinterest in observance of an exacting code *usque and finem*. Only through that consolatory action might Jim assert his own being, affirming his honor.

Meyers, however, shows no grasp of the motto Conrad borrowed from Tadeusz. He calls Conrad's headstone epitaph "moving" (357), apparently with no sense of the irony of Spenser's knight errant hearing it spoken by Despayre as temptation to self-termination, the sham of self-determination. Conrad chose the quotation as epigram for *The Rover,* clearly because Peyrol, having been greatly pleased with living death at Escampobar as his port after stormy seas, resumes his patriotic struggle. Carrying off a consummate ruse that a Pole could identify readily with the glorious deception worked by Konrad Wallenrod, his defeat and death are a victory of spirit, precisely because he surmounts the temptation to despair. Whatever R. B. Cunninghame Graham and Jessie's odd reasons for that epitaph, Meyers's withholding of comment is at least as odd.

Tabloid-style reportage from the Norman Douglas scandal and voyeuristic innuendo about Conrad's friendship with Jane Anderson appear more familiar shallows for this salacious biography, where we may leave it as epigram for a prurient decade. Three years later, biographical criticism rose again to redeeming seriousness with John Batchelor's *The Life of Joseph Conrad: A Critical Biography* (1994); its compelling idea being that Conrad wrote his best works as neurasthenic diversions from what he was duty-bound by his publishers to produce. The psychological astuteness of Batchelor's thesis was matched by his prudent reliance in his introduction on Najder's *Joseph Conrad: A Chronicle* for much of his summary of Conrad's *szlachta* tradition.

But, to acknowledge traditional values on the one hand, and on the other, to interpret text in light of Conrad's intuitions proceeding from them, are entirely different matters. In his discussion of Jim's death, Batchelor jettisoned Conrad's Polonism, adverted to the revival of stoicism in the English Renaissance evinced in *Hamlet*, and concluded that Captain Brierly's jump is a "Stoic's suicide: he opts for death rather than dishonour." Jim, he claimed, takes the other stoically acceptable course: he "does, *of course* [italics mine], in effect kill himself by surrendering to Doramin for execution" (Batchelor, 108).

However, Conrad's secular Polish Catholicism, derived from his classical education and upbringing, should make itself felt throughout the canon and correspondence. In Conrad's worldview despair is the ultimate crime against self. Remorseful at his own folly resulting in destitution, and his prospects for a splendid future dashed, the youthful Conrad despaired and attempted suicide. Conrad knew the unforgiving moment, and lived on to learn that mortification is only a metaphor. Brierly's jump proceeds from the same despairing failure to bear anxiety, when Jim's crime holds a mirror to the imperfection (like original sin) that he will have to face for the rest of his life. Jim's dishonoring jump also is in passive obedience to the anxiety of doubt, triggered by an infelicitous congruence of character and circumstance that finds him out. As Conrad himself had learned and the French Lieutenant observes, one doesn't die of dishonor; and to endure it is itself honoring. By facing Doramin, Jim at last faces the inscrutable consequences of his choices, a Boethian apotheosis fulfilling the dream of self without counting the cost, and without an audience.

Despite much western opinion, exaltation of tragic death (like the Teutonic *Heldentod*) has not been a Polish cultural tradition. Also, Conrad's own childhood, with its memories of the tragic but purposive deaths of family members, may have had much to do with his rejection of Schopenhauerian ideas of sacrifice and expiation if no practical moral purpose was served; he had no patience with sentimentality, and abhorred the grand gesture along with honor's other shams.

Yet, despite Conrad's own words and works showing his Polonism as an inheritance of centuries, it usually has been described as his sharing the *esprit* of a nation deprived of its political existence, its people engaged in a hopeless cause, either through stoic quietism or self-destructive idealism. Conrad's individuality within that context has been seen as a torn personality, wrestling with feelings of guilt for desertion of his nation's glorious and doomed cause. This emphasis is plainly wrong.

The tragedy of Polish history from partition to recent times has obscured the importance of Conrad's *szlachta* tradition, which, admittedly with lapses, sustained him. He knew his conscience, his honor, "[t]hat heirloom of the ages, of the race, of the group, of the family," (*PR*, 94) was still nurtured by his past. His convictions as a Polish gentleman, given their due, will show that his dark side as tormented skeptic is of less significance than his expressions of the timeless ideals of a past "known to [him] and a little *de visu*" (31).

Now Polish scholars have their chance not only to free critical theory from ideological strictures and resurrect Conrad's reputation among Poles, but also to define the Conrad canon against a cultural background of an earlier past which for too long has been a heart of darkness for western scholarship.

NOTES

1. To John Galsworthy, 29 October, 1907, *CL*, II, 504.
2. To Kazimierz Waliszewski, 5 December, 1903, *CL*, III, 87-8.
3. In reality, Stanisław was a soldier in the Grodno Hussars, not Guards.

His brother Kazimierz was an officer in the Russian army. See Morf, *The Polish Shades and Ghosts of Joseph Conrad*, 40 ff.

4. See also Wit Tarnawski, *Conrad the Man, the Writer, the Pole*, trans. Rosamond Batchelor (London: Polish Cultural Foundation, 1985).

5. For Tadeusz Bobrowski's *Pamiętniki* [Memoirs] (1900) see also Gustav Morf, *The Polish Heritage of Joseph Conrad* (New York: Richard R. Smith, 1935).

6. To John Galsworthy, 29 October, 1907, *CL*, II, 17-18, 504. (See also n. 1, above.)

WORKS CITED

Allen Jerry. *The Thunder and the Sunshine: A Biography of Joseph Conrad.* New York: G. P. Putnam's Sons, 1958.

Allen Jerry. *The Sea Years of Joseph Conrad.* Garden City, NY: Doubleday, 1965.

Baines Jocelyn. *Joseph Conrad: A Critical Biography.* London: Weidenfeld and Nicolson, 1960.

Batchelor John. *The Life of Joseph Conrad: A Critical Biography.* Oxford: Blackwell Publishers, 1994.

Bradbrook Muriel. *Poland's English Genius* [1941]. New York: Russell & Russell, 1966.

Busza Andrzej. "Conrad's Polish Literary Background and Some Illustrations of the Influence of Polish Literature on His Work," *Antemurale*, 10 (1966), 109-247; Rome-London: Institutum Historicum Polonicum – Societas Polonica Scientiarum et Litterarum in Exteris.

Conrad John. *Joseph Conrad: Times Remembered. "Ojciec jest tutaj".* Cambridge: Cambridge U.P., 1981.

Davies Norman. *God's Playground: A History of Poland,* vols. I-II. New York: Columbia U.P., 1982.

Follett Wilson. *Joseph Conrad.* New York: Russell & Russell, 1966.

Gillon Adam. *The Eternal Solitary: A Study of Joseph Conrad.* New York: Bookman, 1960.

Gillon Adam. *Joseph Conrad.* Boston: Twayne, 1982.

Guerard Albert J. *Conrad, the Novelist.* Cambridge, MA: Harvard U.P., 1966.

Gurko Leo. *Joseph Conrad: Giant in Exile.* London: Frederick Muller, 1965.

Hewitt Douglas. *Conrad: A Reassessment.* London: Bowes & Bowes, 1969. [First published in 1952. See "Introduction" to this 1969 edition.]

Hodges Robert F. *The Dual Heritage of Joseph Conrad.* The Hague: Mouton, 1967.

Jean-Aubry Georges. *The Sea Dreamer: A Definitive Biography of Joseph Conrad,* trans. Helen Sebba. London: George Allen & Unwin, 1957.

Karl Frederick R. *Joseph Conrad: The Three Lives*. New York: Farrar, Straus and Giroux, 1979.

Krajka Wiesław. "Conrad and Poland: Under the Eyes of My Generation," in *Contexts for Conrad,* eds. Keith Carabine, Owen Knowles, Wiesław Krajka. New York–Boulder–Lublin: Columbia U.P. – East European Monographs – Maria Curie-Skłodowska University, 1993; *Conrad: Eastern and Western Perspectives,* ed. Wiesław Krajka, vol. II.

Meyer Bernard C. *Joseph Conrad: A Psychoanalytic Biography*. Princeton: Princeton U.P., 1967.

Meyers Jeffrey. *Joseph Conrad: A Biography*. London: John Murray, 1991.

Morf Gustav. *The Polish Shades and Ghosts of Joseph Conrad*. New York: Astra Books, 1976.

Moser Thomas. *Joseph Conrad: Achievement and Decline*. Cambridge, MA: Harvard U.P., 1956.

Najder Zdzisław: "Conrad and the Idea of Honor," in *Joseph Conrad: Theory and World Fiction. Proceedings of the Comparative Literature Symposium,* January 23-25, 1974, eds. Wendell M. Aycock, Wołodymyr T. Żyła, vol. 7, Lubbock: Texas Tech, 1974, 103-14.

Najder Zdzisław. *Conrad's Polish Background: Letters to and from Polish Friends,* trans. Halina Carroll. London: Oxford U.P., 1964.

Najder Zdzisław. *Joseph Conrad: A Chronicle,* trans. Halina Caroll-Najder. New Brunswick, NJ: Rutgers U.P., 1983.

Retinger Joseph. *Conrad and His Contemporaries*. New York: Roy Publishing, 1943.

Sherry Norman. *Conrad's Eastern World*. London: Cambridge U.P., 1966.

Tennant Roger. *Joseph Conrad: A Biography*. New York: Atheneum, 1981.

Vigny Comte Alfred de. *Livre Troisieme, Souvenirs de grandeur militaire,* I [1835], in *Oeuvres completes,* ed. Paul Viallaneix. Paris: Editions de Seuil, 1965.

Watt Ian. *Conrad in the Nineteenth Century*. Berkeley: U. of California P., 1979.

Zabel Morton. "Introduction," in *The Portable Conrad*. New York: Viking Press, 1947.

Susan Jones,
St. Hilda's College, Oxford University,
Oxford, England

Conrad's Women and the Polish Romantic Tradition

I

In his reminiscences of a literary friendship with Joseph Conrad, Ford Madox Ford took occasion to remark on Conrad's distinctive evocation of his mother. According to Ford: "Of his father he always spoke deprecatorily...it really pained him to think that his father had been a revolutionary," while on the other hand: "Oddly but comprehensibly, when he spoke of his mother as revolutionary he was full of enthusiasm. For him the Polish national spirit had been kept alive by such women as his mother" (Ford, 76-7).

Ford's observation calls into question some traditional associations in Conrad criticism in which a greater emphasis has fallen on the influence of the father, Apollo Korzeniowski. The strong male presence of Conrad's early life in Poland has been used by critics to support his traditional image as author of a man's world. The early death of Conrad's mother in 1865, when he was only seven, has precipitated much commentary on his close ties, first with his father, Apollo Korzeniowski, and later his uncle Tadeusz Bobrowski, who became his guardian and father figure after Apollo's death in 1869.[1] Apollo's letters, which describe Conrad's brief but intensely emotional years spent with his father, as well as Conrad's intimate correspondence with his uncle, have prompted an examination of the paternal influences on Conrad's writing.[2]

Zdzisław Najder represents the prevailing view that Conrad inherited opposing moral values from his father and his uncle, a conflict which reappeared in his novels as the dilemmas of conscience associated with his male protagonists (Najder, *Conrad's Polish Background: Letters to and from Polish Friends,* 19).

In this school of thought, Conrad's romanticism originated in the lessons of his father, who introduced him to Polish romantic literature, and who taught him high standards of loyalty to the homeland, an ethic steeped in the chivalry and patriotism of the *szlachta*.[3] Conrad's skepticism, however, shows the influence of his Uncle Tadeusz, who deeply mistrusted a tradition which only led to false idealism and futility.[4]

Najder's arguments are persuasive, but they do not fully account for the added complexities suggested by Ford's remarks on the female influence on Conrad's early life. With the exception of a few passing references, critics have never thoroughly examined the impact on Conrad of the women of his years in Poland, nor have they fully considered the genesis of his female protagonists from within the Polish tradition. The suggestive analogies between his presentation of women in his fiction, and those of the Polish romantics, have hardly been noticed.

Yet women played a vital role during Conrad's formative years. Without the sacrifice of a devoted mother during the initial period of the Korzeniowskis' exile it is doubtful whether the sickly infant Conrad would have survived. After Ewa Korzeniowska's death, Apollo relied heavily on the support of Conrad's maternal grandmother Teofila Bobrowska. She continued to nurture the orphaned Conrad for long periods when in 1869 Apollo also died (11-12). In 1900 Conrad himself remarked on how he had benefited from the close bond established amongst the Bobrowski women. In a letter to Edward Garnett of 20 January 1900 he wrote: "There was an extraordinary sister-cult in that family, from which I profited when left an orphan at the age of ten" (*CL*, I, 291).

Although Conrad spent a relatively isolated childhood – "my young days...have been rather familiar with long silences"[5] – he spoke affectionately of his intermittent female companions during those early years. In *A Personal Record* (1912), he vividly recalled his affection for a French governess, Mlle. Durand, who had taught him to speak and read French simply by being "an excellent playmate" (*PR*, 65). He was very close to his cousin Józefa, his Uncle Tadeusz's daughter, a "delightful, quick-

-tempered little girl," who died when she was only fifteen (in 1871), but with whom Conrad had spent "the very happiest period of my existence" (24). Najder tells us that other childhood friends included Janina and Karolina Taube, whom he met between 1870-73, when he was sent to the Georgeon pension in Cracow. He established a lasting friendship with Janina, with whom he corresponded (as Baroness de Brunnow) later in life, and when Uncle Tadeusz sent him to Lvov in August 1873, under the care of his cousin Antoni Syroczyński, he supposedly came into conflict with his new guardian by flirting with his daughter Tekla Syroczyńska (Najder, *Joseph Conrad: A Chronicle,* 32-6).

Najder shows us that Conrad's earliest years were filled with the presence of women, yet in relation to Conrad's creative development he draws little significance from this fact. Most of all, Conrad poignantly recalled the intensity of feeling for his mother, however dimly remembered. His brief sketch of her in *A Personal Record* in itself provides the basis for a re-evaluation of an elusive, but powerful influence on his writing. In the "Author's Note" he recalled how he could still remember her loving presence above all other memories of the many people who wandered through the Korzeniowski household in Warsaw in 1861:

> Amongst them I remember my mother, a more familiar figure than the others, dressed in the black of the national mourning worn in defiance of ferocius police regulations. I have also preserved from that particular time the awe of her mysterious gravity which, indeed, was by no means smileless. For I remember her smiles, too. Perhaps for me she could always find a smile. She was young then, certainly not yet thirty. She died four years later in exile. (*PR,* x)

Beginning with a closer examination of Conrad's relationship to his mother, and drawing on the evidence of Conrad's early experiences and reading, I will show that his childhood recollections, both personal and literary, constituted a fundamental source for his later presentation of women in the fiction.

II

In 1930 Gustav Morf, early critic of Conrad's Polish heritage, drew a brief analogy between Conrad's memory of his mother and his fictional women:

> Most critics of Conrad have remarked that his women have something unfinished, something shadowy, something elusive about them. It is, indeed, as if the memory of her that flitted like a shadow through his infant life prevented him from drawing his women with the same sure stroke which characterises his portraits of men. (Morf, 41)

Conrad's "shadowy" and "elusive" sketch of his mother in *A Personal Record* supports Morf's thesis. It also reminds us of Edward Said's reference to the "fiction of autobiography" in relation to Conrad's work.[6] For not only did Conrad draw closely on personal experience to create his novels, he presented his autobiographical writing, conversely, as a form of partially fictionalized narrative. Conrad relied heavily on the Bobrowski memoirs, especially in compiling the Polish episodes of *A Personal Record,* but he nevertheless produced a highly selective and carefully wrought account of his early life, presented with his individual humor and with considerable restraint. The text is characterized throughout by its episodic nature, by its omissions as much as its inclusion of personal detail, and by its many digressions from a continuous narrative of his own experience. We are made doubly aware of Conrad's pertinent remarks on self-projection in "A Familiar Preface" to this work, where he claims that a novelist's writing is always to some extent autobiographical, but that "the disclosure is not complete."[7]

Conrad presented the partially disclosed portrait of his mother (with the help of his Uncle Tadeusz's memoirs), as a nobly spirited, gentle figure in black, most clearly remembered from the time of their three months' leave from the exile imposed on the Korzeniowskis by the Russians (summer 1863). Like many of the female characters of his novels, he described Ewa as an observant figure, captured in a moment of stillness, framed by the architectural features of his uncle's house in Ukraine: "I seem to remember my mother looking on from a colonnade in front of the dining-room windows as I was lifted upon the pony" (*PR*, 23). We might think of Captain Whalley's daughter at the close of "The End of the Tether," in her plain black bodice, "leaning her forehead against a window-pain," as "the image of her husband and her children seemed to glide away from her in the gray twilight" (*YS*, 339).

Conrad described this time at his uncle's house as the year in which "I first begin to remember my mother with more distinctness than a mere loving, wide-browed, silent, protecting presence, whose eyes had a sort of commanding sweetness" (*PR*, 23). The image of "the grey heads of the family friends paying her the homage of respect and love" (24) bears reminders of the gentle, nurturing qualities of the benevolent Mrs. Gould and her "humanizing influence" as the European hostess of Sulaco in *Nostromo*.

Conrad's most striking reference to Ewa shows her taking leave of her relations for the last time on the steps of her brother's property in Ukraine: "my grandmother all in black gazing stoically, my uncle giving his arm to my mother down to the carriage" (64). Conrad recounts the poignant details of this departure, as Ewa was forced by the Russian authorities to return to exile even though she was barely fit to travel. Yet he only briefly mentions his mother by name. The passage consists chiefly of a report (given in direct speech), of the Russian orders to escort mother and son from the house. As if Conrad were scarcely able to recount this most painful of memories, he avoids any direct interpretation of his mother's position in the scene ("Author's Note," *PR*, x, 64-7). Indeed the tragic memory of his mother's bravery, as she embarked on her final journey into exile must surely account for some of Conrad's difficulty in finding comic resolution to the plots of his self-sacrificing, but ill-fated heroines. The devotion of both Winnie Verloc and Lena, for example, is ultimately rewarded with tragedy and death.

Although Conrad devoted little space to anecdotes of his mother in his autobiographical work, she nevertheless constituted a forceful presence, suggesting an intensity of character that belied the physical frailty so often associated in literature with the moral weakness of the female (Shakespeare, *Hamlet*: "frailty thy name is woman"). Conrad's unqualified praise of his mother as "the ideal of Polish womanhood" (*PR*, 29) suggests that her image exerted an enduring influence on him throughout his life, one which discretely entered the fiction by way of a number of cameo roles of notable impact. Mrs. Verloc's mother, Mrs. de Barral and Mrs. Haldin sustain an unflinching poise in the face of Conrad's predominantly sceptical mode of presentation, offering the only measure of moral certitude within his narratives of pessimism and doubt. The evidence strongly indicates that Conrad's shadowy memories of his mother represented a model for the presence of the self-sacrificing mother figure in his fiction.

Conrad's relationship to his mother needs to be understood in the context of an enduring Polish tradition which idealized and sanctified the mother figure socially, politically, and theologically. Indeed the importance of the role of the mother in both the history of Polish nationalism and within the Polish family dynamic cannot be underestimated. Polish Catholicism privileges the image of the Mother of God rather than that of the Virgin Mary, thus emphasizing her nurturing qualities rather than her chastitiy.[8] A famous hymn of 1407 *Bogurodzica* (Mother of God) supports a legendary history dating back to the tenth century, when it was presumed to have been wirtten by St. Wojciech (St. Adalbert). A tiny fragment surviving from the original mansucript provided a powerful influence on Poland's subsequent political and literary history, as the Mother of God now becomes the Mother of the State. The hymn was transformed into a battle song and was adopted as the national anthem in 1506 (Krzyżanowski, 16). In the seventeenth century it was translated into other languages by a Jesuit (Maciej Kazimierz Sarbiewski) and in the nineteenth century it entered the Polish romantic tradition, when Juliusz Słowacki adapted it for his cycle of lyric poems connected with November 1830 Rising. Słowacki's *Hymn* merges the chivalric tradition associated with *Bogurodzica* with the revolutionary traditions of contemporary nineteenth-century Poland. The great piety associated with the presentation of the "Mother of God" perhaps accounts for the pathos and sincerity of the sacrificing mother figures of Polish romantic literature.

Conrad's later recollections of his mother remind us that Ewa herself represented precisely this figure of integrity and noble self-sacrifice which had been idealized throughout Polish national history. Judging by Ewa's surviving letters to her husband during the time of their separation in 1861, her fervent and practical devotion to her family represented the same exemplary sacrifice that could so often be found in the presentation of the Polish mother in the previous generation's literature.

When Apollo left his wife and young son in Ukraine in 1861, he joined a group of intellectuals in Warsaw which was hoping to incite the longed-for insurrection against Russian hegemony. During this period of separation Conrad was growing up in an atmosphere steeped in the dimensions of tragedy, marked by images of an almost gothic darkness, as, one by one, the Korzeniowskis' neighbors lost their loved ones in the fight against Russian domination – "everyone is in black here, *even the children*" – his mother once wrote during a protracted period of mourning.[9]

Ewa corresponded frequently with Apollo during his absence, although many of her letters were intercepted by the Russians, and, tragically, they later provided evidence for his arrest. Those of her letters that survive overflow with lavish affection and an eager expression of her desire for maternal, domestic, and intellectual activity: "Give me something to do while we are separated....Make me do some translations. Find something new and readable. I should so like to carry at least a small proportion of the cost of living."[10]

While Ewa bravely accepted her responsibilities, she conveyed a strong sense of the anxieties and isolation she suffered under the ubiquitous threat of the Russian authorities. She often referred to the inadequacy of the written communication of her feelings: "How we miss you at home, you cannot imagine and I should probably be unable to express it."[11] Yet she did express her sentiments with a graceful, romantic style: "You miss me; and I do not want to speak of my longing for I know that even without words you must feel it. Besides, what is longing in comparison with the constant fear of danger that, they say, threatens you?"[12]

Even through the medium of translation we can hear a similar sensitivity in Conrad's letters to his wife Jessie. Whilst travelling to the United States in 1923 he wrote to her on April 30: "I miss you more and more...it seems ages since I left you...he [their son Borys] is very near to my heart – in which your dear image dwells constantly commanding all my thoughts and all my love" (*CL*, II, 307).

Ewa's capacity for intense emotional response was combined with the Bobrowski pragmatism (often attributed to her brother Tadeusz). Her fears are often masked in the letters by a sense of spirited optimism in her unfailing support of Apollo: "Several women's homes have been searched. I am prepared for it, rest assured."[13] She was also prepared to engineer, single-handedly, the hazardous trip to join her husband in Warsaw (with the young Conrad): "I shall manage the travel expenses" she announced confidently; "I shall carry out all your instructions and shall bear in mind *the warnings*. I have matured a great deal during the several weeks of our separation and of constant longing combined with anxiety."[14]

Despite her extraordinary courage and integrity, Ewa's sacrifices were ultimately futile. Apollo was arrested in October 1861, and Ewa later accused of "unlawful revolutionary activity" (Knowles, 2). The January 1863 Rising failed miserably, and the Korzeniowskis were exiled to northern Russia, where the harsh winters precipitated Ewa's premature death.

We can only speculate on the effect of Ewa's letters on Conrad the writer, especilly since we do not know whether he read the ones that have survived. Those he did read he claimed to have destroyed, and he rarely spoke about his mother. Yet we cannot overlook the importance of the date at which he read them and at which he became fully conscious of his appreciation of his mother. In a letter of January 20, 1900, to Edward Garnett he recalled:

> my mother was certainly no ordinary woman. Her correspondence
> with my father and with her brothers which in the year 1890 I have
> read and afterwards destroyed was a revelation to me; I shall never
> forget my delight, admiration and unutterable regret at my loss
> (before I could appreciate her), which only then I fully understood.
> (Baines, 6)

The date is significant, since in *A Personal Record* Conrad claims
to have begun writing *Almayer's Folly* late in 1889 (*PR*, 9). He
had taken the manuscript of his first novel with him to Poland
when he visited his uncle early in 1890, and it was there that he
first read his mother's letters. At the turning point in his life, as
he initiated the first steps of his transformation from seaman to
writer, he directly relived, through his mother's words, the events
preceding his painful loss.

We need to consider the impact of Conrad's memories of his
mother as he wrote his first novel. It is quite plausible that
Conrad blamed his father for the death of his mother, who had
sacrificed herself for her husband's political cause. If this had
contributed to his desire to leave Poland, then the asertive, active
role of Nina in *Almayer's Folly* could be interpreted as Conrad's
desire to "reinvent" his mother's life in this narrative. Ewa's
father had considered Apollo to be an unsuitable match and had
forbidden her marriage, and in Conrad's novel Almayer responds likewise to Nina's attachment to Dain. Like Dain, who
offered Nina what Jocelyn Baines calls "glamour" (Baines, 155),
Apollo must have cut something of an exotic figure in the eyes of
the young Ewa. Ewa's mother allowed her to marry the man she
loved only after her father's death. But Conrad gives his female
protagonist greater powers of assertion. Nina defies her father
and takes responsibility for her own life and choice of partner.

Biographers have expressed a certain difficulty in explaining
the prominence of the father-daughter relationship in Conrad's
early novels. Baines avoids a direct confrontation with the issue,
suggesting that the father-*son* relationship "was doubtless far
too charged emotionally for Conrad to be able to represent it
directly, whereas his deepest impulses could find a disguised
expression through a portrayal of the father-daughter relation-

ship" (155). But Conrad's "disguises" as the "daughters" of his early fiction warrant further attention, particularly since they suggest the author's close identification with the women of his fiction.[15] Almayer's relationship to Nina does not exclusively reproduce Conrad's conflict with his father. Conrad was also commenting on a longer tradition of familial discord between patriarchal values and "feminine" responses to the father figure.[16]

Indeed Conrad's earliest experiences had been dominated by Ewa's devotion, and after her death, by his father's intense idealization of her memory. The following account of Apollo's grief at the death of his wife encapsulates the spirit of high romanticism which the young Conrad must have perceived surrounding the memory of his mother. Stanisław Czosnowski wrote in 1929 of a visit to the Korzeniowskis a few years after Ewa's death:

> I found Apollo sitting motionless in front of his wife's portrait. He never stirred on seeing us and Konradek who was accompanying me put his finger to his lips and said: "Let us cross the room quietly. Father spends every anniversary of Mother's death sitting all day and looking at her portrait; he does not speak or eat."[17]

Combined with his own painful and distant memories of a self-sacrificing mother, Conrad had, at an early age, witnessed a spectacle reminiscent of his later fictional idealizations of women, characterized, as they often are, by a sense of detachment, distance, and a passive, iconographic element. Something of this aestheticization of women as paintings of artifacts survives in the late romances, where Conrad emphasizes the gap between what a woman "is" and how she is represented. Drawing on this habitual mode of seeing, Conrad recalled, in his "Author's Note" (1920) to *Victory* (1915), the moment when he first observed the woman who served as model for Lena. She had been playing in a café orchestra in the south of France:

> The shape of her dark head inclined over the violin was fascinating, and, while resting between the pieces of that interminable programme she was, in her white dress and with her brown hands reposing in her lap, the very image of dreamy innocence. (*V*, xli)

In the novel itself, however, Conrad ultimately transformed his passive portrait into an active role (in which Lena courageously dies for Heyst). Likewise Davidson describes Mrs. Schomberg as if she were "behaving like a painted image rather than a live woman" (44), yet the woman actively assists Lena in her escape from Schomberg's hotel. In *The Arrow of Gold* (1919), Rita de Lastaola's face was "like some ideal conception of art" (*AG,* 222), but Rita herself resists all attempts to idealize her. Moreover she evades the traditional closure of the romance heroine, ultimately choosing a solitary path.

Apollo had been anxious that Conrad should retain a romantic, idealized view of his mother. He wrote to Kazimierz Kaszewski on June 10, 1865: "He [Conrad] is all that remains of her [Ewa] on this earth and I want him to be a worthy witness of her to those hearts who will not forget her" (Baines, 17). Conrad's minor fictional portraits provide this "worthy witness." Mrs. Verloc's mother in *The Secret Agent* makes a gesture of self-sacrifice in leaving the Verloc household which sets her integrity against Verloc's pose of lazy self-absorption.[18] Mrs. de Barral in *Chance* also selflessly supports her husband's ventures, then languishes in "exile" as de Barral's business claims his attention. Like Ewa, she dies in isolation, leaving behind a grief-stricken husband and child.

While Conrad's limited memories of his mother echo in his briefly sketched fictional mothers, his presentation of women also alluded to the much longer tradition of idealized motherhood and female heroism that permeated Polish culture. But his romantic literary heritage expressed an uneasy ambivalence to the role of the self-sacrificial heroine. In order to understand the impact on Conrad of both the ideal and the ironic in the female component of Polish romanticism, we need to establish the extent to which this literature informed the context of his upbringing.

III

"This is my Polishness," Conrad remarked in an interview of 1917 with Marian Dąbrowski, referring to the influence of Polish romantic literature on his novels. He concluded that it was his early reading of the work of Adam Mickiewicz (1798-1855) and Juliusz Słowacki (1809-1849) which accounted for "something incomprehensible, impalpable, ungraspable" detected by English critics in his writing. Apollo Korzeniowski had passed on the traditions of Polish romanticism to his son:

> My father read *Pan Tadeusz* aloud to me and made me read it aloud. Not just once or twice. I used to prefer *Konrad Wallenrod, Grażyna*. Later I liked Słowacki better. You know why Słowacki? *Il est l'âme de toute la Pologne, lui.* (Najder, *Conrad under Familial Eyes*, 199)[19]

We should not underestimate the extent to which Polish literary traditions were aligned to Polish national identity. The Polish romantics were associated with the Western European tradition through their reading of Schiller, Goethe, and Byron, but they were also strongly affiliated with the politics of partition, which gave impetus to the nationalist risings of 1830, 1848, and 1863 (Conrad's father being involved in the latter).[20] The themes of this literature heavily metaphorized the struggle of Poland and Russia. Yet the romantics of "The Great Emigration" of the 1830s, exiled from home, compensated for their physical absence from the scene of political conflict by producing literature concerned primarily with the topics of loyalty and betrayal.[21] Critics have shown how Conrad, as a displaced individual, reflected the romantics' uneasy response to the distinction between personal and public duty in the presentation of his own male protagonists.[22]

Conrad therefore borrowed from the Polish writers a structure which bore within it the seeds of its own critique of the romantic ideal. But doubts about the efficacy of male heroism were not only expressed by the male protagonists of this literature. Critics have often overlooked the fundamental position occupied by the women of Polish romantic drama, whose roles often function as a critical reminder of the inadequacy of the hero or the futility of his pursuit of an idealist quest. The women of Conrad's preferred poems, Mickiewicz's *Konrad Wallenrod* and *Grażyna,* offer two such examples of the critique of the hero in Polish romanticism.

Grażyna (1823) represents the exemplary sacrifice and bravery of a female knight, who acts effectively in the face of her husband's betrayal of national loyalties. This Polish version of Spenser's Britomart (Book III, Spenser, *The Faerie Queene,* 1590), refuses to acknowledge her husband's alliance with the national enemy, the Teutonic knights, and goes into battle against them. Having sacrificed her life, her husband then confronts his shame and leaps onto the funeral pyre beside her. The most obvious parallel in Conrad is represented by Lena, who dies heroically for her lover Heyst, her selfless action constituting the *Victory* of that novel, where her sacrifice is swiftly followed by Heyst's belated self-recognition and suicide, as he sets fire to their bungalow.[23] Another echo of the Grażyna type appears in Conrad's earlier work, as Aissa in *An Outcast of the Islands* (1896) fights with equal status alongside her father in battle. Conrad himself provides testimony of his preference for a female type whose selflessness is combined with an unquestionable integrity. He had written to Marguerite Poradowska on December 6 or 13, 1894, that "I think only women have true courage," and that in Polish literature "women will have more character than the men, which with us is unquestionably the case" (*CL,* I, 191).[24] In his "Author's Note" to *Nostromo* (1905), he suggests that a childhood sweetheart, the model for Antonia Avellanos, resembled the Polish patriotic ideal of womanhood:

> How we used to look up to that girl just out of the schoolroom herself, as the standard bearer of faith to which we were all born, but which she alone knew how to hold aloft with an unflinching hope! She had perhaps more glow and less serenity than Antonia, but she was an uncompromising Puritan of patriotism, with no hint of the slightest worldliness in her thoughts. (*N,* xlvi)

Indeed Adam Gillon argues convincingly that Conrad's Polish upbringing accounts for the type to be found in the fiction:

> Conrad's attitude toward women and love comes partly from what he
> himself accepted as the romantic chivalrous tradition of the Polish
> gentry in the Ukraine, and from the tradition of Polish romantic
> poetry. (Gillon, *The Eternal Solitary: A Study of Joseph Conrad,* 89)

But Polish romanticism also questioned, as well as idealized, the
position of women in a chivalric tradition, where maids in towers
were not exclusively rescued, but often condemned to a life of
anguish and stasis. Mickiewicz's verse epic *Konrad Wallenrod,* in
which the hero infiltrates the enemy forces in order to betray
them, provides a striking example of the sacrifice of female
identity to the male heroic quest. The curious presentation of
a tortured, solitary hermitess, once a princess, but now locked in
her tower, occupies an uneasy role in the narrative of national
identity. Princess Aldona became the wife of Konrad Wallenrod
before he set out on his adventure of national recovery against
the Teutonic enemies of Lithuania. She reappers in the narrative
as a schematic figure, an archetypal embodiment of loss, a gothic
wraith (like the lonely female with the Medusa's stare of the
shorter poem "The Romantic"[25]), abandoned by the active male
to her passive grief and self-imposed isolation in a lonely tower
– "an unknown woman found in a living grave" (Mickiewicz,
Konrad Wallenrod and Other Writings, 17).

Her pose functions as a register of the hero's movement
between genres. Her change in role from one of domesticity
("Prince's daughter sits by her loom" [43]), to one of marginalized solitude (hermitess in the tower) also signals the
moment of Konrad Wallenrod's transformation from the locus
of domestic comedy and individual happiness to the broader
sweeps of social duty and national epic. Victim of a narrative of
male assertiveness, Mickiewicz's hermitess claims that she has
been reduced, by grief, to a ghostly representation of her former
self, and declines Konrad Wallenrod's invitation to leave her
tower: "Back to the world wouldst thou be bringing whom?
A phantom!" (69). Her story is one of unrelieved anguish, her
presentation that of an identity unfulfilled, since her personal
sacrfice is unable to match that of her husband's crusading
heroism. A similarly tragic victim of male romantic idealism

appears in Zygmunt Krasiński's *The Un-Divine Comedy* (1833). In his bitter critique of romanticism, Krasiński presents a woman's descent into grief and madness after being betrayed and abandoned by the husband to whom she is devoted. We finally view the dutiful wife of Count Henry in a position of permanent enclosure in the garden of an asylum.

Such figures emerge in Conrad's fiction as ghostly repetitions rather than as direct influences, suggestively recalling, rather than directly borrowing from a tradition which often ironizes as well as idealizes the notion of self-sacrifice in women. We might think of Lena at the beginning of *Victory,* a "phantom-like apparition" (*V,* 83), a "white and spectral ghost" (86), eluding the advances of Zangiacomo; the domestic claustrophobia of Mrs. Hervey (and later Winnie Verloc) in "The Return" in her urban bourgeois "grave" (*Tales of Unrest* [1898]); or the sullen Alice, prisoner of a sinister *"hortus conclusus"* in "A Smile of Fortune" (*'Twixt Land and Sea,* 1912); the psychologically isolated Flora, metaphorically imprisoned on *The Ferndale* (*Chance,* 1913). Both late plays, *One Day More* and *Laughing Anne* (1925) explore the issue of female entrapment in the web of domestic relations and the histories of male identity.

Mickiewicz's hermitess, whose personal narrative is unfulfilled, also provides the model for a familiar device in Conrad in which the women characters signal an uneasy gap in the narrative, the shady presence of a woman's story which is hinted at but has not been fully expressed. In "The Tale" (1917), for example, the female auditor, who initially expresses the desire to hear the story, constantly intervenes in the male narrator's account of a wartime experience:

> She interrupted, stirring a little.
> "Oh, yes. Sincerity, frankness, passion, three words of your gospel. Don't I know them!"
> "Think! Isn't it ours, believed in common?" he asked, anxiously, yet without expecting an answer, and went on at once....(*TH,* 64)

The male narrator's expression of discomfort at her response suggests the tantalizing presence of an alternative story – that of the woman. But the narrator briskly suppresses her story, "papers over the cracks" of the text constituted by her reply, and hurries on with his own narrative.

To some extent Conrad's female figures represent the universally recognizable elements of enclosure or exclusion from male plots, the stasis and madness associated with the feminine of many nineteenth-century gothic narratives. But the Polish examples provide a convincing model for his highly schematic mode of presentation. The fate of the hermitess of *Konrad Wallenrod,* or of Krasiński's abandoned wife in *The Un-Divine Comedy,* suggest the elusively defined, yet powerful presence of Conrad's often silent but remarkably forceful heroines.[26]

Conrad's more ironic presentation of female self-sacrifice alludes closely to the Polish tradition, where works of high romanticism are often tempered by a coexistent parody of the form. The Polish romantics experimented widely with genre, combining and fragmenting forms in a way which might be compared loosely to Sterne's experimentation with the novel in England. Mickiewicz's *Forefathers' Eve* mixes folklore and medieval motifs with a lack of linear chronology; Krasiński's *The Un-Divine Comedy* locates its critique of romanticism within a framework of domestic and political drama. Both exemplify the self-reflective nature of the texts and the parody of the strictly romantic form.[27]

Conrad's preference for the work of Juliusz Słowacki can be attributed to his interest in the potentially subversive nature of the romantic quest. Słowacki's less well-known drama *Fantazy* (written between 1830-40) offers an outrageous parody of romantic self-sacrifice. It was first published posthumously in 1866, under the title *Niepoprawni* (The Incorrigible). Since the narrator of "Prince Roman," Conrad's only overtly "Polish" story, refers to "the great exasperation of our enemies who have bestowed upon us the epithet of Incorrigible" (with a capital "I"), perhaps we can assume that Conrad read this play as a boy in its original edition (*TH,* 29).

This play offers suggestive models for Conrad's caricatured revolutionaries, Madame de S– and Peter Ivanovitch in *Under*

Western Eyes (1911). Countess Idalia was "something on the order of a Madame de Staël, a letter-writing steam engine" (Krasiński, *The Un-Divine Comedy,* 264). And Fantazy's portrait of the heroine Diana refers to her experience of exile in Siberia:

> That girl in black, that Diana whitened by the bind of Siberia who with those black eyes of hers sees graves and crosses there, hears chains rattling, and clasps her hands to her bosom like a statue of obedience and pain. (Słowacki, *Fantazy,* 258)

Fantazy's description resonates with the familiar imagery of Peter Ivanovitch's first speech at the Haldin's – as he recalls his escape from prison, "the loose end of the chain" fastened to his leg "to deaden the clanking" and praises the exemplary Russian womanhood which saved him with "the sacredness of self-sacrifice and womanly love" (*UWE,* 121).

Yet of all Conrad's allusions to the women of Polish romanticism, his reference to the mother figure remains, as in the Polish drama, untainted by skepticism. Again we are reminded of the portrait of his mother in *A Personal Record,* and of Ewa's letters, where her sacrifice to her husband's revolutionary idealism reads like the fruitless self-denial of the mothers of Polish romantic drama (Krasiński, *The Un-Divine Comedy,* 182). Count Henry's wife in *The Un-Divine Comedy* retains her status as nobly dutiful mother despite the parody of other characters, sacrificing both her reason and her life to her husband's highly exaggerated romantic ideals (182). Mickiewicz's Mrs. Rollinson, the blind mother, who in scene viii of *Forefathers' Eve* III (1832) (Mickiewicz, *Forefathers' Eve,* III, 162), pleas for the life of her son, a Polish patriot imprisoned by the Russians, suggests the heroic self-sacrifice of the few mothers of Conrad's fiction. The *gravitas* of this scene contrasts jarringly with a scene in which sham intellectuals conduct a flippant discussion about the suitability of the idyll as a genre for national poetry. Their superficial posing offers an ironic juxtaposition with Mrs. Rollinson's tragic scene, since they claim to prefer the pastoral mode to the stark realism in which poets describe "bloody scenes of violence and stress" (the Polish political reality, of which Mrs. Rollinson's son is a victim).

Mickiewicz's use of the figure of Mrs. Rollinson as a moral gauge of events suggests a method adopted by Conrad in his presentation of female self-sacrifice in *Under Western Eyes*. Mrs. Haldin's marginal but powerful presence on the periphery of the action in Geneva constitutes just such a standard or medium of interpretation, reminiscent of the unwavering moral status of Mickiewicz's Mrs. Rollinson or Krasiński's wife of Henry. A closer reading of this novel reveals the close analogies between the presentation of the mother figure of the Polish tradition and Conrad's personal tribute to his mother's memory in the fiction.

IV

In December 1907 Conrad began working on "Razumov," a short story which developed into the novel *Under Western Eyes* (1911). Simultaneously he was writing "Some Reminiscences" (*A Personal Record*). As Conrad addressed his most poignant memories of the homeland in the autobiographical work, he was also producing his most painfully wrought fictional presentation of betrayal. The story of Razumov's betrayal of his friend Haldin, set in the context of revolutionary resistance to Russian autocracy, constitutes one of Conrad's bleakest confrontations with the issues of private and public loyalties. But this novel also reflects the author's personal conflict surrounding the memories of his parents' revolutionary activity in Poland. The enthusiasm for the cause displayed by Haldin and his sister Natalia is reminiscent of his father's idealistic sacrifice, while Conrad's cynical presentation of Peter Ivanovitch and Madame de S— indicates his own emphatic mistrust of revolutionary values. The attenuated role of Mrs. Haldin, who hovers anxiously on the periphery of the action in Geneva, awaiting news of her son, perhaps represents Conrad's closest tribute to his own mother, whose letters to Apollo expressed so intensely her agony of uncertainty.

Conrad's presentation of Mrs. Haldin initially bears a close resemblance to the description of his mother in *A Personal Record*: a figure dressed in the perennial black of mourning, a "loving, wide-browed, silent, protecting presence" (*PR,* 23). The English teacher, narrator of *Under Western Eyes,* describes Mrs. Haldin as if she were Conrad's own mother, now aged: "a tall woman in a black silk dress," whose "wide brow, regular features...testified to her past beauty," and who "received me very kindly" and spoke "in a gentle voice" (*UWE,* 101). Like Conrad's mother, Mrs. Haldin also displays a capacity for the traditional, maternal self-sacrifice: "I have an idea that Mrs. Haldin, at her son's wish, would have set fire to her house ...without any sign of surprise or apprehension" (100). But she maintains no romantic ideals about Russia, like her daughter's conviction that "concord is not so very far off" (104). "That is what my children think" she tells the English teacher with steady scepticism (104). Thus she embodies one of the few detached political perspectives of the novel.

She repeatedly appears, in the teacher's account, seated in the familiar pose of the portrait painter, passive and watchful in her armchair in the window of the Haldins' apartment in Geneva.[28] Without the guide of a reliable narrator in the novel, her presence, or her noted absence from this pose, indicates the moral direction of the novel. When the English teacher encounters Peter Ivanovitch (Conrad's caricatured revolutionary mystic) at the Haldin's for the first time, he significantly observes that "Mrs. Haldin's armchair by the window stood empty" (118). This is the only reference made to her during this section of the narrative, as if the empty chair signalled both the moral redundancy of Ivanovitch's bogus feminism, as well as the generic slip from realist domestic drama to parody.

Mrs. Haldin's steady psychological decline throughout the space of the novel is registered by the subtle changes of her posture in the armchair – her "immobility" (200) as she waits for news of her son, is transformed into "the poignant quality of mad expectation" (319) once she hears news of his death and is gripped by the notion of his betrayal. Here she most closely resembles Krasiński's mother figure, Count Henry's wife, whose descent into madness follows her betrayal. After Razumov's confession we catch a final glimpse of Mrs. Haldin, "her whole figure had the stillness of a sombre painting" (355). Once more the pose signifies the generic shift. The initially confident image of the formal portrait, reflecting Mrs. Haldin's domestic harmony, is transformed into the iconography of the *Pietà*. The English teacher records how Natalia "pointed mournfully at the tragic immoblity of her mother, who seemed to watch a beloved head lying in her lap" (355). Razumov's "redemption" after his public confession is confirmed by a repetition of this very image – as the lady companion Tekla takes Razumov's head on her lap in the tram after his final accident (371).

Throughout *Under Western Eyes* the image of the self-sacrifice of three women, of Mrs. Haldin, Natalia, and Tekla, is set against the single act of Razumov's betrayal of Haldin. All three are in some way sacrificed to his *story,* since it is after his confession that Mrs. Haldin dies, Natalia gives herself to the poor of Russia, and Tekla saves him. But Razumov himself realizes in his confession that "In giving myself up, it was myself, after all, whom I have betrayed most basely" (361). The search for self-knowledge in this novel seems to be inextricably bound to the concept of self-denial.

We may be reminded that Razumov achieves his anagnorisis in Geneva, the birthplace of Rousseau, under whose statue he writes the reports of his observations (290). The significance of this choice can be glimpsed by reflecting on Claude Lévi-Strauss's interpretation of Rousseau's anthropological thesis (*The Discourse on the Origin of Inequality* [1754]). Lévi-Strauss comments that "the ethnographer must learn to know himself," to discover "a self who reveals himself as *another*" (Lévi-Strauss, 36). The work of the ethnographer is, accordingly, a confession of that compassionate identification with the other (implicit in which is a refusal to identify with the self). If we substitute Razumov, the spy, the observer, for ethnographer, we can see how, in the context of Geneva, he had failed to know himself until he wrote his narrative of identification with the other, the final confession. Yet as Zdzisław Najder has pointed out in his "Introduction" to *A Personal Record,* Conrad himself "specifically scorned the 'confessional' form of reminiscences and taunted its most eminent practitioner Jean-Jacques Rousseau in 'A Familiar Preface' to this work."[29] Indeed the affirmation afforded by Rousseau's "compassionate" philosophy is at odds with Conrad's sense of self-restraint, his "distrust of unbridled emotionalism" (*PR*, xviii) in revealing details of his personal life. Besides, his characterization of Razumov shows that confession often buys redemption at a high price. The appalling cost of Razumov's revelation results in physical disfigurement and loss of identity. What is more, Conrad's own exploration into the past also brought with it physical and psychological breakdown.

We have seen that Conrad began work on *Under Western Eyes* while writing his personal reminiscences. As if compelled to relive and confront all the old memories of Poland, the accusations of guilt associated with leaving his native land, and writing in a foreign language, Conrad devised, in *Under Western Eyes,* his most harrowing narrative of loyalty and betrayal, with Poland's traditional enemy itself as protagonist. The personal cost of exhuming these memories was considerable.

It therefore seems reasonable to identify Conrad with Razumov, who achieved his painful anagnorisis at a price. But what of the women of the novel, who seem to accept self-denial and who sacrifice themselves to Razumov's narrative without a fight? Must we agree with Terence Cave's view, that Natalia is not "an individual" at all, but "a symbol of transcendent value" in which she functions as an uncomplicated two-dimensional figure?" (Cave, 482).

Keith Carabine's extensive work on the texts of "Razumov" and *Under Western Eyes* has shown that Natalia Haldin's role had initially captured Conrad's interest to a much greater extent. Miss Haldin's final characterization, however, expresses less of the depth and nuance of the earlier story, and Conrad himself drew attention to the unfulfilled potential of his heroine. He admitted in a letter to Olive Garnett of October 11, 1911, that he could have done more with the female role:

> That girl does not move. No excuse can be offered for such a defect but
> there is an explanation. I wanted a pivot for the action to turn on. And
> I had to be very careful because if I had allowed myself to make more
> of her she would have killed the artistic purpose of the book: the
> development of a single mood....No doubt if I had taken another line
> the book would have been richer....Still I need not have made Miss
> Haldin a mere peg as I am sorry to admit she is. (Garnett, 234)

Even so, the vital presence of the self-sacrificing women in *Under Western Eyes* does seem to offer moral continuity in a world of epistemological uncertainty (like the role of the mother in Polish romanticism). Jocelyn Baines talks of Natalia Haldin as "Conrad's most effective portrait of a woman," perhaps because, as he sees her, she fits the model of selflessness already mentioned above: "a noble, intensely idealistic girl" who acts as a catalyst for Razumov's self-discovery (Baines, 362). Mrs. Haldin also provides a compelling presence which challenges Razumov on his path to confession: "Must I go then and lie to that old woman!" (*UWE*, 190). However, like their Polish counterparts, these women fade from the narrative, marginalized, destined to a lifetime of self-sacrifice. Only Sophia Antonovna survives intact, and her last words on the subject of the bogus feminist: "Peter Ivanovitch is an inspired man," leaves the question open (382).[30]

There may be more than one story behind Conrad's denial of Natalia's part. I believe that Conrad's presentation of the self-sacrifice of women in this novel offers an alternative perspective on his own position as a writer at this time in his career, one which shows a greater identification with the feminine than is generally assumed. His mental health was sacrificed during the novel's completion, and the book he had put aside (*Chance*) had to wait until 1912 for its initial serialization. In *Under Western Eyes* the tragedies of Natalia Haldin, Tekla, and Mrs. Haldin, all pivot on a denial of the self which Conrad presents later in a very different genre (with the implied comic closure of romance), in the sacrifice of Flora de Barral to her possessive father. The women of *Under Western Eyes,* seen against a bleak philosophical landscape, where their final sacrifices are all in some way associated with Razumov's act of betrayal and confession, might be identified closely with Conrad himself at the time of writing. If their sacrifices to Razumov's story are read as an extended metaphor for Conrad's sacrifice to his text, a powerful model for interpretation emerges in which these emblematic figures signify the immense anguish and energy of self-destruction that represented Conrad's input into this novel.

As the Polish material has shown, the full significance of Conrad's identification with the women of his early life and reading has so far been unrecognized. By tracing this influence on his presentation of women in the fiction, we perceive a sense of continuity in his career denied by the traditional bifurcation of the canon into early and late works. It has been customary to see Conrad's breakdown, following the completion of *Under Western Eyes* in 1910, as the end of his achievement, but from another point of view his illness freed him to produce the first work in which the woman protagonist dominates the narrative. Conrad's interest in women and the "feminine" in *Under Western Eyes* (particularly his emphasis on the bogus feminism of Peter Ivanovitch), prefigures the central theme of the later novel *Chance* and its narratorial obsession with defining "woman." Like Natalia Haldin, Flora de Barral makes her sacrifices. But it is she, and not the male protagonist, who commands the central role of *Chance*. Having confronted the ghosts of his Polish life and the tragic loss of his mother, Conrad produced the first novel in which a woman finally achieves the status of the mysterious and "unknowable" Conradian hero.

NOTES

1. See Z. Najder, "Introduction," in *Conrad's Polish Background:....;*C. Miłosz, "Joseph Conrad in Polish Eyes;" A. Busza, "Conrad's Polish Literary Background...;" A. Gillon, "Conrad in Poland;" G. Morf, "Apollo Korzeniowski (1820-69);" "Ewa Korzeniowska (1833-65)," in G. Morf, *The Polish Heritage of Joseph Conrad.*

2. See Z. Najder, *Joseph Conrad: A Chronicle,* 6-13; *Conrad's Polish Background:...,* 19.

3. See Z. Najder, *Conrad's Polish Background:...,* 2: "The term cannot be adequately rendered in English because there was no difference in Poland between nobility and gentry."

4. Z. Najder, *Conrad's Polish Background:...,* 19. In Conrad's presentation of *Lord Jim* (1900) we can detect the conflict of romantic idealism and doubt in the heroic ideal.

5. "A Familiar Preface," *PR,* xx.

6. See E. Said, *Joseph Conrad and the Fiction of Autobiography.*

7. "A Familiar Preface," *PR,* xiii.

8. In spite of Conrad's sceptical presentation of religious faith in his later texts, it is interesting to note that he had learned early on to identify himself as a Catholic. His oldest existing autograph, now in the Beinecke Library, Yale University, is inscribed on the back of a photograph: "To my beloved Grandma who helped me to send cakes to my poor Daddy in prison – grandson, Pole, Catholic, nobleman – 6 July 1863 – Konrad."

9. June 20-July 2 in *Conrad under Familial Eyes,* ed. Z. Najder, 51. All references to Ewa Korzeniowska's letters to her husband are from this edition. Date and page numbers given in the notes.

10. June 19-July 1, 1861, 48.

11. June 20-July 2, 1861, 51.

12. June 19-July 1, 1861, 48.

13. June 9-21, 1861, 46.

14. June 20-July 2, 1861, 50; undated, 52.

15. See also Conrad, letter to Mrs. E. L. Sanderson, February 26, 1899, *LLI,* 271. Commenting on his relationship with his young son, Borys (born in 1898), he wrote: "I don't mind owning I wished for a daughter. I can't help thinking she would have resembled me more and would have been perhaps easier to understand."

16. See also Karl, 76. He also suggests that Conrad substituted "daughter" for "son" in this novel: "Conrad creates a dying, broken Almayer, with a daughter, not a son, anxious to survive a breaking away. Conrad may have been writing of Malayans, but his memories are also of Poles, of his father and of his home in those last days."

17. Stanisław Czosnowski, "Conradiana," *Epoka,* 136 (Warszawa, 1929). Reprinted in *Conrad under Familial Eyes,* ed. Z. Najder, 136.

18. See Conrad, letter to Edward Garnett, October 1, 1907, in which he referred to Mrs. Verloc's mother: "She *is* the heroine" (*CL,* III, 487).

19. Conrad referred to three patriotic poems by Adam Mickiewicz, *Pan Tadeusz* (1834), *Konrad Wallenrod* (1828), and *Grażyna* (1823). See also A. Busza, "Conrad's Polish Literary Background...", 171, who cites Roman Dyboski, "Z młodości Józefa Conrada," *Czas* (Kraków, December 1927). Dyboski quotes Jadwiga Kałuska, a friend of the Korzeniowskis in Lwów

in 1867, who remarked that the young Conrad "astonished everyone by reciting whole passages of *Pan Tadeusz* as well as Mickiewicz's ballads from memory."

20. Mickiewicz also owed something to Walter Scott's ambivalent presentation of nationalism.

21. Nearly a hundred years later Eliza Orzeszkowa accused Conrad, in an open letter of April 23, 1899, published in *Kraj,* of betrayal of the homeland by leaving Poland and writing in English.

22. See A. Gillon, *The Eternal Solitary:...,* 92. Like Conrad's Lord Jim, Słowacki's Kordian (*Kordian,* 1834) fails to act at the fundamental moment when confronted with the moral test.

23. See A. Busza, "Conrad's Polish Literary Background...," 216. Busza also suggests the close affiliation of *Victory* (especially the penultimate chapter) with Stefan Żeromski's *Dzieje grzechu* [The history of a sin], 1908. Żeromski was highly influenced by Zola and the French sensationalist school.

24. Conrad may also have been reminded of the Grażyna type from Marguerite Poradowska's *Popes et popadias* (1892), which he read while working on *An Outcast of the Islands* (letter to Poradowska, May 20, 1895, *CL,* I, 221). In her novel Poradowska makes several references to the heroic suicide of the Polish Queen Wanda.

25. See C. Miłosz, *The History of Polish Literature,* 208.

26. See also Hermann's niece in "Falk."

27. See A. Busza, 208. Busza draws attention to the influence of the Polish *gawęda* or literary yarn – a traditional narrative technique – on Conrad's fiction (especially in *Lord Jim, Under Western Eyes,* and *Chance*): "a loose, informal narrative, told by a speaker in the manner of reminiscing. It is often involved and full of digressions. Little attention is paid to chronology. At first, seemingly important details and fragmentary episodes come to the fore, then gradually a coherent picture emerges. By the time the speaker has finished everything has fallen into place."

28. *UWE,* 101, 107, 177, 182, 196, 335, 338-9. See J. Hillis Miller, 6 (and Jakob Lothe for a critique of Miller). Miller makes use of Gilles Deleuze's theories to account for repetitions occurring in Western literature: "Positing a world based on difference...the Nietzschean mode of repetition assumes that each thing is unique, intrinsically different from every other thing...it is a world not of copies but of what Deleuze calls 'simulacra' or 'phantasms'." There is, according to Miller, "something ghostly about the effects of this...kind of repetition." Given the variety and character of the English teacher's use of Mrs. Haldin's pose as a repetitive narrative trope, it presents a strong example of the Nietzschean mode of repetition in Conrad's work. However, Miller only discusses *Lord Jim* in this context.

29. Z. Najder, "Introduction," *PR,* xviii.

30. See Carabine, "From 'Razumov' to *Under Western Eyes*: The Case of Peter Ivanovitch." Carabine provides detailed textual evidence to show how Conrad sacrificed Natalia's role in order to preserve Ivanovitch's credibility as an influence on the women of this novel.

WORKS CITED

Baines Jocelyn. *Joseph Conrad: A Critical Biography*. London: Weidenfeld and Nicolson, 1969.

Busza Andrzej. "Conrad's Polish Literary Background and Some Illustrations of the Influence of Polish Literature on His Work," *Antemurale* 10 (1966), 109-247; Rome-London: Institutum Historicum Polonicum – Societas Polonica Scientiarum et Litterarum in Exteris.

Carabine Keith. "From 'Razumov' to *Under Western Eyes*: The Dwindling of Natalia Haldin's 'Possibilities'," *The Ugo Mursia Memorial Lectures: Papers from the International Conrad Conference, University of Pisa, September 7th-11th 1983*, ed. Mario Curreli. Milano: Mursia International, 1988, 147-71.

Carabine Keith. "From 'Razumov' to *Under Western Eyes*: The Case of Peter Ivanovitch," *Conradiana*, 25 (Spring 1993), 3-29.

Cave Terence. *Recognitions*. Oxford: Clarendon Press, 1988.

Ford Ford Maddox. *Joseph Conrad: A Personal Remembrance* [1924]. New York: Ecco Press, 1989.

Garnett Edward, ed. *Letters from Conrad*. London: Nonesuch Press, 1928.

Gillon Adam. *The Eternal Solitary: A Study of Joseph Conrad*. New York: Bookman Associates, 1960.

Gillon Adam. "Conrad in Poland," *Polish Review* 19:3-4 (1974), 3-28.

Karl Frederick R. *Joseph Conrad: The Three Lives*. New York: Farrar, Straus and Giroux, 1979.

Knowles Owen. *A Conrad Chronology*. London and Basingstoke: Macmillan, 1989.

Krasiński Zygmunt. *The Un-Divine Comedy*, in *Polish Romantic Drama*, ed. and trans. H. B. Segel. Ithaca NY: Cornell U.P., 1977.

Krzyżanowski Julian. *The History of Polish Literature* [1972]. Warsaw: Polish Scientific Publishers, 1978.

Lévi-Strauss Claude. *Structural Anthropology*, vol. 2, trans. M. Layton. Harmondsworth: Penguin, 1978.

Lothe Jakob. "Repetition and Narrative Method: Hardy, Conrad, Faulkner," in *Narrative: From Malory to Motion Pictures*, ed. J. Hawthorn, London: Edward Arnold, 1985.

Mickiewicz Adam. *Forefathers' Eve*, in *Polish Romantic Drama*, ed. and trans. H. B. Segel. Ithaca NY: Cornell U.P., 1977.

Mickiewicz Adam. *Konrad Wallenrod and Other Writings*, trans. G. R. Noyes and others. Berkeley: U. of California P., 1925.

Miller J. Hillis. *Fiction and Repetition: Seven English Novels*. Oxford: Blackwell, 1982.

Miłosz Czesław. "Joseph Conrad in Polish Eyes," *Atlantic Monthly*, 200:5 (1957), 219-28.

Miłosz Czesław. *The History of Polish Literature* (1969). Berkeley: U. of California P., 1983.

Morf Gustav. *The Polish Heritage of Joseph Conrad*. London: Sampson Low, Marston, 1930.

Najder Zdzisław, ed. *Conrad's Polish Background: Letters to and from Polish Friends*. London: Oxford U.P., 1964.

Najder Zdzisław. *Joseph Conrad: A Chronicle*. Cambridge: Cambridge U.P., 1983.

Najder Zdzisław, ed. *Conrad under Familial Eyes,* trans. Halina Carroll. Cambridge: Cambridge U.P., 1983.

Najder Zdzisław. "Introduction," in Joseph Conrad, *A Personal Record*. Oxford: Oxford U.P., 1988.

Said Edward. *Joseph Conrad and the Fiction of Autobiography*. Cambridge MA: Harvard U.P., 1966.

Słowacki Juliusz. *Fantazy,* in *Polish Romantic Drama,* ed. and trans. H. B. Segel. Ithaca NY: Cornell U.P., 1977.

Addison Bross,
Lehigh University,
Bethlehem, USA

The January Rising and Its Aftermath: The Missing Theme in Conrad's Political Consciousness[1]

How Conrad thought and felt about Poland and his Polish heritage has been an enduring question for students of his life and work. Equally significant, however, are the Polish themes that do *not* figure in Conrad's consciousness, the ways in which Conrad did *not* think about his Polishness. Certain concepts and issues that became for many Poles of Conrad's generation vital for understanding the Poland of their era never appear in Conrad's references to his native land. Whether the absence of these matters from his consciousness is an inevitable result of his long absence from Poland, or whether subtler factors were at work, this omission must be seen as a significant trait of Conrad's grasp of things Polish, with consequences for his political thinking and for his imaginative rendering of political struggles in his novels.

For whatever reason, Conrad failed to absorb the historical lessons of the period following the defeated January Rising when his compatriots were debating two irreconcilable interpretations of Polish history – one pragmatic-materialist and the other romantic-idealist. The years within this period that Conrad spent in Galicia (occupied Poland's Austrian sector) after his return at age ten with his father from their Russian exile, saw the rise of the positivists, who urged economic development and conciliation of the occupying powers, and of the Kraków school of historians, who tried to demythologize Polish history. Both movements challenged the traditional, romantic form of Polish patriotism and rejected the conspiracies and armed risings it had long sanctioned. The January 1863 Rising, prepared by his conspirator parents – the event that would determine the conditions of Conrad's life – was one focus of the debate, for it seemed to dramatize the flaws of romantic patriotism.

Apparently the youthful Conrad came up with no definite response either to the specific condemnation of the Rising by various revisionists or to the more general questions the debate introduced about Polish history, the Polish temperament, the national myths, or the revisionists' hope to change Poland's destiny through "organic work." By default Conrad accepted the romantic-idealist position of his father – a less desirable outcome for a novelist who would someday write about the influence of "material interests" in the life of societies.

I believe a lacuna exists in Conrad's understanding of "Poland" that is at least as interesting as those Polish elements and themes that are embraced by his vision of the homeland. Despite the immense importance of the January Rising in Conrad's personal experience, any reference to that great upheaval in Polish life of the late nineteenth century and the subsequent debates of the 1860s and 1870s is almost totally absent from Conrad's fiction, essays, letters, and from records of his conversations. Conrad mentions the Rising only rarely; nothing he has written suggests that he was aware of the controversy that followed it. His reading of a book he admired, *Pamiętnik mojego życia* [Memoirs] of his uncle Tadeusz Bobrowski – given the importance it places on themes central to his debate – was necessarily shallow because of this lacuna.[2]

In Conrad's best-known references to Poland, the January 1863 Rising does not appear. In *A Personal Record* it remains on the periphery, and when his Polishness arises in less formal writings to non-Poles, the Rising yields to more general explanations of his nationality. When troubled, for example, by H. L. Mencken's reference in a review to his alleged "Slavonism," Conrad wrote to a friend to correct the misperception he found in Mencken's remark. In his letter he pointed to the ancient and continuing role of Poland as "an outpost of Westernism." This self-definition had been invoked by Poles for centuries. Oddly, Conrad does not refer to a more recent event focussing a few years after his own birth – the January Rising – in which Poland, the West's savior, had confronted that "Slavo-Tartar Byzantine barbarism" (as he called tsarist Russia) and in which his parents and other family members played heroic roles.[3] The same omission of any reference to the Rising occurs in the "Author's Note" to *Nostromo,* where Conrad recalls a relationship dating obviously from his school years in Kraków – precisely the time when quarrels were raging about the wisdom of the Rising; and Poles were debating the nature of Polish patriotism and the potential good that might come from laying aside armed revolt, conciliating the partitioning powers, and developing Poland economically. In the "Author's Note" Conrad describes a girl, an ardent patriot (the prototype, he calls her, of Antonia Avellanos), who shamed him as an unworthy son of Poland. Though at that time the most recent example of Poles' witness to the sacred cause – the example best known to Conrad and his young friend – was the January Rising, the occasion of his own parents' sacrifice, Conrad fails to mention it.[4]

Conrad's personal links with the January 1863 Rising against tsarist Russia are intimate and numerous. This most tragic effort of the Polish national-liberation movement, crushed by 1864 (but in Conrad's native region wiped out in a single week), was the cause to which his parents dedicated their energies, fortune and health, the calling for which they became national martyrs. Their conspiracy and agitation for the Rising led to their fatal exile with their son to Vologda in northern Russia in 1861, before the Insurrection broke out. Severe conditions there meant early deaths for the parents and orphanhood for their child. During the Korzeniowski family's exile and after Apollo's release with his son to Galicia, Poles in "right-bank" Ukraine west of Kiev – the family's ancient locale – suffered the tsar's vengeance: a program of devastating Russification – severe limitation or cancellation of the few freedoms they still enjoyed under tsardom before the Rising; confiscation of property owned by participants; banning of Poles from most professions; extortion through taxes specifically levied against the Polish nationality (upon participants in the Rising and those who had refused to join it); and tight restrictions on Poles' right to buy land. The process would end in total annihilation – long hoped for by Alexander II – of the Polish culture that since the fifteenth century had flourished in Ukraine. The openly anti-Polish policies that tsarist officials had followed there before the Insurrection were now for the first time – thanks to the Rising – echoed by widespread animosity against Poles on the part of ordinary Russians. At the time of the father and son's release from deportation, given their poor health, this locale would have presented insurmountable hardships. The Rising and its aftermath had made any homecoming impossible. It was this Insurrection, and the ideology of Polish romanticism that had served it, that were under discussion in the press and elsewhere when two Korzeniowskis left exile and arrived in Lwów and later in Kraków.

In *A Personal Record,* it is true, Conrad recalls childhood memories from the years around the Rising, incidents that have as their cause and conditions the January 1863 Rising and the penalty of exile that the young Conrad and his family were paying. Nowhere in that volume, however, does Conrad link these childhood impressions of the Rising with an analytical grasp of the event of the sort that Poles pursued in the debates of the 1860s and 1870s. Conrad does recall here his family's flat in Warsaw, where – he supposes – conspirators met; his forced departure with his ailing mother to their place of exile in northern Russia after a sojourn at her brother Tadeusz's estate in Ukraine; the lonely sorrow Conrad shared with his widowed father; his vigil as a young boy outside his father's sickroom in Kraków; and the crowds in that city's streets at Apollo Korzeniowski's funeral.

But in print and talk, despite its impact on his life and all other lives of his generation, Conrad kept an almost perfect silence about the Insurrection.[5] He never named the January Rising as an important event conditioning his Polishness, nor did he reflect on the parts of himself formed under the pressure of this historical phenomenon, even though in his best fiction, Conrad attempts to trace just such links between the personal and the political in the lives of his characters (e.g., between Decoud's upbringing amid the nihilistic world of cynical emigrés in Paris and his pathetically ambiguous commitment, formed under the influence of Antonia Avellanos, to the Costaguanan cause).

Whatever its cause may have been, the absence of the major intellectual and political issue of Conrad's youth in Galicia from his conceptual framework set him outside the main current of thought of his generation in his home country. It can be described as the greatest intellectual loss resulting from his lifetime exile from Poland. For example, in Zakopane in 1914, the mature emigré novelist Conrad met a Pole whose work he admired (with reservations), Stefan Żeromski, author of an appreciative essay on Conrad. Here were two literary artists who had felt compelled to ponder and represent in fiction the ambiguous role of economic development in a society's struggle for stability, feedom, and justice – i. e., the uncertain effects of "material interests." But the difference between them, resulting from their unequal experiences of the post-1863 era when the value of "material interests" came under debate in Poland, was striking. Through these debates Żeromski had become aware of the delusions of Polish messianic romanticism as a political guide, as well as the strength of its appeal. He knew also the promises and pitfalls of the "organic work" movement then challenging romantic patriotism. Żeromski had thus won a firm grasp, through concrete historical experience personally endured and pondered, of the relative value, in Poland in the 1860s and 1870s, of the human tendencies to idealism and to materialism. His novel *Popioły* (Ashes) – on which Conrad offered varied opinions at different times – has been described as presenting "a modern type of patriot [i. e., non-romantic], a disciplined citizen and soldier, in contrast to the established patriotism of the old style, burdened with the sins of backward, obscurantist landowners."[6]

Conrad, lacking either experience or guidance for analyzing the debates of his youth, and having few other sources for his renderings of idealist-materialist conflicts in societies, produced political fiction in which such issues are blurred. For example, in *Nostromo,* the figure who might have developed a sense for his and his fellow dock-worker's situation is arbitrarily rendered by the author too alienated from his class to grasp what "material interests" are, what miracles they accomplish for the wealthy, and how, unbeknownst to him, these material possessions can be used to drastically alter the conditions of his own life. In fact, the novel conceives of Costaguanan society's flaw as simply "material interests" – as if the problem were the materiality of wealth and not the capacity it affords its owners to control the lives of others.

Conrad's reservations about Żeromski's work[7] seem to have their source in his inadequate understanding of Żeromski's goals as a novelist, goals drawn precisely from these debates of the post-Insurrection era that were still current in Żeromski's and in Conrad's youth.

Again, the Polish novelist Eliza Orzeszkowa in "The Emigration of the Talents" complained that Conrad had developed his talent abroad among Englishmen, where it could never – as Polish writing should, she believed – nourish the hearts of young Poles for the work of building up the Fatherland. Unware of the controversy that had stirred Poland in this era – about the role of literature in society, about writing as a powerful transforming force that must serve a people's needs as readily as any other resource (a theory Orzeszkowa expounded in her "Remarks on the Novel")[8] – Conrad could not grasp the rationale of her complaint or confront her charge with any meaningful response. When his cousin Aniela Zagórska innocently offered him one of Orzeszkowa's books, he could only turn away in rage and disgust. Conrad could experience the movement called positivism in his native land, which had its rise during his residence in Lwów and Kraków, not through any understanding of the debate surrounding it or for the opportunities and dangers it might hold for his nation's future, but only on a personal, emotional level – as enmity toward Orzeszkowa.[9]

The wide-ranging debate that began among the Polish intelligentsia in the middle 1860s had (to describe it briefly) three main concerns: (1) the value of those romantic notions of patriotism which shaped the popular conceptions of the national cause, prompting the recent disastrous Rising; (2) the assignment of blame for Poland's suffering – even for the Partitions – not simply to Poland's greedy invaders, but to certain flaws in Poland's own social and political structure, long in developing, for which Poles themselves were responsible; and (3) the possible advantages to the homeland of rejecting armed revolt as a method, conciliatng the occupiers, and accepting, if only temporarily, subject status as a national minority within the three separate Empires, striving to win, meanwhile those material, economic advances that in the West seemed to be the key to social and political stability.

Both movements – to revise Polish history and to build the economy – rejected traditional Polish political thought, but they were distinct. The new version of Polish history written by the Kraków school of historians was at bottom a critique of the myth formed by romantic historiography of a wholly innocent Poland slain by its neighbors. The group took the name of a skeptical court jester from the Renaissance – Stańczyk – calling themselves the Stańczycy. They entiled their famous pamphlet *Teka Stańczyka* (The Stańczyk Papers). The other movement, the program to create a new Poland by economic and cultural achievements, was called positivism, or "work on the foundations" (*praca u podstaw*), or "organic work" (*praca organiczna*). Its adherents, the *organicznicy* or *pozytywiści,* insisted that societies are like living organisms in the mutual dependence and interrelatedness of their many elements. They claimed therefore that Poland's independence could never be a feasible objective if it were separately pursued; certainly not if it were placed ahead of the basic material needs of the society. They held that the good of a society is achieved by its internal development along economic lines, more than by its relation to other nations as dominant or subservient. Both movements redefined Polishness and included warnings against useless and destructive insurrections. Their difference was that the Stańczycy were rewriting history while the positivists were urging economic advance that would, they believed, improve conditions for all classes – as an end in itself, but also as lessons in cooperation, "civic virtue," and society-building that positivists thought Poles most needed.

In the course of this controversy, issues, terms, and categories emerged that advocates of every contemporary position would accept as crucial to the debate, along with concepts that for decades to come would define the debate about Polish history. This cultural process continued to stir in the press and in informal political discussions, particularly in Warsaw and in the two Galician cities Lwów and Kraków, where Apollo Korzeniowski lived with his son between their release from exile at Chernikhov in January 1868 and the elder Korzeniowski's death in May 1869. It continued well beyond the young Conrad's period of residence with his grandmother as guardian in Kraków and his time at a boarding school in Lwów in 1873. It raged for some two decades after the 16-year-old youth had departed from Kraków for Marseilles and a seaman's career in 1874. The debate was by far the dominant concern among the intelligentsia during Conrad's approximately six-year residence in these two major cities of Galicia.

The public controversy over the January 1863 Rising and over the new critiques should be taken into account when considering any aspect of Conrad's early years. For example, it has been claimed that Conrad's faith in his father, in the Polish cause, and in the January Rising specifically, was destroyed by his uncle Tadeusz Bobrowski's disapproval of all three of these. But given the frequent and open condemnation in the Galician press of all uprisings, Bobrowski's negative judgments of Apollo Korzeniowski's politics were not at all needed for this outcome. If Bobrowski had never uttered a word to Conrad about his father or the Insurrection, the debates raging in all sophisticated circles in Kraków and Lwów in Conrad's youth would have been quite sufficient to shake any young person's belief in the soundness of the insurrectionists' cause and its inevitable victory.[10]

In reading the history of the post-Insurrection period in both Warsaw and Galicia (the Austrian sector of occupied Poland), one is continually confronted with valuable lessons for writing about political quarrels and confusions, lessons which, had Conrad pondered them, might have provided useful hints for handling the theme of "material interests" (e.g., in *Almayer's*

Folly, "Heart of Darkness" or *Nostromo).* For the era saw intense cultural labor by publicists, thinkers, and literary artists, out of which a new, powerful reading of Polish history and Polishness was devised, an interpretation that altered the balance established in Polish thought after the Partitions between ideal and material realities; the relative roles and relative value of imaginative, spiritual phenomena on one hand, and economic and social development on the other. A quarter century earlier, the poet Adam Mickiewicz lectured at the Collège de France on the Slavic literatures. He spoke perhaps as the ultimate Polish idealist when he declared to his audience that the so-called real world (that realm in which one would have to acknowledge that the insurrection of his own generation, 1830, had failed) was after all unreal;[11] furthermore, that no thought should be given to such merely practical questions as the polity by which Poland would be ruled after its deliverance from foreign powers, for if Poland is Christian, any political system will serve its need.[12] Apollo Korzeniowski's writings show that he accepted Mickiewicz's anti-materialist metaphysics and politics. He wrote that Providence had denied to Poles success in embodying their noble ideas in reality, but Muscovites had been fully capable of rendering their thoughts real, because material reality by its nature is far more receptive to evil than to good.[13]

Korzeniowski also violently rejected all forms of industry, which in his eyes could serve nothing but greed. Choosing a Dickens novel to translate, he picked *Hard Times,* probably for its scathing picture of captains of industry Gradgrind and Bounderby.[14] In a letter to the press responding to an unapproving essay on the novelist J. I. Kraszewski, Korzeniowski branded the conservative critic, Michał Grabowski (who was pursuing unsuccessfully the industry of beet-sugar refining) "a reptile of industry." In the same letter he praised Kraszewski for one of his books, *Choroby wieku* [The illnesses of the age], with which "he has striven, as with our Holy Patrons' relics, to exorcise that Jewish cloud, industrialization; with [this book] he holds us back, as behind a sanitary cordon, from that plague that is the piling-up of wealth in total neglect of all things else, a pestilence now spreading among us, killing everything of ours that is honest, God-fearing, and sacred; that plague that upon our very immortality itself exhales a whiff of mortality."[15]

This rejection of industry and of the entire material world was strong in the thought of some planners of the January Rising. It was perhaps through a denial of meaning to immediate physical reality that Poles were able to keep faith in their nation's ultimate revival.

Despite strong resistance from traditional, romantic Poles, between 1863 and the middle 1880s, the January Rising and its roots in the concepts of Polish romanticism – of which Mickiewicz's and Korzeniowski's remarks are examples – were brought under critical scrutiny, and the new, pragmatic faith was expounded. This was a labor performed chiefly by younger intellectuals to criticize their elders' vision, to construct alternatives to it, and to defend their own ideas and programs against charges of betrayal leveled by ardent patriots of the traditional type.

In Galicia the positivist revolt began almost before the Rising was totally quelled. Many of its adherents, as well as of the Stańczycy, had earlier supported the Rising as conspirators or combatants. In 1864, in the Insurrection's last moments, with Conrad and his parents still in Vologda, a young Pole named Ludwik Powidaj was serving time in an Austrian jail for conspiracy. There he wrote an essay lodging a wide range of complaints against the national-liberation tradition, under the title "Polacy i Indianie" [Poles and Indians]. His work, published in two journals at Lwów, immediately and throughout the period evoked strong affirmation from some quarters, but angry counter-critiques of positivism from insurrectionists and conservatives. In the essay Powidaj compared his compatriots, surrounded by predatory neighbors, to American Indians forced to flee before the advance of European settlers in order to preserve their existence as a race. Poles, he claimed, must likewise either accept extinction or adopt equally stringent measures. Particularly they must cease to gamble their dream of independence against possible annihilation in that "lottery" called insurrection. Powidaj identified romantic ideas as the culprit. Like Tadeusz Bobrowski, he deplored the sad state of affairs in the years before the Rising, when older, more experienced citizens had allowed fiery youths to plot the nation's course toward armed conflict with Russia's armies.[16] He blamed his own society for continuing, even after the recent disaster had struck, to scorn useful knowledge – of industry and business – and to feed itself on poems. Powidaj presented his remedy in a formula that made material progress the prerequisite to cultural and spiritual consciousness: "After wealth is accumulated, learning will arise; after learning will come national consciousness; and then political consciousness will start to grow. Above all, we must strive to increase national wealth; then all will be added unto us." [17]

In 1872, two years before Conrad's departure for Marseilles, came the anniversary of the First Partition of Poland. During the observance a conservative lecturer in Lwów insisted that "Poland's native wisdom does not yield place to English Positivism." A positivist columnist in Kraków's journal *Kraj* (for which Apollo Korzeniowski, but for his bad health, would have covered English and Russian events)[19] responded: "Why, then has this wisdom led us into disaster?"[19] In 1876 various ideas from the continuing anti-romantic critique that had fermented in earlier decades were gathered in a powerful article by Franciszek Krupiński, entitled "Romanticism and its Consequences." There Krupiński mocked the arch-romantic Mickiewicz's lines from his popular "Ode to Youth:" "Reach beyond where sight extends; / Break what reason cannot break." Krupiński wrote: "It has taken us half a century [since the November 1830 Rising] to realize that if something proves unbreakable to reason, then youth's emotions can offer no help."[20] Still later, in 1884, the novelist Henryk Sienkiewicz published what became a widely--known fable expounding the virtue of *praca organiczna*. The story was entitled "Legenda żeglarza" [The sailor's legend]. It features a ship, long favored by clear skies and calm seas, whose sailors have grown lax and neglectful of mundane duties. When a storm arises and the vessel is near foundering, they rush for their guns and fire volley after volley at the threatening waves and winds. Having exhausted their shot, they begin beating the ocean with whatever comes to hand. Suddenly an idea arises: their method must change. Some of them relinquish these intrepid attacks on their nonhuman enemy, go below, and start repairing the ship's underside. Readers quickly understood that the vessel is Poland, the heroes firing at the forces of nature are Polish insurrectionists, and the sailors who set about patching the hull are *organicznicy*.

Clearly positivism had its problematic side. Those who advised turning from insurrection to legal, economic development could give no guarantee that "material interests" would serve the whole society and not just a few capitalist entrepreneurs. According to Stefan Kieniewicz, even those *organicznicy* who were most benevolent toward the lower classes knowingly or unknowingly blocked any impulses from below toward active, self-directed development. "Leaders of the bourgeoisie always saw in *praca organiczna* only a tool for securing the dominance of their class. All organic-work enterprises that were inspired with the altruism of their noble initiators awaited defeat or decay from the indifference of the crowd or from the partitioning powers' repressions, or from distraction from their intended goals."[21] Henryk Markiewicz suggests that many positivists found it necessary to alter their doctrines as Poland's industrialization progressed. He identifies the positivist as one "who trusted that with the growth of capitalism, education and democratic freedoms would come a general increase in welfare, morality and happiness; one who later, disappointed in this optimistic view, continued to repeat positivist slogans, with one or another corrective, while categorically rejecting revolution." Those were still positivists "who in the 1880s sounded an alarm against poverty among the common masses, persisting ignorance, and glaring incidents of exploitation and degeneration among the bourgeoisie; who saw and exposed the deepening social antagonisms." They continued to seek "refinements to the development of capitalism."[22]

Kieniewicz notes that the programs of the *organicznicy* in

Galicia, compared with those of their colleagues in the Russian and Prussian sectors, were ineffective. Though Austria granted autonomy to its Polish subjects, this native authority was controlled by landowners who cared little either for industrialization or for educating the masses.[23]

Galicia, specifically Kraków, was the site where Polish history was being rewritten. The conservative attack on the romantic tradition in Poland was powerfully formulated there in the work of Józef Szujski as publicist and historian at Jagiellonian University. He claimed that Poland had succumbed first to dangerous manipulation by foreigners through the freedom of powerful magnates and their client members of the lesser *szlachta,* particularly through the freedom they had taken to wring privileges for their class from monarchs dependent upon them for election as king and hence defenseless before their demands. The nation ultimately succumbed, the contended, to foreign invasion and domination because of such flaws in its state system. Szujski researched the path by which the magnate class in Poland came to domination. Their exclusive power occasioned the underdevelopment of their rival class, the townspeople, and Poland became a nation of landowners on widely-separated estates. Ultimately it was this magnate class that would ratify the annexation of Polish territory by the three eastern powers in the Partitions.

Szujski examined the impulse toward extreme individualism in the history of the Polish polity, especially the egotism of the magnates and the lesser *szlachta* who imitated them. Szujski studied the origins of the rule called *liberum veto,* which permitted a member of the *szlachta* as parliamentary delegate, if displeased by some part of a sessions's legislation, to cancel by his single veto all measures passed in that session. He showed that in the famous Four-Year Parliament of 1788-92, an event proudly cited as proof of Poles' love for freedom, not only patriotic reformers participated. A strong obscurantist faction there opposed reform in the name of "the ancient freedoms" of their class. But Szujski redefined the concept "freedom:" "To be free is to be capable of forming a government." He angered many Poles with his warning that the same individualist, anarchic tendency embodied in *liberum veto* was still present in modern times in the form of *liberum conspiro* (the freedom to conspire). With others of the Stańczycy, Szujski produced a strident, strongly influential counter-interpretation of Poland's past.

Conrad's silence about these great debates of positivism and the new historiography is particularly striking when we recall his close relation with Tadeusz Bobrowski, the maternal uncle who became his guardian, his mentor, and correspondent through all his twenty years at sea. Conrad's tie with the author of the famous *Pamiętnik mojego życia* [Memoirs] is noteworthy because, while Conrad had no grasp of these issues, Bobrowski's strongest beliefs link him to the positivists – for example, his scorn for "ardent patriots" and his insistence that the renewal of Polish society must begin not with an armed rising but with the emancipation of the peasantry (i.e., with land grants to peasants, which he believed would unite the classes of the *szlachta* and peasantry, then mutually hostile, into a homogeneous society of landowners with varying degrees of wealth. In this way, like the positivists, Bobrowski identifies Poland's salvation with a specific plan of economic reform. The most intense of his personal efforts at reform came when he was chosen as delegate to two of the regional committees set up all over the Russian Empire in 1857 to debate the terms of the coming law to abolish serfdom in the Russian Empire.

Bobrowski was quick to see a damaging contradiction in the insurgents' program. His critical description of Apollo Korzeniowski in *Pamiętnik mojego życia* – as self-deluded in his claim to be a democrat, actually hesitant to take land from his own class and grant it to peasants – is by and large the same complaint that contemporary positivists in Galicia were launching against the national-liberation movement generally: it lacked grounding in economic and social realities. The social realities here at issue were not abstractions. After all, advocates of insurrection were (or their families had been) members of the *szlachta,* possessors of the exclusive privilege of ownership and control of farmland. They were naturally reluctant to sacrifice their class advantage, even though this seemed the only method by which peasants might be persuaded to march with their Polish masters against the Russians.

Korzeniowski often wrote as if this dilemma did not exist. His easy reference to "*szlachta* democracy"[24] suggests that this ancient landowning class could remain what it had always been – the sole controller of arable land – and yet at the same time promote "democracy." Korzeniowski and his colleagues among the "Red" faction of insurrectionists often overlooked the incompatibility between the democratic principles they professed and the strong traditions – and economic interests – of their class. Stefan Kieniewicz in his history of the Rising observes that democrats among the insurrectionists, especially those from the Kiev region, planned to restore the Polish state within its old boundaries, embracing in its governmental authority those territories occupied by non-Polish minorities (Ukrainians, etc.), even though nationalist movements had recently sprung up among them. Democratic principles required granting these peoples' self-determination, but the so-called democrats' firm intention, if need be, to "mark the [pre-Partition] boundaries with blood" questioned this plan. Kieniewicz calls this internal conflict "the dilemma of the Kiev democrats."[25] Here Korzeniowski as romantic insurrectionist offers probably the best possible contrast to his brother-in-law Bobrowski as positivist. The difficulty for all *szlachta* democrats lay in accepting the economic losses that the material embodiment of their ideals demanded. In his *Pamiętnik mojego życia* Bobrowski acknowledges his brother-in-law's compassion for the poor, but points precisely to the confusion that apparently clouded Korzeniowski's mind when he began to consider what difficult material changes his "democratic" movement would require of Polish society. While identifying this internal contradiction in Korzeniowski's mind, Bobrowski openly denies that he himself ever had any pretensions to be a democrat.[26]

Bobrowski had strong connections to the positivist movement. He was not a publicist and never joined the fray in the journals; nevertheless, his judgments of persons and events and the social actions he pursued were consistently informed by positivist ideas. He harshly condemns, as they did, the January Rising for its basis in false ideas. He identifies as a new trend of sanity and "civic virtue" the work he and his compatriots had begun on regional Committees for the Peasant Question (established throughout the Empire by Alexander II, to devise the terms of emancipation), and he curses the Rising for interrupting and destroying the movement. Yet he is hopeful that rational *praca organiczna* will begin again among Poles and he describes with gratification the beet-sugar refineries and credit unions that have been established. He sees nothing wrong in cooperating in a reform movement at the Tsar's command; he holds that the occupying powers, knowing their own interests, will approve modernization in the territories they have annexed. He uses in his text the positivist watchword *praca organiczna* and he urges Poles to develop in themselves the trait they have hithero lacked: "civic virtue."

His closest personal tie with the movement was his friendship with the Russified Pole Włodzimierz Spasowicz, an attorney and professor of penal law at Petersburg, associated there with the conciliatory journal *Kraj,* and author of a history of Polish literature published first in Russian in a collection on Slavic literatures. Spasowicz's best remembered work in literary criticism from the period of the debates is a positivist treatment of romantic poet Wincenty Pol. In his opening remarks Spasowicz reveals that for him the prophet-poets were not sacred figures, but subject to pragmatic critique: "In criticism lies our guarantee of intellectual independence; it assures self-direction to a society confronted by the great monarchs of thought, whose rule is extremely longlasting and powerful, often enduring through many generations. Yet their work can be effective not when taken simply on blind faith, but only when submitted at intervals to critical review."[27] Spasowicz also wrote a preface to the *Memoirs* of his friend Tadeusz Bobrowski.

Through both the letters and the *Memoirs* of his uncle, Conrad was exposed to opinions generally similar to the new movements of thought that were challenging the Januarists' notion of patriotism. For example, Bobrowski's frequently cited letter of 28 October 1891, offering Conrad advice for conquering his pessimistic moods, rings with positivist doctrine: Work for the common good must replace mystical brooding. "Everyone may and even ought to contribute [to one's society's development] his hand or head, according to his strength and talents." One should not, however, imagine oneself "the chosen Apostle of the people [as did the poet-mystic Konrad in Mickiewicz's play *Dziady* (*Forefathers' Eve*), for whom Józef Konrad Korzeniowski was named], but rather [think] of himself as a modest tiny ant which by its insignificant toil in fulfilling its modest duty secures the life and existence of the whole nest!"[28]

During his ten-week visit to Bobrowski's estate, Kazimierówka, in Ukraine in 1890, while engaged in writing *Almayer's Folly*,[29] Conrad read most of the *Memoirs* in mansucript. (Their handwritten state did not mean that they were then unfinished, for Bobrowski wanted them published no sooner than five years after his death.)[30] As is widely known, Conrad admired the *Memoirs* sufficiently to take whole passages from Bobrowski and set them, translated, into *A Personal Record.*

The strange lacuna that I am describing here in Conrad's awareness of things Polish shows up perhaps most surprisingly in his remarks on Bobrowski's *Memoirs*. The many passages in Bobrowski's text that exemplify the new direction of Polish thought and undermine traditional patriotism seem to have passed lightly through Conrad's mind, arousing no sense of their actual import. For Bobrowski's thinking totally inverts the basic assumptions of the insurrectionists. Though he does not downplay the necessity of emotional commitment for effective reform, Bobrowski implies that pragmatic measures, not spiritual force, is to relieve the plight of the Fatherland. Bobrowski rejects the opposition of a diabolic Russia and a sainted Poland. He claims that Poles, not Russians alone, have exploited the peasants, who, despite the wishful thinking of their landlords, are quite hostile toward the Polish *szlachta*. He mercilessly mocks the conspirators' faith – cherished by Korzeniowski – that their serfs will support the Rising. His conception of peasant relations obviously implies that the blame for the Poles' plight lies partly at their own door.

Finding the *Memoirs* of his uncle pervaded by distinctly positivist notions, Conrad should have been profoundly disturbed, given his own quite different conception of Polish history and given the nearly total absence from his consciousness of certain of its issues. Crucial here are Conrad's characteristic responses, emerging strongly in his fiction, his essays and letters to political and economic matters, especially to any Polish themes that bear upon the debates about *praca organiczna*. Whenever Conrad's thoughts moved in this direction, one of his responses would be to fall back into romantic-insurrectionist patriotism, into its unswerving loyalty to an idealized Fatherland. Or he would translate the whole realm of politics into metaphysics: when he begins discussing socialism with Cunninghame-Graham, for example, suddenly he is writing not about whether workers might someday control their own destinies by controlling the conditions and the results of their labor, but whether the entire structure and processes of human existence, conceived as a great knitting-machine, may be changed so that it will embroider, instead of knitting.[31] Or again, he would confess deep fear and mistrust of "material interests" – not, be it noted, fear of capital wealth that is used by its owners to control the powerless, but of material resources simply because they are material.

Somehow Conrad was not disturbed by the problems that Bobrowski's *Memoirs* pose for the traditional patriot. For example, when Bobrowski looked at the relations of his class with the peasantry, he found his own people guilty of an "ancient wrong." He considered the future health of his society to depend on a solution to the peasant question, which to him seemed to lie in a set of new economic relations to be devised pragmatically in terms of yield of land by hectare, of sums to be paid landowners in return for farmland ceded to peasants, etc. It would lie in compromise between the *szlachta*'s right to its property, and the emancipated peasants' need for land, i.e., for some of the *szlachta*'s property. But when we turn from Bobrowski's pages to the "Author's Note" to *A Personal Record,* Conrad's unproblematic vision of the relation between classes in his homeland is striking: "The mental and moral atmosphere" of his native region was marked, he writes, by "a special regard for the rights of the unprivileged of this earth."[32]

Bobrowski and the publicists engaged in debate between 1863 and 1890 encountered thorny problems not only with the January 1863 Rising and the peasant question, but also with the linkage of these two that had come about by the vagaries of Polish history. For although the ultimate goal of the insurrectionists was to free Poland from foreign rule, their political program for a successful insurrection was grants of land and freedom to the serfs – their emancipation. Although committed to this goal, the *szlachta* was often hesitant to adopt this prescribed method, so that at times the meaning of the Insurrection seemed to embrace political and economic change, but at other times it appeared to be merely an attempt to restore Poland's independence. In Galicia at the time of Conrad's sojourn, 1868-74, the peasant question was still alive, and its relation to Poles' political goals under Austrian rule was an issue debated among positivists and insurrectionists.

For Conrad at the time he wrote the "Author's Note" to *A Personal Record,* the question whether the 1863 Rising meant political and economic change, or whether it was a movement only to restore Polish statehood, was not problematic at all. He settles the question unequivocally: "The Polish Risings of 1830 and 1863" were not revolutions but "revolts against foreign domination." What Conrad leaves out is the tangled connections between the cause of national liberation and the plan to change land ownership in Poland. Conrad insists that his father did not work "for the subversion of any social or political scheme of existence" (*PR,* xiv). But certainly when the system of serf-labor on manor farms was at last ended (not by the Polish insurrectionists, but by tsarist ukase), an ancient social scheme had been destroyed.

Conrad's hasty denial of any revolutionary element in the

Januarists' program is a shocking oversimplification of Polish history. Even Bobrowski, with his scorn for the Insurrection, claimed it produced a single positive effect: in the struggle Alexander II was forced to vie with the insurgents for the peasants' favor, and hence to promise peasants a more advantageous agrarian reform than was granted anywhere else in the Empire. This means that though Conrad claimed that his father as Januarist did not plan "the subversion of any social or political scheme of existence," the Rising prepared by Korzeniowski's agitation in Warsaw (1860-61) did in fact radically alter the system of land ownership in right-bank Ukraine. Conrad's downplaying of the Insurrection's revolutionary side is of a piece with his failure to come to terms with the debates pursued in Galicia during his residence there, for these arguments about the relation of the agrarian question to the liberation struggle and their importance for Poland's ultimate destiny lay precisely at the center of the 1863 Rising.

Conrad's mistaken account of the Insurrection is all the more interesting, given his plan (announced in a letter to his agent) to treat in *A Personal Record* exactly this complex historical issue – "to touch in a personal way upon such events...as the liberation of the serfs." He admits this is "a big enterprise;" yet "I feel equal to the work" because of "the intimate nature of the task [!] and of the 2 vols [sic] of my uncle's *Memoirs* which I have by me, to refresh my recollections and settle my ideas."[33] But it is hard to believe that the *Memoirs* could have settled Conrad's ideas. They are instead full of a kind of analysis that would have left in shambles his simplistic account of his homeland in his own early years, in which "a special regard for the rights of the unprivileged of this earth" supposedly prevailed.

Despite Conrad's admiration for his uncle and for his uncle's book, Conrad's vision of his homeland and its plight was wholly incompatible with the one presented in the *Memoirs*. Though Conrad mined the *Memoirs* for material for *A Personal Record,* he seems never to have recognized this discrepancy.

In the story "Prince Roman," drafted during Conrad's work on *A Personal Record,*[34] the uncle's and the nephew's opposing visions of a prominent personage of their era are just as far apart as the two writers' portrayals of the 1863 Rising. Again, Conrad oversimplifies history, but what is oversimplified is the basic subject ot the insurrectionist-positivist conflict. The historical person, Prince Roman Sanguszko, was the scion of a magnate family in Ukraine. He joined the 1830 Rising, was sentenced to Siberia and then to military service in the Caucasus, where he attained officer rank. While serving in the war office in Moscow, he lost his hearing in an accident and ultimately was permitted to return to his native region but forbidden from owning land. Settled as manager of an estate belonging to his married daughter, Sanguszko became as fervent an advocate of *praca organiczna* as he had once been of insurrection. He experimented in beet-sugar refining and built a textile mill and an iron foundry. In each of two eras spanned by his long career, he followed wholly different ideals of patriotism, as Novembrist, then positivist. Conrad's story distorts the 1830 Rising, suggesting warm and respectful relations between landowners and peasants. The Rising becomes here a democratic movement originating with the common people. More significantly, Conrad truncates the prince's career to eliminate his positivist phase, robbing him of the uncommon status he held as an embodiment of the two great, distinct movements that dominated the nineteenth century in Poland. Conrad concentrates almost entirely on the Prince's valor and his endurance in Siberia and the Caucasus. Conrad's prince is a romantic insurrectionist, exiled by tsarist authorities, as were Conrad and his parents, for attempting to liberate his country. Roman Sanguszko holds this place in Poland's history, but he played just as significant a role in the positivist Poland of the 1863 era.

In real life the prince spent time during his exile striving to grasp intellectually the challenging age of mechanical marvels in which he was living. He wrote his parents: "Doesn't today's construction of canals, of railroads, of great mechanical undertakings surpass a thousand times those works accomplished in antiquity, once so much admired, that today seem so trivial? My whole desire is not to fall too far behind my epoch. I can take no

active role in it, nor do I wish one, but I want at least to
understand it."[35] Prince Roman considered his role in the
founding of various industries as "a kind of civic calling, which
he satisfied often at the expense of his own business" (80). On
other occasions the positivist-romantic conflict prompted silence from Conrad; in this story Conrad has responded to the
prince's positivism simply by excising it from his life story.

Józef Ujejski implied that an anachronistic tendency was
apparent in Conrad's treatment of things Polish. Reading
Conrad's treatment of Poland's past in "Autocracy and War,"
Ujejski found it easy "to succumb to the delusion that we are
reading the prose of a Polish emigré of the Romantic period in
English translation....[This version of Poland presents] precisely
the same apotheosis that we know so well from the works of the
'prophet-poets' [from the Great Emigration following the
November Rising]."[36]

At no time in his life did Conrad bring under conscious
examination the subjects debated in his youth in Galicia. This
gap in his conceptual world was never filled, and in all of his
representations of Poland, he would flee the complex questions
about material and ideal realities, and their roles in human
political strategies, that lay at the center of certain disturbing and
crucial quarrels, conflicts in which his countrymen, on the eve of
Konrad Korzeniowski's second departure from his homeland,
were seeking to resolve its destiny.

NOTES

1. For aid from two agencies beyond my base at Lehigh University as
well as from campus sources, which made possible the research for this
essay, I am grateful – to the National Endowment for the Humanities for
a research award from their Translations Division in 1991-92; also, for
funds to visit libraries in Warszawa, Wrocław, and Kraków in the summer
of 1994, to the International Research and Exchanges Board, to Lehigh
University's Henry Gipson Institute, and to the Dean of Lehigh's College
of Arts and Sciences. To the family of Władysława and Jerzy Oczkowicz of
Wrocław I am especially grateful for their warm hospitality, as well as for

help in gaining access to library materials. Of course it is not implied that any of these persons or agencies espouses the views presented in this essay.

2. Conrad's most pointed remarks on the January Rising appear in the "Author's Note" to *A Personal Record*. Here he puzzlingly describes the Rising as strictly a revolt against foreign domination, lacking any revolutionary element. But all serious historians from Conrad's time to our own have acknowledged that the Rising, as envisioned by many of its promoters – including Korzeniowski – meant not only restoring Poland's independence, but dismantling its system of land ownership and hence its class system by enabling peasants to posses farmland. Conrad, however, wholly overlooks this essential aspect of the Rising. He insists that by policy and temperament, Apollo Korzeniowski was incapable of giving his life for a movement that would have overturned one social order and set up another. Hence, he implies, that the cause for which his father was a chief conspirator must not have been revolutionary. *A Personal Record* (London & Toronto: J. M. Dent and Sons, 1919), xiv.

3. Letter to George T. Keating, 14 December 1922, in *Joseph Conrad: Life and Letters,* ed. G. Jean-Aubry, vol. II (Garden City, NY: Doubleday, Page, 1927), 289.

4. "Author's Note," *N,* xx-xxi.

5. Ford Madox Ford cites a rare mention of the Rising. Conrad told him, he says, that on the journey to Vologda with other exiles, the male prisoners – including Conrad's father – were separated at some road-station from their wives, fed on red herrings and given no water. According to Ford, Conrad described his father as "less effectual" than his mother. Conrad, Ford claims, "deprecated" his father's role as "the prime mover of an abortive revolution." "[I]t really pained him....[But] when he spoke of his mother as revolutionary he was full of enthusiasm." F. M. Ford, *Joseph Conrad: A Personal Remembrance* (Boston: Little, Brown, 1924), 75-7.

6. Zbigniew Żabicki, "Stefan Żeromski," *Mały słownik pisarzy polskich,* część I [A short dictionary of Polish writers, 3rd edition] (Warszawa: Wiedza Powszechna, 1972), 243.

7. Letter to Edward Garnett, 2 September 1921, in *Letters from Joseph Conrad 1895-1924,* ed. Edward Garnett (Indianapolis: Bobbs-Merrill, 1928), 280-1.

8. "Kilka uwag nad powieścią," *Gazeta Polska,* 285-8 (1866).

9. Aniela Zagórska, "A Few Reminiscences of Conrad," in *Conrad under Familial Eyes,* ed. Zdzisław Najder, trans. Halina Carroll-Najder, (London: Cambridge U.P., 1983), 214 (originally published as "Kilka wspomnień o Conradzie," *Wiadomości Literackie* [Literary news], 51 [1929]).

10. Zdzisław Najder has blamed a psychological malaise in Conrad upon Bobrowski's allegedly distorted and negative account of Korzeniowski's character and political views, and on the young man's painful

discovery of his two mentors' ideological conflict. This malaise supposedly became "the curse of Conrad's inner life and the bitter inspiration of his art: his deep scepticism, frequently tinged with pessimism," *Conrad's Polish Background: Letters to and from Polish Friends,* ed. Zdzisław Najder (London: Oxford U.P., 1964), 19.

11. *Literatura słowiańska wykładana w Kolegium Francuzkiem przez Adama Mickiewicza...rok trzeci, 1842-1843* [Slavic literature: lectures presented at the College de France by Adam Mickiewicz...year three, 1842-1843] (Poznań: Księgarnia Jana Konstantego Żupańskiego, 1865), 71.

12. Wiktor Weintraub, "Adam Mickiewicz, the Mystic-Politician," *Harvard Slavic Studies,* I (Cambridge: Harvard U.P., 1953), 147.

13. "Polska i Moskwa: pamiętnik***, zaczęty 186-" [Poland and Muscovy: a memoir by***, begun in 186-], *Ojczyzna* [Fatherland], 28 (4 June 1864), 1.

14. The translation originally appeared in *Gazeta Polska,* 1866-7.

15. "Korrespondencya," *Gazeta Warszawska,* 23 (1857), 4.

16. Cited in Halina Kozłowska-Sabatowska, *Ideologia pozytywizmu galicyjskiego 1864-1881* [The ideology of positivism in Galicia, 1864-1881] (Wrocław: Zakład Narodowy imienia Ossolińskich, 1978), 92. Powidaj's article appeared in an abridged version in *Dziennik Literacki* [Literary daily], 53, 56 (1864). The full text is in *Gazeta Narodowa* [National gazette], 285, 293 (14, 23 December) (1864) (Kozłowska-Sabatowska, 92). Cf. Tadeusz Bobrowski, *Pamiętnik mojego życia* [A memoir of my life], vol. II, ed. Stefan Kieniewicz (Warszawa: Państwowy Instytut Wydawniczy, 1979), 443-4.

17. Kozłowska-Sabatowska, 92.

18. Zdzisław Najder, *Joseph Conrad. A Chronicle* (New Brunswick: Rutgers University Press, 1984), 26. The possibility of Korzeniowski working on the staff of *Kraj* is surprising, given the journal's positivist stance and Korzeniowski's fervent, traditional idealist viewpoint.

19. Kazimierz Chłędowski, "Kronika Lwowska" [Lwów Chronicle], *Kraj,* 111 (1872); cited in Kozłowska-Sabatowska, *Ideologia pozytywizmu galicyjskiego 1864-1881,* 127. Karol Kosek has concluded that the Korzeniowskis, father and son, were quite current with the Galician press, for which the father was then writing. "Nieznane listy Apolla Korzeniowskiego do Władysława Łozińskiego i kontakty obydwu Korzeniowskich w Galicji w latach 1868-1874" [Unknown letters of Apollo Korzeniowski to Władysław Łoziński, and the contacts of both Korzeniowskis in Galicia, 1868-1874], *Rocznik Przemyski,* 24-25 (1986), 509-14.

20. *Ateneum,* 4 (1876); reprinted in *Programy i dyskusje literackie okresu pozytywizmu,* [Literary programs and debates of the positivist period], ed. Janina Kulczycka-Saloni (Wrocław: Zakład Narodowy imienia Ossolińskich, Biblioteka Narodowa, Seria I, 249, [1985]).

21. Stefan Kieniewicz, *Dramat trzeźwych entuzjastów: o ludziach pracy organicznej* [The drama of the sober enthusiasts: the proponents of organic work] (Warszawa: Wiedza Powszechna, 1964), 210.

22. "Pozytywizm a realizm krytyczny" [Positivism and critical realism], in *Tradycje i rewizje* [Traditions and revisions], (Kraków: 1957), 162, cited in Tadeusz Bujnicki, *Pozytywizm*, 3rd edition (Warszawa: Wydawnictwo Szkolne i Pedagogiczne, 1994), 34.

23. *Historia Polski 1795-1918* (Warszawa: Państwowe Wydawnictwo Naukowe, 1987), 327.

24. As editor of a new journal, *Dwutygodnik* [Fortnightly], Korzeniowski used the phrase to define for a potential contributor the spirit he wanted the journal to convey (Zdzisław Najder, *Joseph Conrad. A Chronicle*, 15).

25. *Powstanie Styczniowe* [The January Rising] (Warszawa: Państwowe Wydawnictwo Naukowe, 1983), 42.

26. *Pamiętnik mojego życia*, I, 427. Korzeniowski's most surprising blindness to the conflict emerges in his narrative of a disturbance near Kiev in 1855. Incredibly, he claims that a mass of Ukrainian peasants – serfs who had long wanted farmland of their own – had relinquished this demand and made a compact with their Polish landlords by which they would perform their usually hated labor duties gladly without supervision of a bailiff; also, that these Ukrainian peasants requested that their Polish lords lead them in an attack on the tsarist armies. What Korzeniowski presents as a faithful report is the wishful thinking of a member of the Polish *szlachta*. His vision of peasant relations dispels the *szlachta*'s two paramount fears – that peasants will more aggressively demand land of their own, and that they will not ally with the *szlachta* against the tsar (Korzeniowski, "Polska i Moskwa:...," *Ojczyzna*, 51, 1 July [1864], 1). The part of "Polska i Moskwa:..." containing Korzeniowski's report is not among the parts of the treatise translated in *Conrad under Familial Eyes*, ed. Zdzisław Najder, 75-88. See Addison Bross, "Apollo Korzeniowski's Mythic Vision: 'Poland and Muscovy,' A Note," forthcoming in *The Conradian*. Noting the positivist slant to Bobrowski's account of Korzeniowski, it is interesting that certain Polish critics have recognized the positivist element that pervades Bobrowski's worldview. Stefan Zabierowski identifies this trend as beginning with Róża Jabłkowska's discussion of Bobrowski's letters to Conrad (1956) and lists other "positivist" scholars on Bobrowski – Maria Danilewiczowa and Stanisław Helsztyński: *Conrad w Polsce: Wybrane problemy recepcji krytycznej w latach 1896-1969* [Conrad in Poland: Selected problems concerning his critical reception, 1896-1969] (Gdańsk: Wydawnictwo Morskie, 1971), 35-8.

27. *Ateneum*, 2 (1878), 104-40; partially reprinted in *Programy i dyskusje literackie okresu pozytywizmu*, ed. Janina Kulczycka-Saloni, 196.

28. *Conrad's Polish Background:...*, ed. Zdzisław Najder, 154.

29. Owen Knowles, *A Conrad Chronology* (Boston: G. K. Hall, 1990), 14.

30. A letter from Marguerite Poradowska attests to Conrad's reading, at least in part, of Bobrowski's manuscript of the *Memoirs* during his visit in Ukraine. Her letter was to request that copies of the published *Memoirs* be sent to Conrad. Her addressee was Józef Korzeniowski, librarian at Czartoryski Library, Kraków. Professor J. H. Stape kindly called my attention to this letter and provided me with a photocopy of it. On 14 February 1901 Conrad acknowledged receipt of the published *Memoirs*. *CL*, I, 322.

31. *CL*, I, 425.

32. *PR*, xiii.

33. *CL*, IV, 138.

34. The first four chapters of *A Personal Record* included a draft of this story (Knowles, 73).

35. Quoted in Janusz Poray-Biernacki, *Z przekonania: Roman Sanguszko w oczach Conrada i historii* [From conviction: Roman Sanguszko as seen by Conrad and by history] (London: PCA Publications, 1979), 72, 80.

36. Józef Ujejski, *O Konradzie Korzeniowskim* [On Konrad Korzeniowski] (Warszawa: Dom Książki Polskiej, 1936), 55.

WORKS CITED

Bobrowski Tadeusz. *Pamiętnik mojego życia*, ed. Stefan Kieniewicz, 2 vols. Warszawa: Państwowy Instytut Wydawniczy, 1979.

Bujnicki Tadeusz. *Pozytywizm,* 3rd ed. Warszawa: Wydawnictwo Szkolne i Pedagogiczne, 1994.

Ford Ford Maddox. *Joseph Conrad: A Personal Remembrance*. Boston: Little, Brown, 1924.

Garnett Edward, ed. *Letters from Joseph Conrad 1895-1924*. Indianapolis: Bobbs-Merrill, 1928.

Jean-Aubry Georges. *Joseph Conrad: Life and Letters,* 2 vols. Garden City: Doubleday, 1927.

Kieniewicz Stefan. *Dramat trzeźwych entuzjastów: o ludziach pracy organicznej*. Warszawa: Wiedza Powszechna, 1964.

Kieniewicz Stefan. *Historia Polski 1795-1918*. Warszawa: Państwowe Wydawnictwo Naukowe, 1987.

Kieniewicz Stefan. *Powstanie Styczniowe*. Warszawa: Państwowe Wydawnictwo Naukowe, 1983.

Knowles Owen. *A Conrad Chronology*. Boston: G. K. Hall, 1990.

[Korzeniowski Apollo] "Polska i Moskwa: pamiętnik***, zaczęty 186-," *Ojczyzna*, 27-29, 31, 34-36, 42-52 (1864).

Korzeniowski Apollo. "Korrespondencya." *Gazeta Warszawska* 23, (1857).

Kosek Karol. "Nieznane listy Apolla Korzeniowskiego do Władysława Łozińskiego i kontakty obydwu Korzeniowskich w Galicji w latach 1868-1874," *Rocznik Przemyski*, 24-25 (1986).

Kozłowska-Sabatowska Halina. *Ideologia pozytywizmu galicyjskiego 1864--1881*. Wrocław: Zakład Narodowy imienia Ossolińskich, 1978.

Kulczycka-Saloni Janina, ed. *Programy i dyskusje literackie okresu pozytywizmu*. Wrocław: Zakład Narodowy imienia Ossolińskich, 1985; Biblioteka Narodowa, Seria I, 249.

Mickiewicz Adam. *Literatura słowiańska wykładana w Kolegium Francuzkiem przez Adama Mickiewicza...rok trzeci, 1842-1843*. Poznań: Księgarnia Jana Konstantego Żupańskiego, 1865.

Najder Zdzisław, ed. *Conrad's Polish Background: Letters to and from Polish Friends*. London: Oxford U.P., 1964.

Najder Zdzisław, ed. *Conrad under Familial Eyes,* trans. Halina Carroll--Najder. London: Cambridge U.P., 1983.

Najder Zdzisław. *Joseph Conrad. A Chronicle*. New Brunswick: Rutgers U.P., 1984.

Orzeszkowa Eliza. "Kilka uwag nad powieścią," *Gazeta Polska*, 285-288, (1866).

Poray-Biernacki Janusz. *Z przekonania: Roman Sanguszko w oczach Conrada i historii*. London: PCA Publications, 1979.

Ujejski Józef. *O Konradzie Korzeniowskim*. Warszawa: Dom Książki Polskiej, 1936.

Weintraub Wiktor. "Adam Mickiewicz, the Mystic-Politician," *Harvard Slavic Studies*, I, Cambridge: Harvard U.P., 1953.

Zabierowski Stefan. *Conrad w Polsce: Wybrane problemy recepcji krytycznej w latach 1898-1969*. Gdańsk: Wydawnictwo Morskie, 1971.

Zagórska Aniela. "A Few Reminiscences of Conrad," in *Conrad under Familial Eyes,* ed. Zdzisław Najder, trans. Halina Carroll-Najder. London: Cambridge U.P., 1983, 210-23. Originally published as "Kilka wspomnień o Conradzie," *Wiadomości Literackie,* 51 (1929).

Żabicki Zbigniew. "Stefan Żeromski," in *Mały słownik pisarzy polskich,* 3rd ed. Warszawa: Wiedza Powszechna, 1972.

Keith Carabine,
University of Kent,
Canterbury, England

"Irreconcilable Antagonisms:" Reflections on Conrad, Poland, and the English Political Novel

I

The relation between Conrad's Polish heritage and his work has sponsored a variety of conflicting approaches and interpretations. Gustav Morf and Bernard Meyer take a psychoanalytic approach and accept Conrad's conviction that "a novelist lives in his work."[1] Thus Morf searches for the "figure behind the veil" in Conrad's guilt over his betrayal of Poland, when he left her shores and became an English novelist, and detects ramifications of these obsessive concerns in every cranny of Conrad's work.[2] Bernard C. Meyer canvasses "the phenomena of mental conflict, unconscious intention, or the psychological kinship between art, fantasy, and the dream" (Meyer, 6) in order to show that Conrad's "variegated cast" of characters "were virtually all cast from the same mould – a mould that was assuredly the writer himself" (280). Robert F. Hodges and Peter Stine both begin with the notorious divisions in Conrad's Polish heritage and reach opposite conclusions. Apollo Korzeniowski, Conrad's father is for Hodges the source of all the presuming, defeated heroes in Conrad's fiction who seek to reform or redeem their worlds, such as Kurtz, Jim, and Haldin; whereas Stine believes that a single crime "energizes all of Conrad's fiction," namely "his sense in exile, of having betrayed the revolutionary ideals that martyred his parents and earned his life-long respect" (Stine, 95). Conrad's great Polish biographer, Zdzisław Najder, however, is convinced that we can understand the relationship of Conrad to his Polish background neither in his personal reactions to it nor in his unconscious, but through a study of his culture, which reveals, for example, that the themes of guilt and betrayal that so preoccupy his critics are a common-place in Polish literature and history. Because Najder is a convinced logical positivist he is disinclined to relate Polish culture to Conrad's work other than in suggestive, general terms.[3] As I hope to show, however, it is possible to demonstrate that Conrad's Polish heritage informs his sense of the writer's task, of his fictional aesthetic, and consequently, of the presentation of his narratives – all of which help explain why his work is so different from that of English novelists.

At the risk of oversimplification, the four most significant aspects of Conrad's Polish heritage are that: 1) he was from birth simultaneously a subject of the vast, oppressive Russian empire and a member of the *szlachta* who had constituted the hereditary ruling class of Poland since feudal times, and who had cherished and fought to defend the lost freedoms of the Old Polish Commonwealth after the three partitions in the last third of the eighteenth century; 2) the Russian Ukraine of Conrad's birth was multiethnic, multireligious, and multilingual; 3) his own "closest parentage suffered," like Razumov's in *Under Western Eyes* (1911), from the throes of "internal dissensions" (*UWE*, 11); 4) the two most significant decisions of his life – his departure from Poland to go to sea and his subsequent career as an English novelist – replayed on a personal level the great public themes of Polish literature and history, namely "duty abandoned, of betrayal, and above all – desertion" (Najder, "Conrad and the Idea of Honor," 104).

Before the partitions, Ukraine had been part of the loose federation of the Old Polish Commonwealth. When Conrad was born in 1857 Ukraine for over two generations had been annexed and occupied by Russia. After the abortive Polish Risings of 1830 and 1863, which led to the banishment of the insurgents and the wholesale confiscations of their lands, severe political and cultural repression occurred. Conrad's historical knowledge and youthful experience of the horrors of a lawless tsarist imperialism was supplemented and confirmed by his subsequent exposure as a mariner in the British merchant service to English and Dutch modes of imperialism. Moreover, in the Belgian

Congo, to which he went both as an adventurer hoping to make his fortune and to fulfil childhood dreams of visiting the "very heart of Africa," Conrad witnessed the disintegration of a western imperialism based on the Christian mission into "the vilest scramble for loot that ever disfigured the history of human conscience and geographical exploration" ("Geography and Some Explorers," *LE*, 17).

The population of the province of Podolia when Conrad was born consisted of a tiny but powerful Russian (orthodox Christian) bureaucracy and standing army; Polish (Roman Catholic) landowners and landlords; German (Protestant) colonists; a vast underclass of Ukrainian (Uniate Christian) serfs, and in the town of Berdichev, a large Jewish population. Crucially, as Paul Hostowiec has noted, "each of these groups had their own truth, separated from others by religion, customs, tradition, profession," and of course by language (Berka, 10). The Polish romantic nationalists such as Korzeniowski presumed to speak for all these groups when they appealed to the liberal traditions and lost freedoms of the Jagiellonian period. Their failure to realize that they were divided from their serfs by race, class, religion, culture, and language was a major factor in the failure of both Risings in 1830 and 1863. Conrad mordantly acknowledges these divisions in Chapter Three of *A Personal Record* (1912), when "less than forty-eight hours after the beginning of the rebellion" of 1863 in Podolia (*PR*, 57), a "bucolic mob" (62) of local Ukrainian serfs for whose freedoms the Polish romantic nationalists claimed to be fighting united with the Cossacks to sack the manor house of Conrad's grand-uncle Mr. Nicholas B.

Born into a region repressed by the Russians and characterized by groups who "were not linked by common institutions nor by recognition of common laws and interests," it was Conrad's peculiar fate to experience as a youth two opposed ideologies within his own family on how to live as a Pole within the repressive Russian empire (Berka, 10). Conrad's ancestors on his father's side were committed insurrectionists. "My paternal grandfather," Conrad wryly notes in *A Personal*

Record, was "of that type of Polish squire whose only ideal of patriotic action was to get into the saddle and drive them out" (*PR,* 57). His father Apollo Korzeniowski was an ardent messianist and fighter for "the great and godly cause of Poland" and was one of the leading spirits behind the 1863 Rising (Najder, *Conrad under Familial Eyes,* 88).[4] Korzeniowski was a member of the radical "Reds" party. When it split over the moral issue of terrorism as a political weapon against individual members of the State, he sided with Chmielenski who advocated random terrorism" (Davies, II, 351). Apollo trained Conrad during their exile in northern Russia to "Be a Pole!:" (32)[5] that is to define himself in permanent opposition to Muscovite oppression; to resist the enemy within, namely the bourgeoisie and the conciliators among the *szlachta,* who placed money and comfort before love of their country; and to affirm a democratic faith in the spiritual purity and insurrectionary potential of the peasantry.

In marked contrast the orphaned Conrad's maternal uncle and guardian Tadeusz Bobrowski was a conciliator who scorned both the impractical political aims and the inflammable temperament of his insurrectionist kin. He was a positivist who believed in the need to develop the material resources of Ukraine; and he sought "the attainment of a fairly tolerable modus vivendi" with the loathed and feared Russian autocracy "that would find its expression in a complete autonomy of the (Polish) kingdom, a recognition of our basic needs and, in time, an acknowledgement of certain national rights" to the territories of the Old Polish Commonwealth (Davies, II, 36). Andrzej Busza after a careful survey rightly concludes that these clashing sincere loyalties which Conrad inherited and internalized "were representative of the political possibilities and modes of action open to the nation as a whole and gave him a great start as a writer" (Davies, II, 36).[6]

Conrad's feelings of guilt and betrayal inform his famous self-ascription "homo duplex." Though "both at sea and on land my point of view is English," he trusted his Polish correspondent would understand that the phrase had in Conrad's case more than one meaning (*CL,* III, 89), not least that the true Poland survives in his heart and mind. Conrad, therefore, could sincerely affirm that he never separated himself from his country. Hence, also, his tormented recognition that whatever he achieved as an English novelist, because he had declined his Polish "palm of martyrdom" he was fated to lead "a double life one of them peopled by shadows" (491).[7]

The four factors I have outlined, together with his twenty-year career in the British Merchant Service, during which he shared the lives of working class British and foreign seamen and encountered a great variety of cultures, truths, faiths, languages (including Dutch, Malay, African, Indonesian and Chinese) and a range of imperialisms, constitutes the richest and most extraordinary life of any major English novelist.

II

Given the loathing of Russia by Conrad's nation, and given his multiethnic, multilingual background and his experience of a variety of competing cultures, truths and faiths, it is hardly surprising that from the moment Conrad began his first novel *Almayer's Folly* (1895) with Mrs. Almayer's disconcerting Malayan screech "Kaspar! Makan!" (*AF,* 3) – which startled Almayer, a Dutch trader, from his dreams of a "splendid future" in Amsterdam – the central informing idea of his fiction should be "the essential difference of the races" (*CL,* II, 402): with, we might add, its attendant offspring; the clash and interaction between the various races' histories, cultures, values, faiths, and languages, and their existence in and effects upon the (often) divided minds and lives of his characters.

Conrad's most succinct and compelling definition of the role of the artist and the fate of mankind is to be found in his great letter of August 2, 1901, to *The New York Times,* which was written shortly after he composed "Amy Foster" – a pure illustration of his key idea:

> Fiction at the point of development at which it has arrived, demands from the writer a spirit of scrupulous abnegation. The only legitimate

> basis of creative work lies in the courageous recognition of all the
> irreconcilable antagonisms that make our lives so enigmatic, so
> burdensome, so fascinating, so dangerous – so full of hope. They exist!
> And this is the only fundamental truth of fiction. Its recognition must
> be critical in its nature, inasmuch that in its character it may be
> joyous...sad...angry with revolt, or submissive in resignation....But,
> whatever light he flashes on it, the fundamental truth remains, and it is
> only in its name that the barren struggle of contradictions assumes the
> dignity of moral strife going on ceaselessly to a mysterious end. (*CL*,
> II, 348-9)

The "courageous recognition of all irreconcilable antagonisms" is central to Conrad's work, and as generations of
commentators have attested, to any appreciation of its power,
ambivalence, and authority. Conrad's fictional worlds discon-
cert us because they are constructed out of and explore a play of
opposites that are never finally resolved. These (famously)
include heart and head, emotion and reason, solidarity and
isolation, idealism and scepticism, piety and scorn, loyalty and
betrayal, heroism and contingency, fidelity to a code composed
of "a few very simple ideas" (*PR,* xix) and truth to one's own
sensations, and, finally, competing beliefs that an individual has
the capacity to create order and that the world is a cosmic joke.

These oppositions are also evident in Conrad's sense of his
audience and his views on the power and value of language. On
the one hand, he believes that the artist works through language
for a direct grasp upon humanity, that "one writes only half the
book: the other half is with the reader" (*CL,* I, 370), and that
"the control of the public (audience, readers' attention) is in
a sense the beginning and end of artistic method" (*CL,* IV, 422);
and on the other, he distrusts his reviewers, thinks his audience
elusive and fickle, feels with the narrator of *Under Western Eyes*
that "words are...the great foes of reality" (*UWE,* 3), and that
"half the words we use have no meaning whatever and of the
other half each man understands each word after the fashion of
his own folly and conceit" (*CL,* II, 17). On the one hand he
advocates in his "Preface" to *The Nigger of the "Narcissus"*
a Flaubertian "unremitting never-discouraged care for the shape
and ring of sentences" and in "A Familiar Preface" proclaims

"Give me the right accent and I will move the world" (*PR*, xii); and on the other he claims "words blow away like mists" (*CL*, II, 17) and both fears and distrusts, as Kurtz's case supremely exemplifies, humankind's "gift of expression" because it is simultaneously "the bewildering, the illuminating, the most exalted and the most contemptible" (*YS*, 113).

At different moments and moods and in relation to different audiences and correspondents, and in the complex interplay of opposing scenes, characters, images, and reflections in his fictions, Conrad emphasizes one set of values and possibilities as against another: but, essentially, and this sets him apart from English political novelists such as Mrs. Gaskell, Kingsley, Eliot, Trollope, Galsworthy, Bennett and Wells, the conflicting values and attitudes remain irreconcilable. Critics, of course, according to their own predispositions, preoccupations, and theories, are prone to emphasize one set of values and attitudes as against another.

Conrad's vision of irreconcilable antagonisms sponsored his search for a correlative form, for what the narrator of *Under Western Eyes* called a "living form" (*UWE*, 3) that would register, negotiate and both give free play to and shape the competing languages, perspectives, and points of view on the world. Reviewing this search late in life Conrad remarked on "my unconventional grouping and perspective...and wherein all my art consists...it is fluid depending on (grouping) sequence, which shifts, and on the changing lights giving varied effects of perspective" (Jean-Aubry, II, 317). Hence, famously, Conrad's fondness for multi-layered, multi-voiced, and multi-mediated fictions, and for dazzling switches of chronology and perspective, which oblige us as in *Nostromo* (1904) to build up the picture and history of Costaguana for ourselves, or as in *Under Western Eyes,* demand we negotiate between the Janus eyes of the narrator and Razumov's tormented diary. Hence Conrad's persistent manipulation of the reader, who is often puzzled by the opposing, criss-crossing viewpoints on and interpretations of either a given event, such as Jim's jump and MacWhirr's storm strategy, or of totemistic commodities such as ivory in "Heart of

Darkness" or silver in *Nostromo,* from both of which "there is no escape in this world" (*Nostromo,* xi). Hence Conrad's fondness for tellers, who in James's elegant formulation enact "a subjective hovering flight" over "the case of the ground exposed" (James, *French Writers, Other European Writers, The Prefaces to the New York Edition,* 149) – radically uncertain hoverings we might add, that are often greatly disturbed, even circumvented, by the cases they scan. Hence as his narratives spiral around his subjects, we are aware that they are "long" as Conrad told Garnett, "because my thought is always multiple" (*CL,* III, 492). Hence in Watt's fine formulaton our sense as we read Conrad "of the almost unmanageable inclusiveness of what we are being left to piece together" (Watt, 210).

Led by Garnett, Conrad's reviewers once they realized he was Polish persisted in viewing his imagination and "psychological insight," "his tender, and sombre vision of life" as Slavic, and constantly comparing him to the great Russian novelists.[8] Conrad was enraged by such comparisons not only because he loathed being associated with the Russians, but also because as he told Garnett, he felt the reviewers presented him "as a sort of freak, an amazing bloody foreigner writing in English" (*CL,* III, 488). But, as James recognized, he was set apart from his Edwardian contemporaries because "No one has known – for intellectual use – the things you know: and you have as the artist of the whole matter, an authority that no-one has approached" (Edel, II, 397). James alluded specifically to Conrad's knowledge and mastery of life at sea. As the factors I have outlined suggest, however, the differences between Conrad and his Victorian forbears and contemporaries can be traced to things he knew stemming from what he called in his "Author's Note" (1920) to *Under Western Eyes* "my peculiar experience of race and family" (*UWE,* viii).

III

These differences are most apparent in *Under Western Eyes,* because it is the only novel which directly engages "the political conditions" (117) in Russia within whose huge empire he was born, and because in it Conrad also returns to the ur-source of the "irreconcilable antagonisms" he inherited and internalized. In marked contrast to his English narrator and English readers, Conrad shares with Razumov an immense and divided parentage and "an hereditary and personal knowledge of the means by which a historical autocracy represses ideas, guards its power, and defends its existence" (25). Whereas Conrad escaped, Razumov is embroiled: "crystallized by the shock of his contact with Haldin" (67), and after his betrayal of him, conscious of the brutality of tsarism, Razumov stabs to "the lath and plaster wall at the head of his bed" (66) what Mikulin later calls "a sort of political confession of faith" (99):

> History not Theory
> Patriotism not Internationalism
> Evolution not Revolution
> Direction not Destruction
> Unity not Disruption. (66)

Razumov's secular "conservative convictions, diluted in a vague liberalism" (67) of tradition, compromise, gradualism, and slow change are familiar to "western" readers. Indeed, in varying degrees, they underpin and sustain both English political life and praxis and the social and political novel from Gaskell, Dickens, Eliot, and Trollope, through to the Edwardians. Moreover they inform the narrator's western point of view in *Under Western Eyes*. Forged out of the depths of Razumov's anguish and out of his sense that he is being crushed between the clashing forces of revolutionary idealism, the intoxication of the peasants and the brutality of tsarism, his political principles – and this is the foundation of his tragedy – are precisely those that are unobtainable and unrealizable in Russia and the oppressed lands of her vast empire such as Poland. (And we might add, in the East Indies of *Almayer's Folly* and *An Outcast of the Islands* [1896], and in the Congo and Costaguana.)

Desperate to stop the revolving cycle of violence that is tearing his nation and himself apart, Razumov, the man of reason (*razum* is the root of reason in Russian), strives to graft liberal values onto the stock of autocracy, which naturally rejects and systematically opposes the fusion. Russian "autocracy in mystic vestments, engendered by the slavery of a Tartar conquest" (*UWE*, 142) has no historical experience of the institutions and legal freedoms that inform and sustain western political life. Moreover because the tsarist system, based on autocracy, nationalism, and orthodoxy, was imposed both within Russia and throughout her empire, its principles remained inorganic and "lawless."[9] Thus both Razumov and the warring factions in his nation may yearn and search for "some form of peace," and liberty but are obliged to settle, as *Under Western Eyes* demonstrates, only for "some formula" (5).

As a Pole Conrad knew that the absence of the middle ground which is taken for granted in English political life meant that "Evolution," which he called "precisely the expression of the highest intellectual hope," was a "gruesome pleasantry" in Russia (*NLL*, 99). He was also aware that tsarism's inability to countenance the notion of loyal political opposition drove all dissidents underground and thereby ensured that revolution, "a short cut in the rational development of national needs," was the only alternative response to despotism (101). Thus both revolution and tsarism were forms not of "Direction" but of "Destruction." These factors combined with the scorn of both revolutionaries and tsarists "for all the practical forms of liberty known to the western world" (*UWE*, 104) – such as freely-elected assemblies and parliamentarianism – meant that theories of every utopian variety (whether anarchist, communist, or the messianisms of the Russians in the novel and of his own father) flourished unchecked by practical experience of government and therefore remained, in the narrator's words in *Under Western Eyes*, "disembodied" and abstract (106).[10] Relatedly, as the son of a messianic nationalist, Conrad knew that "with us religion and patriotism go hand in hand," and he turned "this complex feeling to good account" (*CL*, I, 174) in *Under Western Eyes*. Thus in the novel speakers of all theoretical persuasions blend the discourses of politics and religion thereby confusing the spiritual and temporal realms. Both the tsarists' view of autocracy as the manifestation of "Divine Intention" on earth (*UWE*, 8) and the revolutionaries' belief that "Destruction" will lead to a "new revelation" (22) scorn and reject "the irremediable life of the earth as it is" (104) and ensure that Russian national life is an endless cycle of repression and violence.

As Conrad's negative presentation of Geneva shows he distrusts the "hypocritical respectability" (332) and complacency of the bourgeoisie; and as his withering critique of the ramifications of "Material interests" (*Nostromo*) upon the inhabitants of the Congo and Costaguana show, he shares and intensifies the English novel's distrust of capitalism and of "the lack of idealism in English" (and western) politics, which left, in George Eliot's formulation, "all mutuality between distant races to be determined simply by the needs of a market" (George Eliot, *Daniel Deronda*, I, 179). But Conrad differs markedly from English novelists in his abiding distrust of all searches for forms of "Unity" to heal or transcend the divisions of race and class, because like Russian thinking, they fall into "mysticism."

These forms of unity include Charles Kingsley's Christian socialism in *Alton Locke* (1851), which would "claim universal suffrage only on the grounds of the universal redemption of mankind" (Kingsley, *Alton Locke*, 368); Mrs. Gaskell's attempt in *North and South* (1855) to graft through the convenient marriage of Margaret and Thornton the Christian values of compassion and forgiveness upon the stock of capitalism, thereby "cultivating some intercourse with the hands beyond the mere 'cash nexus'" (Mrs. Gaskell, *North and South*, 525); George Eliot's enthusiastic interpretation in *Daniel Deronda* of Zionism's belief in "a fusion of the races" (George Eliot, *Daniel Deronda*, I, 179) through "the divine Unity" to be found in "the soul of Judaism" (II, 400, 553); and finally Galsworthy's appeal in *Fraternity* (1909) to "the wild force which turns form to form...this great wild force of universal life" (Galsworthy, *Fraternity*, 232) manifest in the seasonal round dwarfing ideas of fraternity and "Universal Brotherhood" (346).

Placed alongside Conrad's devastating critique of the confusions at the heart of the messianic spirit that informs the
thinking of all the Russians in *Under Western Eyes,* Eliot's
fondness for Zionism's messianic vision of "the ultimate unity of
mankind" (George Eliot, *Daniel Deronda,* 553) and Kingsley's
eschatological theocratic Christian State are revealed as both
fatuous and dangerous. Like the Russians in *Under Western
Eyes,* we cannot "defend" ourselves, "from the suspicion that"
these novelists "really understand what they say" (*UWE,* 4),
because they do not consider the inevitable disruptive consequences of their beliefs. Again the melioristic fusion of
Christian compassion and capitalism advocated by Mrs. Gaskell
as the solution to class antagonism confuses the spiritual and
secular realms as surely if not as dangerously as the variety of
Russian messianisms in *Under Western Eyes.* Galsworthy like
his close friend Conrad may have been a secularist, but his "wild
force" expresses an English whimsy and sentimentality which
riddles his novel and is completely alien to Conrad's sensibilities.
   Conrad's knowledge in *Under Western Eyes* of "the shadow
...stretching across the middle of Europe" (184), of the absence
of a middle ground – which all English novelists presume and are
concerned to protect – and his experience of the oscillations of
autocracy and revolution link him to twentieth century central-
-European writers such as Kafka, Tadeusz Borowski, Bruno
Schulz, Miłosz, and Škvorecký, and make him in Najder's
formulation "exceptionally conscious of the sinister brutalities
hidden beneath the richly ornate facade of *bourgeois* political
optimism" (Najder, "Conrad's Polish Background,..." 30).
Conrad in Bertrand Russell's marvellous image in *Portraits from
Memory,* "thought of civilized and morally tolerable human life
as a dangerous walk on a thin crust of barely cooled lava, which
at any moment might break and let the unwary sink into fiery
depths" (Russell, *Portraits from Memory,* 82).[11] This thought is
most movingly expressed in the narrator's meditation upon Mrs.
Haldin, the stricken victim of the destructive struggle between
autocracy and revolution:

> I won't say liberty, but the mere liberalism of outlook which for us is
> a mere matter of words, of ambitions, of votes (and if of feelings at all,
> then the kind that leaves our deepest feelings untouched) may be for
> other beings very much like ourselves and living under the same sky,
> a heavy trial of fortitude, a matter of tears and anguish and blood.
> (*UWE*, 318)

Such knowledge also sets Conrad apart from English novelists
and helps explain his fascination with and compassion for
characters such as Razumov, Kurtz, Jim, Nostromo, and
Winnie Verloc, who fall through the "crust" and have to
negotiate and live with new and disturbing forms of feeling and
knowledge about themselves and their relationship to their
fellows and society. Even more importantly this awareness
sponsored Conrad's very un-English serious engagement with
and sympathy for revolutionary idealists such as Haldin, Sophia
Antonovna, who is "the true spirit of destructive revolution"
(261), and for the fanatical professor in *The Secret Agent* (1907).
All three idealists want to "move mankind" and strive like
"artists" "to make a direct grasp upon humanity" through either
revolutionary disturbances of the social order or through
eloquence and propaganda (*UWE*, 67). Haldin's and the revolutionaries' faith in "blood and violence" as a means of
reconciling "the antagonistic ideas" (105) that are tearing their
nation apart are shown to be deluded, but they are also inspired
by, as the narrator compassionately notes, "the noblest aspirations of humanity," such as "the desire of freedom, an ardent
patriotism, the love of justice," which are "prostituted to the
lusts of hate and fear, the inseparable companions of an uneasy
despotism" (7). Conrad understood, whereas English novelists
could not, that this desire for freedom is unappeasable. When
you struggle "under the net" (139), like Natalia Haldin, you
"would take liberty from any hand as a hungry man would
snatch at a piece of bread" (135). Conrad quotes her fierce words
on the flyleaf of the first edition of the novel and they have
axiomatic force in his fiction. Because the desire for liberty is an
appetite, which will always sponsor heedless behaviour, it can
neither (as in English political novels) be contained, sidelined,

fudged, or appeased, nor can or should it be satisfied on earth by
the other-worldly consolations of religion of whatever faith, or
by "Internationalism" in any of its varieties, including those of
messianism, imperialism, and socialism.[12]

In English political novels a faith in law, an acceptance of
"Evolution" and "Direction," and a fear of and a determination
to contain (at whatever cost to their fictions), what Carlyle in the
opening words of *Chartism* (1839), called the "ominous matter"
of "the condition and disposition of the working classes," ensure
that revolution is never seriously entertained. English novelists,
unlike the characters in *Under Western Eyes,* can always take the
long view and see even *failed* attempts at instituting radical
change, such as Phineas Finn's hopes for tenants' rights in
Ireland, as encouraging and, indeed, as necessary if change is to
occur:

> Many who before regarded legislation on the subject as chimerical,
> will now fancy that it is only dangerous, or perhaps not more than
> difficult. And so in time it will come to be looked on as among the
> things possible, then among the things probable; – and so at last it will
> be ranged in the list of those few measures which the country requires
> as being absolutely needed. That is the way in which public opinion is
> made. (Trollope, *Phineas Finn,* II, 341)

Phineas then, from the evolutionary, parliamentarian perspective outlined by the radical M. P. Joshua Monk, is neither
a dreamer nor misguided like Alton Locke, the militant miners in
Felix Holt, the Radical (1866), and the striking mill workers in
Mary Barton (1848), *North and South,* and *Hard Times* (1854).
The great tragedy of Razumov's life and of Russia as a nation is
that in a country devoid of legislative checks and balances, and
"where an opinion" in the old teacher's formulation, "may be
a legal crime visited by death" (*UWE,* 6), a devotion to
gradualism and to "Evolution" is itself as fantastic as a commitment to revolutionary "Destruction" as a means of progress, or
to tsarism as a form of "Unity."

Conrad's racial and historical experience of the long "shadow
of autocracy" and his exile with his parents in northern Russia

informed his overriding sense that politics constitutes "the great spring of modern tragedy" (Hay, 80). In the old teacher's comprehensive and tragic assessment, "the shadow of autocracy" tinges the Russians' "thoughts, their views, their most intimate feelings, their private life, their public utterances – haunting the secret of their silences" (*UWE,* 107). The sweep and passion of such formulations penetrate areas and sound notes that are new to the English novel, wherein the "most intimate feelings" of characters remain either untinged by politics or are protected from its "shadow," as in Gaskell, Kingsley, and Eliot by their blatant manipulations of plot and by their bias against radical politics; or as with Hilary Dallison of *Fraternity,* the very security of his class sense both blinds and saves him from the encroachments of political forces; or in Wells's *Tono Bungay* (1909) "the crumbling and confusion" at the heart of politics, commerce and industry in London and the Empire yield to misty affirmations that "Something comes out of it," and "Sometimes I call this reality Science, sometimes I call it Truth" (Wells, *Tono Bungay,* 377); or as in *Ann Veronica* (1909), the heroine's feminism and revolt against the constraints and complacencies of her middle class family dwindle into the gushy escapism of submission to her lover Capes, who finally becomes her husband.[13]

Thus Alton Locke writes his cockney autobiography from the perspective of a Christian convinced his childhood poverty and sufferings and his subsequent espousal of Chartism are to be understood neither as the natural protest of the down-trodden, nor as an instinct for "liberty" in this world, as with Natalia in *Under Western Eyes,* but as "God's gift." Hence, from the moment he puts pen to paper the radical legislative aims of the chartists are both bleached of their political content and displaced by Alton's aim "to vindicate democracy as the will and gift of God" (Kingsley, *Alton Locke,* 368). Similarly Eliot's anxiety to protect Felix Holt from any imputation of causing a riot during polling day (chapter 33) results in a blatant plot manipulation, which inadvertently renders Felix, said to be a man of "rapid senses and quick thoughts," a patent fool. Once

in jail, however, he disappears for a fifth of the novel, and the
political issues of workers' rights, the vote, and their representation in Parliament disappear with him.

Galsworthy's *Fraternity,* as Conrad acknowledged, is a novel
which conscientiously examines "the moral evil of class feeling"
(Galsworthy, *Fraternity,* 4, 120) through the aptly named Ivy,
the artist's model and inspirer of a painting called "The
Shadow."[14] Throughout the novel she is compared either to "a
little ghost, the spirit of the helpless submerged world for ever
haunting with its dumb appeal the minds of men" (186)
threatening to disrupt the social order; or to "some unlawful
spirit" anxious to embroil the wealthy writer Hilary Dallinson in
"the marshy ground of feeling" (315), wherein the English (as
Conrad dramatizes in the old teacher in *Under Western Eyes*),
are always likely to sink. Hilary finally resists Ivy's entwining
because he claims "Class has saved me; it has triumphed over my
most primitive instincts" (Galsworthy, *Fraternity,* 342).

Conrad's critique of Galsworthy's portrayal of "the pure
spirit" Hilary, because though "thrown amongst impure conditions," he is not shown to end in "some base betrayal of
himself" (*CL,* IV, 119), summarizes why his protagonists are so
different from, and meet such different ends to, those in English
fiction. Thus, Hilary escapes the shadow of "this girl of the
people" (Galsworthy, *Fraternity,* 168) because of his fastidious,
aesthetic sense of class differences; while a succession of
characters in Victorian political novels escape the pollution of
mass agitation because they are either dispatched to Texas like
Alton Locke, or because like Felix, they find a temporary haven
in prison, or like Margaret and Thornton, a permanent one in
marriage in *North and South.* Galsworthy is, as Conrad told him,
a moralist and "A moralist must present us with a gospel – he
must give counsel not to our reason or sentiment but to our very
soul" (*CL,* IV, 116). In Conrad's fiction there is no gospel of
Judaism as in *Daniel Deronda,* or of altruism as in *Felix Holt, the
Radical,* or of Christianity as in Kingsley and Gaskell, or of
social engineering as in Wells to rescue his characters from
"under the shadow" of tsarism: or we might add from under the

shadow of either the ivory in "Heart of Darkness," or the silver in *Nostromo,* which also tinge the private lives, the public utterances, the secret actions, and silent thoughts of all the characters.

In Conrad's novels nobody 'scapes tingeing. Haldin is executed in prison, and his spirit, unlike Ivy's, truly haunts Razumov because he is shown to be a secret sharer of his most intimate feelings and silences. Marriage and reconciliation are anticipated by the narrator of *Under Western Eyes* and desired by Tekla even after Razumov's confession to Natalia; but both protagonist and heroine resist a romance ending to the love plot. The latter at the end returns to the shadow-ridden land of Russia. The "pure spirit" in *Under Western Eyes,* she accepts Razumov's charge that her very innocence and unselfishness rendered her "defenceless." Unlike Hilary who flees England, and unlike Jem and Mary in *Mary Barton* and *Alton Locke* who are packed off to Canada and Texas respectively, Natalia returns to Russia with her "simple human dignity intact," because, unlike Galsworthy with his protagonist, Conrad ensures she knows what it is like to "sit down in the mud" (*CL,* IV, 120). Having read Razumov's diary, which he passed to her wrapped up in her veil, she feels "My eyes are open at last and my hands are free now" (*UWE,* 376). She shares a knowledge unavailable to Galsworthy and Kingsley, that human dignity is "made up of good and evil faced openly, grasped with full knowledge" (*CL,* IV, 120): faced openly without the consolations of Christian understanding as in Mrs. Gaskell and Kingsley, and without a faith in "the precious estate of society," as in George Eliot.[15]

Unlike English political novels such as *Mary Barton* which end with assurances that the sufferings and actions of the characters generated "improvements now in practice in the system of employment in Manchester" (Mrs. Gaskell, *Mary Barton,* 460), the political conditions to which Natalia returns in Russia are no different from those that obtained when the novel began. We learn at the end that she shares "her compassionate labours between the horrors of overcrowded jails, and the heart-rending misery of bereaved homes" (*UWE,* 378). Her good service, however, is as powerless to resolve the irreconcilable antagonisms ripping her nation apart, as Mrs. Gould's sympathetic imagination is to protect Costaguana from the imminent communist revolution stemming from and attendant upon the triumph of "Material interests." Moreover, at the very end of *The Secret Agent* the fanatical professor "passed on unsuspected and deadly, like a pest in the street full of men" (*SA,* 231),[16] poised to spread his poison yet again; and the last words of *Under Western Eyes* are spoken by the most admirable and sympathetic of the revolutionists, Sophia Antonovna, who assures the incredulous English narrator that Peter Invanovitch, the revolutionary leader, whom he regards as a charlatan, is an "inspired man" (*UWE,* 382).

Conrad's presentation of the inescapable shadows of politics and of "Material interests," together with his sympathy for the range of voices canvassed, coexistent, and inextinguishable, explains why he sounds so foreign placed against his Victorian forbears and Edwardian contemporaries. Thus Conrad strikes new, intense, and precarious notes in English political fiction when he demonstrates that we walk "on a thin crust of barely cooled lava;" that "sinister brutalities" lurk beneath the social surface, and that the desire for liberty is as compelling as the need for bread; that so long as it is in Stevie's words in *The Secret Agent* a "bad world for poor people" (*SA,* 132), "Destruction" and "Revolution" are inevitable alternatives; that the middle ground cannot be taken for granted bacause, as Razumov discovers, "in a period of mental and political unrest," it is impossible to "keep an instinctive hold on normal, practical everyday life" (*UWE,* 10); and that, lastly, the secular values of parliamentarianism, as Don José Avellanos's case in *Nostromo* illustrates, are extremely fragile concepts, and only one among many competing alternatives, such as oligarchy, class war, revolution, and dictatorship.[17] In comparison to Conrad's comprehensive and tragic sense of "the deepest feelings" and "the noblest aspirations of humanity" corrupted and perverted by political conditions, even George Eliot's famous appeal to the reader's feelings of "pity and terror" for "some hard" and inescapable "entail of suffering" and for "pain that is quite noiseless" in all human affairs and actions in her "Author's Introduction" to *Felix Holt,...*(George Eliot, *Felix Holt, the Radical,* 83-4) sounds merely worthy; and even her austere maxim in *Middlemarch* that "there is no creature whose inward being is so strong that it is not greatly determined by what lies outside it" (George Eliot, *Middlemarch,* 896), sounds positively bracing.

NOTES

1. "A Familiar Preface," *PR,* xiii. A letter, 13 September, 1911, confirms that this Preface – his finest meditation on the relationship between his life and his art – was written "to explain (in a sense) how I came to write such a novel" as *Under Western Eyes,* the only one to "seek discourse with the shades" of his Polish past (*UWE,* xv). Conrad wrote the Preface in the summer of 1911; the novel was published 5 October, 1911. For the letter see *CL,* IV, 477.

2. "A Familiar Preface," *PR,* xv. The old English teacher of languages, as Conrad acknowledges in his "Author's Note" (1920) to *Under Western Eyes,* functions as a screen, working for "impartiality" and "detachment from all passions, prejudices and even from personal memories" (*UWE,* viii).

3. This is one of Najder's prevailing themes in all his writing on Conrad. Cp. especially, his essay in *Conradiana* (1986). My account of Conrad's Polish heritage is necessarily sweeping and general. Readers interested in this huge and controversial subject should begin with Najder's biography and the documents he gathers in *Conrad's Polish Background:...*and *Conrad under Familial Eyes.* The latter includes Eliza Orzeszkowa's infamous accusation (1899) that Conrad betrayed Poland when he emigrated and then proceeded to drain away "the life blood of the nation" by writing popular and lucrative novels in English (187). The most balanced account of Conrad's Polish background is still Busza's.

4. Korzeniowski's screed written during his exile in Vologda in Northern Russia is a cry of pain and a bitter denunciation of Muscovite tyranny. Conrad secretly rehearses aspects of his father's case against Russia through the old English teacher's "digressions" and commentary in *Under Western Eyes* (cp. for example *UWE,* 3, 25, 67).

5. Taken from Korzeniowski's extraordinary poem, "To My Son Born in the 85th Year of Muscovite Oppression, a Song for the Day of his Christening." In it he outlines both his own romantic, messianic faith in Poland's future and his pilgrim son's spiritual and political inheritance.

6. The fairest historical account of these clashing loyalties which were representative of the political possibilities and modes of action open to the nation as a whole and which Conrad inherited and internalized is Davies II. He carefully surveys the respective values, hopes and actions of these opposing nationalistic traditions, and then in an elegant aphorism suggests: "If the Insurrectionists were the high-priests of the nation's soul, the Conciliators were the guardians of its Body" (Davies, II, 46). As Busza, among many, has noted this clash manifest in the romantic literature Conrad read at his father's knee and in the positivist letters Bobrowski wrote to him, "gave him such a magnificent start as a writer" (Busza, 161). Bakhtin, incidentally, charts precisely such a start for Dostoevsky, and his account of the complex relationship of a writer's art to his life could fruitfully be applied to Conrad's. Thus, briefly, like his *bête noire* and *semblable*, Conrad was a "social wanderer," aware from childhood on of "the extensive and well-developed contradictions which coexisted among people" (27) and of the "objective complexity, contradictoriness and multi-voicedness" of his heritage (30). The Edwardians, as we shall see, found Conrad's work foreign and labelled it "Slavic:" from this perspective they were right. Cp. Carabine, "'Irreconcilable Differences:'...," especially 198-202.

7. This letter of 7 October, 1907 was written just two months before Conrad began *Under Western Eyes*. Cp. Carabine, "The Figure behind the Veil:..." for the ways Conrad's double life and his dialogue with the "shadows" of his parents enters the novel.

8. Garnett, "The Genius of Mr. Conrad," *The Nation*, 3, London 22 August 1908 (of *A Set of Six*), in *Joseph Conrad: Critical Assessments*, ed. K. Carabine, I, 333. Cp. also the "Anonymous Review" of *Typhoon and Other Stories* (*Speaker*, 8, 6 June 1903); Garnett's "Mr. Conrad's Art" on *Nostromo* (*Speaker*, 11, 12 November 1904) and "Unsigned Review" of *Under Western Eyes* (*Nation*, 10, 21 October 1911); Robert Lynd's unspeakably stupid "Review" of *A Set of Six* wherein he says that "without country or language" Conrad should write in Polish and find a translator as good as Mrs. Garnett to translate his novels into English (*Daily News*, 10 August 1908); and "Anonymous Review" of *Under Western Eyes* (*North American Review*, December 1911, 935), in *Joseph Conrad: Critical Assessments*, ed. K. Carabine, I, 303, 314, 332, 337, 338). For Conrad's outraged reaction to Lynd and for his critique of Garnett's view of him see his letters to the latter of 21 and 28 August 1908 and 20 October 1911 (*CL*, IV, 107-8, 111-12, 488).

9. These charges dominate Korzeniowski's "Poland and Muscovy...," Conrad's most important political essay "Autocracy and War" (1905), and the end of his "Author's Note" to *Under Western Eyes*.

10. He replies to Natalia's Slavophile platitudes: "We Russians shall find some better form of national freedom than an artificial conflict of

parties – which is wrong because it is a conflict and contemptible because it is artificial" (*UWE,* 106).

11. Russell, incidentally, finally broke with Lawrence for reasons that echo the old teacher's critique of Natalia's messianism. In Lee Horsley's account, "Russell met in Lawrence the full implication of the doctrine which held that 'facts' are of no account in comparison with 'truths,' and was exasperated beyond bearing by the 'dream-like,' impractical quality of Lawrence's responses to contemporary history: 'He never let himself bump into reality'" (Horsley, 124).

12. This huge subject is, of course, too big for a note. For a scathing rejection of "International fraternity" and socialism, and a defense of patriotism, see Conrad's letter of 8 February 1899, to Cunninghame Graham who wanted him to attend a peace meeting run by "the Social Democratic Federation" (*CL,* II, 157-61).

13. Thus Ann tells her married lover, "I want to put myself into your hands....It's a pure joy of giving, giving to *you*" (H. G. Wells: *Ann Veronica,* 240), and the colluding narrator assures us "She loved to be told to do things" (243). In marked contrast to Conrad (witness the fates of Winnie Verloc and Natalia), the personal, as ever in English fiction, subsumes and surmounts the political. Cp. Catherine Gallagher's superb exploration of these oft-discussed issues: "the tendency to dissociate the family from society is prevalent in both social paternalism and domestic ideology. Both assume the separation of the public and private spheres they attempt to integrate" (Gallagher, 148). *The Secret Agent* literally detonates such comfortable assumptions.

14. Conrad read *Fraternity* (then called *Shadows*) in manuscript in September 1908. His letters to Galsworthy are among the finest he ever wrote because they combine a brilliant critique of the limitations of vision and presentation of his friend's novel and, correspondingly, an implicit account of his own very different concerns and fictional aesthetic – manifest in the novel he was struggling to write, namely *Under Western Eyes.*

15. *Felix Holt, the Radical,* Appenix A, 621, from "Address to Working Men," written in the *persona* of Felix at the request of John Blackwood who was "excessively anxious" that the Second Reform Bill (1867) pass peaceably.

16. Joseph Conrad, *The Secret Agent: A Simple Tale,* ed. Bruce Harkness and Sid W. Reid (Cambridge: Cambridge U.P., 1990).

17. After completing the last draft of this essay, I read Najder's "Conrad in His Historical Perspective:" "A part of Conrad's legacy as a political novelist consists simply of the themes he raised for the first time:...of ineffectual liberalism and degenerating revolution, of 'material interests' corrupting both their exploited victims and their supposed beneficiaries, of political provocation and terroristic idealism...." (Z. Najder, "Conrad in His Historical Perspective," 163). The first time in English novels as I have

suggested: but surely the first theme is one of Turgenev's great subjects. The last is inseparable from Conrad's critique of Dostoevsky, who strained to deny the symbiotic relationship between what Conrad called in his "Author's Note" to *Under Western Eyes*, "The ferocity and imbecility of an autocratic rule rejecting all legality" and "the no less imbecile and atrocious answer of a purely Utopian revolutionism encompassing destruction by the first means to hand" (*UWE*, x).

WORKS CITED

PRIMARY:

Eliot George. *Felix Holt, the Radical* [1866], Oxford: Oxford U.P., 1980.

Eliot George. *Middlemarch* [1871-2]. Oxford: Oxford U.P., 1986.

Eliot George. *Daniel Deronda* [1874-76]. London: Everyman's Library, 1964.

Galsworthy John. *Fraternity* [1909]. London: William Heineman, 1920.

Gaskell Elizabeth C. *Mary Barton* [1848], ed. Stephen Gill. London: Penguin English Library, 1970.

Gaskell Elizabeth C. *North and South* [1855], ed. Dorothy Collin. London: Penguin English Library, 1970.

Jean-Aubry Georges. *Joseph Conrad: Life and Letters*, 2 vols. New York: Doubleday, Page, 1927.

Kingsley Charles. *Alton Locke, Tailor and Poet: An Autobiography*. Oxford: Oxford U.P., 1983.

Najder Zdzisław, ed. *Conrad's Polish Background: Leters to and from Polish Friends*. Oxford: Oxford U.P., 1964.

Najder Zdzisław, ed. *Conrad under Familial Eyes*, trans. Halina Carroll--Najder. London: Cambridge U.P., 1983.

Russell Bertrand. *Portraits from Memory*. New York: Simon and Schuster, 1956.

Trollope Anthony. *Phineas Finn* [1869]. Oxford: Oxford U.P., 1973.

Wells Herbert George. *Tono Bungay* [1909]. Boston: Houghton Mifflin, 1966.

Wells Herbert George. *Ann Veronica* [1909]. London: J. M. Dent, 1943.

SECONDARY:

Berka F. P. "Zhitomir and the Ukrainian Background in the Early Childhood of Joseph Conrad," *The Conradian*, 8:2 (Summer 1983), 4-11.

Bakhtin M. M. *Problems of Dostoevsky's Poetics*, ed. and trans. Caryl Emerson. Minneapolis: U. of Minnesota P., 1984.

Busza Andrzej. "Conrad's Literary Background and Some Illustrations of the Influence of Polish Literature on his Work," *Antemurale* 10 (1966), 109-247; Rome-London: Institutum Historicum Polonicum – Societas Polonica Scientiarum et Litterarum in Exteris.

Carabine Keith. "'The Figure behind the Veil:' Conrad and Razumov in *Under Western Eyes*," in *Joseph Conrad's "Under Western Eyes:" Beginnings, Revisions, Final Forms*, ed. David R. Smith. Hamden: Archon Books, 1991, 1-37.

Carabine Keith, ed. *Joseph Conrad: Critical Assessments*, 4 vols. Robertsbridge: Helm Information, 1992.

Carabine Keith. "'Irreconcilable Differences:' England as 'An Undiscovered Country' in Conrad's 'Amy Foster,'" in *The Ends of the Earth*, ed. Simon Gatrell. London: The Ashfield Press, 1992, 187-204.

Davies Norman. *God's Playground: A History of Poland,* 2 vols. New York: Columbia U.P., 1982.

Edel Leon. *The Life of Henry James,* 2 vols. London: Penguin Books, 1977.

Gallagher Catherine. *The Industrial Reformation of English Fiction, 1832-1867*. Chicago: Chicago U.P., 1988.

Hay Eloise Knapp. *The Political Novels of Joseph Conrad: A Critical Study*. Chicago: Chicago U.P., 1963.

Hodges Robert F. *The Dual Heritage of Joseph Conrad*. The Hague: Mouton, 1967.

Horsley Lee. *Political Fiction and the Historical Imagination*. London: Macmillan, 1990.

James Henry. *French Writers, Other European Writers, The Prefaces to the New York Edition*. New York: The Library of America, 1984.

Meyer Bernard C. *Joseph Conrad: A Psychoanalytic Biography*. Princeton: Princeton U.P., 1967.

Morf Gustav. *The Polish Heritage of Joseph Conrad*. London: Sampson Low, 1930.

Najder Zdzisław. "Conrad in His Historical Perspective," *English Literature in Transition*, 14:3 (1971), 157-66.

Najder Zdzisław. "Conrad and the Idea of Honor," in *Joseph Conrad: Theory and World Fiction, Proceedings of the Comparative Literature Symposium,* January 23-25, 1974, eds. Wendell M. Aycock and Wołodymyr T. Żyła. Lubbock: Texas Tech U.P., 1974.

Najder Zdzisław. *Joseph Conrad: A Chronicle*. Cambridge: Cambridge U.P., 1983.

Najder Zdzisław. "Conrad's Polish Background, or from Biography to a Study of Culture," *Conradiana,* 18:1 (1986), 3-8.

Stine Peter. "Joseph Conrad's Confession in *Under Western Eyes,*" *Cambridge Quarterly,* 9 (1980), 95-113.

Watt Ian. *Conrad in the Nineteenth Century*. Berkeley: U. of California P., 1979.

Noel Peacock,
University of Western Ontario,
London, Canada

The Russian Eye: Surveillance and the Scopic Regime in *Under Western Eyes*

"My task which I am trying to achieve is, by the power of the written word to make you hear, to make you feel – it is, before all, to make you see." Thus Conrad summarizes his aesthetic aims in the 1896 "Preface" to *The Nigger of the "Narcissus"* (*NN,* x). The assertions made here are notable for their proclamation of what Edward Said has called a "faith in the supremacy of the visible" (Said, 95) in Conrad's work. Vision in the "Preface" is given a revelatory power in relation to truth that is implicitly denied or not fully available to the other senses. As Conrad defines it, art is the "single-minded attempt to render the highest kind of justice to the visible universe" (*NN,* vii), and the task of the artist, whose first act must be to "snatch...from the remorseless rush of time, a passing phase of life," is to:

> hold up...the rescued fragment before all eyes in the light of a sincere mood. It is to show its vibration, its colour, its form; and through its movement, its form, and its colour, reveal the substance of its truth – disclose its inspiring secret: the stress and passion within the core of each convincing moment. (x)

In his emphasis on light, color, and form here Conrad conforms to a longstanding Western tradition of what Martin Jay and others have called "ocularcentrism," in which notions of truth or reality are conveyed through metaphors of the eye and of vision.[1] Conrad indeed is a particularly subtle practitioner within this tradition, one concerned with revealing a truth "obscured by mists" (xi) or as in "Heart of Darkness," in showing the delicate form of the mist itself that does not veil the truth but is "the meaning of an episode...enveloping the tale which brought it out only as a glow brings out a haze, the likeness of one of these misty halos that sometimes are made visible by the spectral illumination of moonshine" (*YS,* 48). Vision and its precondition, light, is thus intricately linked in Conrad to the disclosure of truth.

It is far from clear that this is always the case, however. Ocularcentrism, as Jay notes, denotes a range of attitudes to vision within which, and running parallel to the tradition that associates vision with truth, is an alternate tradition that distrusts the power of sight. This second tradition regards corporeal vision as responsible for leading the mind away from truth – hence, for example, Plato's arguments in *The Republic* against the mimetic arts as imitations of imitations that are at a third remove from truth and therefore "appearances and not realities" (Plato, 426-7). Visual skepticism or scopophobia often remains ocularcentric to the extent that it insists, as an alternative to the fallible bodily eye, on the power of inner spiritual vision, the "eye of the mind," to perceive the truth that the sensual eye obscures (Jay, 29). Thus the perception of truth, metaphorized as a form of vision, survives in the distinction between intellectual and corporeal sight the attack on the very sense which forms its basis.

The possibility for this kind of complex interplay between variants of visual metaphors is important for Conrad, particularly in *Under Western Eyes,* his novel that is most saturated with images of eyes, sight, and vision. Vision here is rarely the kind of revelatory sight that Conrad speaks about in his famous "Preface," though it does, as we will see, involve disclosure. I wish here to interrogate the novel's use of visual metaphors with an end to showing how vision is aligned with both falsehood and truth, though not along the classical lines of intellectual versus corporeal sight. In "Author's Note," after all, Conrad claims that aesthetic insight is resolutely sensual: "All art...appeals primarily to the senses, and the artistic aim when expressing itself in written words...also makes its appeal through the senses" (*UWE,* ix). Instead, falsehood and truth correspond to two orders of corporeal sight: that of the gaze, which is associated with the surveillance practiced by Russian autocrats and revolutionaries, and in a different form, with the ineffective eye of the Western narrator; and that of the glance or glimpse into which the moral reality of Russian life upon occasion emerges clearly.

Under Western Eyes devotes much of its attention to the first of these modes of vision, one that is associated in the novel with Russia because it is shared by both revolutionaries and the state. This visual mode, however, is constantly mediated by the imperfect sight of the narrator, the teacher of languages, whose attempts to penetrate to the heart of things Russian are baffled by a screen of received popular opinion that flattens knowledge of the East into the stereotypes of popular entertainments, "ideas of political plots and conspiracies [that] seem childish, crude inventions for the theatre or a novel" (109). Such hazy, imperfect knowledge of Russia is metaphorized ironically by Conrad in the "Author's Note" to the novel as a form of naive vision. He describes the assassin Nikita there, for example, as having "been exhibited to the public eye for years in so-called 'disclosures' in newspaper articles, in secret histories, in sensational novels" (xxxii). For the teacher of languages, however, vision does occasionally prevail, penetrating beyond this screen of appearance to witness images "which astonish and puzzle the average plain man who reads the newspapers, by a glimpse of unsuspected intrigues...the stir of vaguely seen monstrosities" (305). Russia, as revealed by such a "glimpse behind the scenes" (330, 339), is a land of "monstrous chimeras and evil dreams" (297), the very sight of which, as we will see, can be harmful to the observer.

What is glimpsed is not a conventional object of sight that, from the perspective of popular opinion can be safely distanced from the gaze of the perceiver. Instead, it is precisely a way of seeing itself, or "scopic regime,"[2] a political mode of perception that is monstrous both in its functioning and in its relationship to the perceiving eye of the narrator. A suggestive insight into the nature of this scopic regime can be found in Mark A. Wollaeger's book *Joseph Conrad and the Fictions of Skepticism*. Wollaeger argues that "Razumov's subjective experience...compresses into the narrative space of an individual life what Foucault has

analyzed as an epistemic shift from punishment to discipline"
(Wollaeger, 188). Wollaeger's comment, however, provides only
a glimpse of the complex system of vision that characterizes
Russian society in *Under Western Eyes.*

This system is characterized by the kind of centralized
surveillance, described by Foucault in *Discipline and Punish,* that
has displaced the spectacle of execution by which punishment
was meted out in the eighteenth century. In lieu of the ritual of
public punishment, by which the power of the sovereign was seen
to exact its vengeance on the body of the condemned criminal,
a system of regulated and reciprocal supervision emerged over
the course of the nineteenth century transforming Europe into
what Foucault calls a "disciplinary society" (Foucault, *Discipline and Punish: The Birth of the Prison,* 193). The metonymic
model for this society of "domination and observation" (305) is
the prison, the emblem of which Foucault sees in Jeremy
Bentham's panopticon, an architecture of total surveillance in
which "Visibility is a trap" (220). The Russian state's power in
Under Western Eyes is organized along such a panoptical
principle of "compulsory visibility" (187) as the frequency of
visual metaphors in the novel attests. The field within which the
novel's action occurs can be understood as a visual field. None of
the elements of this field escapes the surveillance represented
literally by the network of "European supervision" (*UWE,* 309)
through which Mikulin and his system of police spies keep track
of enemies of the state. This network obeys a principle of
reciprocity in which each of the observers is himself observed.
Thus Razumov in his capacity as informer is watched and
ultimately punished by the police spy Nikita.

Surveillance also figures symbolically in the novel. The cover
for Razumov's infiltration of the revolutionaries is an oculist's
shop, within whose premises "all...preliminary work was concealed from observation" (307). This reference to a power of
sight that protects itself through its own invisibility suggests
Foucault's account of a central principle of panoptical surveillance, the requirement that "the inmate must never know
whether he is being looked at at any one moment; but he must

be sure that he may always be so" (Foucault, *Discipline and Punish:...*, 201). Mikulin, in this respect, is "simply inconspicuous" (*UWE*, 305), but has forgotten "no one who ever fell under his observation" (306). Razumov begins to experience the possiblity of his own perpetual visibility after Haldin's visit to his rooms. Reflecting on why he did not kick the assassin out on his first appearance, Razumov considers that he was "a noticeable person" (20) about whom "police in their thousands must have had [a] description" (20). By concealing Haldin within the private space of his rooms, Razumov may escape the imagined outcome of exposure, being "shut up in a fortress" or "leading a miserable life under police supervision" (21). Such fears of imprisonment and surveillance increase with the violation of the distinction between personal and public space on which Razumov relies for self-protection. The police raid on his rooms, the intrusion of the public gaze of the state, induces in Razumov a vision of psychological exposure in which his subjective identity is threatened: he "beheld his own brain suffering on the rack – a long, pale figure drawn asunder horizontally with terrific force in the darkness of a vault, whose face he failed to see" (88). In his discussion of surveillance in *The Secret Agent*, Mark Conroy argues correctly that "One crucial reason for the proliferation of suspicion in Conrad's world is the effacement of the border between public and private realms" (Conroy, 142). In the Russia of *Under Western Eyes*, however, surveillance is itself the instrument of this effacement, one that is figured quite literally in Razumov's vision of the effacement of his private identity.

This collapse of the public/private opposition is constructed as abnormal and monstrous – as part of the general monstrosity of Russia – through its inducement of morbid symptoms in its victim. The terrific force exerted upon Razumov to submit to the state's scrutiny manifests itself in the repeated hallucinations of supernatural visitation that he experiences after Haldin's initial intrusion. Trapped in "Russia, the land of spectral ideas and disembodied aspirations" (*UWE*, 34), Razumov is thrust at the stroke of midnight into a "comedy of errors, phantoms, and

suspicions" (99) in which the omnipresence of the scopic regime
is figured in his fears of being watched by specters. The
supernatural here is a threat to self-determination characterized
as a violation of private space: alone in his rooms, Razumov
thinks, "I want to guide my conduct by reasonable convictions,
but what security have I against something – some destructive
horror – walking in upon me as I sit here?" (78). Such shapes are
partly intrusive extensions of the state's gaze, as when Razumov
glimpses in his rooms "the eyes of General T– and of Privy-
-Councillor Mikulin side by side fixed upon him, quite different
in character but with the same unflinching and wary and yet
purposeful expression...servants of the nation!" (302).

Figuring surveillance as supernatural visitation in this way,
Under Western Eyes plays on the paradoxical significance of the
uncanny considered more explicitly by Freud.[3] Ghosts here are
both known and unknown, seen and unseen; their unfamiliarity
becomes familiar as it crosses the threshold of the domestic or
the private, and as Razumov becomes increasingly at home in
a world of "ogres, ghouls, and vampires" (254). The surveillance
exercised by the state, too, works by co-opting the power of
vision of the observed. Feeling himself under suspicion, Razumov shows symptoms of faulty sight, seeing things that are not
there. Hallucination thus signifies a psychological internaliz-
ation of the scopic regime's gaze. The power of the state to induce
spectral hallucinations in its subjects, shown here, is accom-
panied by a complementary power to exorcize them. It is only in
spaces fully observable by the state's gaze that Razumov escapes
being haunted. These also include his rooms, but only after they
have been exposed by the – unseen – police raid, and the oculist's
address where "Haldin...was no longer a haunting, falsehood-
-breeding spectre" (304). Hallucination thus signifies the felt
presence of the scopic regime which, though it has infiltrated the
realm of the private, has not managed to sweep all of its corners.
Pursued by this gaze, Razumov manages to conceal from it his
visit to Ziemianitch, which he confesses later to Natalia Haldin.
His spying, as an extension of the state's power of sight, is thus
conditional upon his remaining opaque to Mikulin's scrutiny,

yet it is also a way of resisting the power of the state's gaze by reserving a portion of that power for himself.

The collapse of the public and private spheres and the resulting proliferation of uncanny hallucination is a phenomenon that is dependent not solely on the visual practice of the state however. The Russian mode of vision, indeed, extends beyond the border of the country both in its observation of the Genevan exiles and in those exiles' espousal of similar methods of surveillance and control. Peter Ivanovitch preaches explicitly the effacement of privacy practiced by the state he condemns, arguing that "We Russians have no right to be reserved with each other. In our circumstances it is almost a crime against humanity. The luxury of private grief is not for us" (127). The "eye of the social revolution" – symbolized by the scrutinizing but inscrutable eyes of the "darkly bespectacled" (125) Peter Ivanovitch and the "big gleaming eyes" of Mme. de S– "rolling restlessly behind a short veil of black lace...[that] resembled a mask" (125) – is dedicated to the end of such reserve; directed toward Razumov, it provokes "an unnamed and despairing dread" (301) like his fear of the unseen back in Russia. The student in St. Petersburg is "a vision out of a nightmare" (75), Peter Ivanovitch a "monster" (124), and Mme. de S–, whose chateau is "haunted, it was said, by evoked ghosts, and frequented, it was to be supposed, by fugitive revolutionists" (212), is "a galvanized corpse out of some Hoffmann's Tale" (215) who declares herself to be "in matters of politics...a supernaturalist" (222). The first intrusion on Razumov's privacy and the first haunting of him are of course by Haldin. The identity of revolution and autocracy, observed by many critics and made explicit by Conrad at the end of the "Author's Note" and in the "queer tale" (381) of the meeting of Peter Ivanovitch and Councillor Mikulin, thus involves not just the shared tyranny of their politics, but the mechanism of exposure and haunting by which autocracy maintains itself. These elements are seen by the teacher of languages as essentially Russian in character: "Whenever two Russians come together, the shadow of autocracy is with them, tinging their thoughts, their views, their most intimate feelings, their private lives, their public utterances – haunting the secrets of their silences" (107).

The identity of revolution with the autocratic state, the collapse of public and private spheres and the maintenance of state power by a regime of intrusive vision are themes which converge in the image of Rousseau, whose "exiled effigy" (291) supervises Razumov's writing of his spy report. That Conrad stands in the political tradition of Rousseau, as Avrom Fleishman suggests (Fleishman, 59), is an argument that more recent critics have ventured to refute, most notably Zdzisław Najder, who characterizes Conrad's relationship to the philosopher as an "opposition-obsession syndrome" (Najder, 83). This opposition, as it is articulated in *Under Western Eyes,* becomes clearer when we consider the centrality of metaphors of vision to Rousseau's revolutionary dreams. In his *Discourse on the Sciences and Arts,* conceived like Razumov's fantasized Silver Medal essay for submission in an essay competition,[4] Rousseau deplores the decline of contemporary morals in terms of social opacity. Lamenting the waning of the uncorrupted past, he writes that:

> Before Art had molded our manner and taught our passions to speak an affected language, our morals were rustic but natural, and differences of conduct announced at first glance those of character. Human nature, basically, was no better, but men found their security in the ease of seeing through each other, and that advantage, which we no longer appreciate, spared them many vices.
>
> Today, when subtler researches and a more refined taste have reduced the Art of pleasing to principles, a base and deceptive uniformity prevails in our morals, and all minds seem to have been cast in the same mold....One no longer dares to appear as he is....Therefore one will never know well those with whom he deals....(*UWE,* 6)

In the face of such degeneration, Rousseau prizes a social ideal of reciprocal transparency, in which the visibility of each subject to the other guarantees the avoidance of social vices. As Martin Jay writes, Rousseau "dreamed...of a new social order in which humans would be utterly open to each other's gaze, a utopia of mutually beneficial surveillance without reprobation or repression" (Jay, 92). This utopia was epitomized in Rousseau's notion of the festival, in which the artificial separation of observer and observed in such phenomena as the theater was eradicated in favour of a celebration of "pure presence...a communion of souls without anything to mediate between them" (93). As Rousseau concludes in his *Letter to d'Alembert*:

> Let us not opt for these exclusive spectacles, which sadly enclose a small number of people in a dark cavern; which restrain them, fearful and immobile, in silence and inaction; and which show nothing but walls, steel blades, soldiers, and other distressing images of servitude and inequality. No! Happy nations, these festivals are not yours. It is in the open air, beneath the sky that you ought to gather and give reign to the sweet sensation of happiness....Let the sun shine on your innocent spectacles. You yourselves are one of those spectacles, the worthiest on which the sun can shed its light. (quoted in Starobinski, 94)

Clear vision, the immediacy of mutual transparency, is thus for Rousseau the antidote to the scopic regime represented by the prison of the theater. As Jean Starobinski observes in his book on Rousseau, the ideal of the festival has its political counterpart in the General Will expressing the will of all in the *Social Contract*. Here, Rousseau advocates the annihilation of public/private distinctions described in such frightening terms in *Under Western Eyes* when he summarizes the rights of association in society as "reducible to a single one, namely the total alienation by each associate and all his rights to the whole community" (*UWE*, 60). As Starobinski observes, this political alienation of rights corresponds to the entry into a state of reciprocal transparency: "Each person is 'alienated' in the gaze of others, and each is restored to himself by means of universal 'recognition.' Having given itself freely, the self...discovers...pure freedom, pure transparency, through its intimate association with other free and transparent souls, indeed, with the 'communal soul'" (Starobinski, 97).

It is as "the author of the *Social Contract*" (*UWE*, 291) that Rousseau is identified in *Under Western Eyes*. The idea of such a communal soul is regarded there, however, with considerable skepticism. Rousseau in Conrad's novel is the emblem not of a benign visual disingenuousness, the coincidence of appearance and reality which eradicates lies and vice, but of an oppressive surveillance – identified with both revolutionaries and the state – that breeds dishonesty. Razumov must live a lie with respect to both the Russian government and the occupants of *La Petite Russie,* and his interviews with Mikulin "wear perhaps the sinister character of old legendary tales where the Enemy of mankind is represented holding subtly mendacious dialogues with a tempted soul" (304-5). Located on the "absurd island" that is the only place where "solitude could ever be secured in the open air" (290), Rousseau's statue presides over Razumov's writing of the spy report, the report that contributes to the illusion of his false identity as Russian patriot and the safe compositon of which requires Razumov's concealment from the eyes of the revolutionaries. The bronze effigy is thus the image of a political power that breeds the need for concealment and opacity in response to its intrusive supervision of individual privacy; the statue seems symbolically to scrutinize, as if from above, Razumov's secret writing, just as the police read "the record of his intellectual life for the last three years" (77) during their raid on his rooms. In its historical association with the French Revolution, Rousseau's image thus further confirms the ironic entanglement of radicalism and autocracy in the novel.

Conrad's hostility to Rousseau's notions of social transparency can perhaps best be seen in his skepticism toward the belief that such a mutual visibility would ensure a pure egalitarianism. For Conrad, suspicious in any case of the claims od democracy, surveillance is based on an absolute asymmetry of power which enforces the autocratic demand of complete obedience. This demand internalizes itself in the state's subjects as the need to confess, the need that torments Razumov in his isolation. Confession in *Under Western Eyes* however is associated not with truth, but with an admission that consolidates the subject's subordination to power. It is thus identified historically as a practice of domination. Mrs. Haldin remarks that "With us in Russia the church is so identified with oppression, that it seems almost necessary when one wishes to be free in this life, to give up all hope of a future existence" (103). Peter Ivanovitch's style of dress and his comments about religion speak to the modern secular extension of this oppression: wearing a "black broadcloth coat [that] invested his person with a character of austere decency – something recalling a missionary" (129), he remarks that "Sin is different in our day, and the way of salvation for pure souls is different too. It is no longer to be found in monasteries but in the world" (128).

In the first volume of his *The History of Sexuality: An Introduction,* Foucault associates confession with the empirical sciences, "the learned methods of observation and demonstration" (Foucault, *The History of Sexuality:...,* 59) that rely on vision as their structuring principle. In Conrad, confession, though it may rely on hearing rather than sight, is implicitly identified with vision through a synaesthetic identification of the two senses. Part of Razumov's mandate as a spy, for example, is to both "see and hear" (*UWE,* 311), and hearing is connected disturbingly with vision in the descriptions of Razumov's encounters with the revolutionaries. Conversing with Sophia Antonovna, Razumov "noticed the vacillation of surprise passing over the steady curiosity of the black eyes fastened on his face as if the woman revolutionist received the sound of his voice into her pupils instead of her ears" (257). To his "startled glance," similarly Peter Ivanovitch's voice "seemed to proceed from under [his]...steady spectacles...rather than from his lips, which had hardly moved" (216). This sensory conflation is placed explicitly in the confessionary context in the case of Razumov's diary, the narrator's translation of which constitutes crucial portions of the narrative. The diary is written and thus composed to be read rather than audited.

Confession is therefore associated with visual exposure in *Under Western Eyes*. The deprivation of sight is also associated with such exposure, signifying the state's power to reappropriate the prerogative of vision it has provisionally permitted its subjects to exercise. This is the power of sight that Razumov has managed to retain by his self-concealment from both Mikulin and the revolutionaries. Exposure for Razumov however culminates in its loss. His deafening, according to the synaesthetic equation of senses just noted, constitutes a symbolic blinding that Razumov experiences immediately after Nikita's assault: "he came to rest in the roadway of the street at the bottom, lying on his back, with a great flash of lightning over his face – a vivid, silent flash of lightning which blinded him utterly" (369).

This blinding is the final moment of Razumov's incarceration within the prison of the Russian scopic regime, an incarceration which is metaphorized quite literally in the description of the hotel room where he confesses to the revolutionaries:

> The walls were white, the carpet red, electric lights blazed in profusion, and the emptiness, the silence, the closed doors all alike and numbered, made me think of the perfect order of some severely luxurious model penitentiary on the solitary confinement principle. (326)

Razumov's exposure to the eye of the social revolution thus does not free him from his intolerable isolation, but confirms this isolation in such a way as to recall the isolating principle of the panopticon. His confession to Natalia Haldin prompts his recognition of this isolation: "to-day I made myself free from falsehood, from remorse – independent of every single human being on this earth" (368). Isolation thus is not freedom but a confinement that is characteristic of things Russian and associated with exposure and blindness, an "alienation" of the power of vision on Razumov's part that is a parody of Rousseau's sense of the term. These themes converge in the narrator's observation of Razumov's confession to Natalia Haldin that takes place in a cell-like space of absolute visual clarity: "The light of an electric bulb high up under the ceiling searched that clear square box into its four corners, crudely, without shadows" (342). The confession ensures their mutual alienation:

> To me, the silent spectator, they looked like two people becoming conscious of a spell which had been lying on them ever since they first set eyes on each other. Had either of them cast a glance then in my direction, I would have opened the door quietly and gone out. But

> neither did; and I remained, every fear of indiscretion lost in the sense of my enormous remoteness from their captivity within the sombre horizon of Russian problems, the boundary of their eyes, of their feelings – the prison of their souls. (345)

This confession, which marks the imprisonment and separation of Razumov and Natalia, also occurs at the moment of the latter's final absorption into the "corrupted dark immensity claiming her for its own" of Russia (356). In this respect, Razumov's confessions to Natalia and the revolutionaries differ significantly from his meetings with Mikulin; Razumov's words to Natalia are self-motivated, rather than coerced by an external power. They are uttered, furthermore, in contexts in which he feels himself not to be under suspicion and constitute a revelation of moral truth. Conrad thus distinguishes between what might be called institutional confession, characterized by duress and by its failure to produce moral truth, and free confession, which does produce such truth. For Razumov however the distinction is finally irrelevant, since free confession is nevertheless exposure to the surveillance of state and revolution. As far as this surveillance is concerned, morality is superfluous.

It is worth noting how this visually-oriented process of incarceration and isolation has analogies in the changing physical description of Razumov's character over the course of the novel. For Foucault the idea of character derives from the emergence of the disciplines of psychology, sociology, and criminology in the nineteenth century, disciplines by which individuality could be isolated and described according to visual criteria. In a tantalizing passage in *Discipline and Punish*:...he associates this emerging "account of indviduality" with the "passage from the epic to the novel" (Foucault, *Discipline and Punish*:...., 193). Such a generalization invites the kind of protest articulated by Edward Said who calls Foucault's theory of power "a form of theoretical overtotalization" (Said, 246). It is certainly true that nineteenth-century realism might be said to have espoused at some level the principle of fixed and clearly definable character disclosed to the eye of an omniscient narrator. Conrad's rejection of such narrative omniscience, demonstrated in his repeated dramatization of the telling and hearing of narrative, not least in *Under Western Eyes,* however, indicates his skepticism of such a principle. This skepticism most often manifests itself in doubts about the truth of personality corresponding to the visible signs of physical appearance. The entirety of *Lord Jim,* for example, after the physical description of Jim in the opening paragraph, represents a lengthy meditation on the mystery of its protagonist's personality. Similarly, *The Secret Agent* parodies Lombrosian criminology's reduction of character to criminal types according to their physiognomy by having such beliefs articulated by Ossipon as a form of superstition. In *Under Western Eyes,* this skepticism can be seen in the way in which Razumov is subjected to precisely such a visual fixing over the course of the novel as he is pulled deeper into the Russian visual net. His initial description is notable for its visually ill-defined quality:

> his good looks would have been unquestionable if it had not been for a peculiar lack of fineness in the features. It was as if the face modelled vigorously in wax (with some approach even to a classical correctness of type) had been held close to a fire till all sharpness of line had been lost in the softening of the material. (*UWE,* 5)

Once Razumov is conscripted into the surveillance system, and he begins the inevitable movement toward his final exposure and incarceration within the scopic regime, the blurriness of his features is replaced by a description much more distinct and clear cut: "His features were more decided than in the generality of Russian faces; he had a line of the jaw, a clean-shaven, sallow cheek; his nose was a ridge and not a mere protuberance" (179). Peter Ivanovitch on the other hand, in his capacity of inscrutable observer, remains visually indistinct: "He had one of those bearded Russian faces without shape, a mere appearance of flesh and hair with not a single feature having any sort of character" (120).

Conrad's construction of character thus defies Foucault's generalizations about the novel. Does Conrad's construction of the Russian scopic regime in *Under Western Eyes* differ in any

other way from Foucault's notion of panopticism? It is important to recognize, in this respect, that while the novel demonstrates the complicity of vision and power, it also shows how the
dominant mode of vision, that of the gaze that attempts to pierce
the opacity of obscure subjects or events, is incapable of
revealing truth. The gazes that crisscross the narrative of *Under
Western Eyes* are either too weak – as in the case of the teacher of
languages' failed attempts to penetrate the screen of illusions
surrounding Russia – or too strong, as in the case of the
authorities' totalizing gaze which breaks its victims as it exposes
them. Indeed the insistently pressing Russian system of vison is
constructed throughout the novel as a moral blindness. Peter
Ivanovitch is an "enormous blind teacher" (329); the eyes of
Sophia Antonovna and Mme. de S–, like the cloud of autocracy
that claims Natalia Haldin at the end of the novel, are described
repeatedly in terms of their darkness; and it is the "true
conspirator's blindness" (283) of Haldin and the revolutionaries
as well as of Mikulin that lands Razumov in his intolerable
circumstances.

For Conrad unlike Foucault surveillance transmits power but
does not produce truth. It is Razumov's faulty vision in fact that
is morally clear in its perception of the monstrous reality of
Russian society. As he remarks to Natalia, "I have had the
misfortune to be born clear-eyed. And if you only knew what
strange things I have seen! What amazing and unexpected
apparitions!" (345). It is in fact amazingly and unexpectedly that
truth emerges into sight in the novel, appearing accidentally and
as if of its own accord, out of the pressure of events rather than
from the acuity of any perceiver's gaze. It is viewed not through
the gaze but in the instant of the glance, the glimpse behind the
scenes so often referred to by the narrator, constituting an order
of vision different from that of the supervising gaze. Such
glimpses characterize the moments of insight in the novel
experienced by both Mrs. Haldin when she reads of de P–'s
assassination and the narrator as he observes Razumov's
confession to Natalia. The very disclosure of the truth of Russia
that is central to both of these instants, however, involves its own

dangers. In the first case, Mrs. Haldin reacts differently to the English newspaper than to the teacher of languages, who merely comes up again against the screen of "theatrical and morbidly affected" (110) images of Russia. She is stricken by her brief vision of monstrosity: "I did not imagine," the narrator remarks, "that a number of the *Standard* could have the effect of Medusa's head. Her face went stony in a moment" (111). He is himself affected by a vision of his own superfluousness that arises out of his witness of Razumov and Natalia's meeting however: "The true cause dawned on me: he had discovered that he needed her – and she was moved by the same feeling. It was the second time that I saw them together, and I knew that next time they met I would not be there, either remembered or forgotten. I would have virtually ceased to exist for both these young people" (347).

The proximity of the glance to the gaze and its power to disclose the truth of the scopic regime causes dangers to arise. Opening visually onto the different order of vision characterized by the state's surveillance, the desultory accidental glance does not actively expose the truth but receives it passively and unexpectedly. This passivity however involves the glance in a dangerous paradox, for its very dissociation from the object-ifying, "fixing" operation of surveillance deprives it of the safety of distance. To oppose the fixing powers of the Russian gaze is also to reject the possibility of containing that gaze within its proper bounds, the "sombre horizon of Russian problems" (345); the glimpsed exposure of Russia to the eye of the West risks the possibility of releasing it. Thus the narrator's glimpse into the heart of Russian affairs threatens to involve him in the dialectics of surveillance. The emergence of the truth of Natalia and Razumov's final meeting occurs simultaneously with a mo-ment of self-reflection in which the teacher of languages' experience is associated with tormenting exposure: "standing thus before each other in the glaring light, between the four bare walls, they seemed brought out from the confused immensity of the Eastern borders to be exposed cruelly to the observation of my Western eyes" (346). To Razumov the narrator appears another incarnation of the proliferating network of lies bred by surveillance: "Could he have been the devil himself in the shape of an old Englishman?" (360).

The narrator's entry into the Russian system of vision is momentary, a sudden access of vision that is sealed by Razumov's exit and by Natalia's return to the center of Russia. Once again distant from Russian affairs, the teacher of languages must rely on Sophia Antonovna's secondhand news to construct the rest of their two stories. The dangerous proximity of the truthful glimpse to the gaze of political surveillance, the ability of the former to be infected by the latter and for the gaze to spread and displace the possibility of truth in the innocent Western eye, however, remain threatening possibilities that lend a cautionary note to the novel. The remark of the narrator's acquaintance's wife about Mme. de S– that "I should not be surprised if she were more dangerous than an Englishman would be willing to believe" (163) thus resonates with Razumov's ominous comment about the imminent shattering of the screen of received ideas about Russia: "What's going on with us is of no importance – a mere sensational story to amuse the readers of the papers – the superior contemptuous Europe. It is hateful to think of. But let them wait a bit!" (189).

These cautionary hints find more explicit echoes in "Autocracy and War," another of Conrad's texts dealing with Russia that was written prior to *Under Western Eyes*. Here referring to the Japanese victory over Russia in 1905, Conrad speaks warningly of "the explosive ferment of a moral grave, whence may yet emerge a political organism to take the place of a gigantic and dreaded phantom" ("Autocracy and War," *NLL*, 86). This organism, at the end of the essay, is shown to be Germany, whose militant threat is described in terms that associate political might with vision:

> The German eagle with a Prussian head looks all round the horizon not so much for something to do that would count for good in the records of the earth, as simply for something good to get. He gazes upon the land and upon the sea with the same covetous steadiness, for he has become of late a maritime eagle, and has learned to box the compass. He gazes north and south, and east and west, and is inclined

> to look intemperately upon the waters of the Mediterranean when
> they are blue. (113)

The threat to England, apparent in the allusion to the British
navy in the last sentence, is associated with the weakness of
Western sight, of "those who gaze half-unbelieving at the
passing away of the Russian phantom" (113).

The fact that the threat remains despite the laying of the
Russian ghost here points to a question central to my reading of
Under Western Eyes, but which I have not yet explicitly
addressed. This is the question of whether Conrad is in fact
concerned in the novel with conveying "the effect produced on
him by Russia," in Edward Crankshaw's words (Crankshaw,
101), or whether as Reynold Humphries argues in a recent
article, "*Under Western Eyes* is not 'about' Russia at all"
(Humphries, 13). Certainly considerable energy has been devoted to freeing Conrad from what Tony Tanner sees as the slur cast
upon him by "[t]oo much insensitive criticism [that] has charged
the book with being a crude and embittered anti-Russian tract"
(Tanner, 198). Crude and embittered it is not, but to detect an
anti-Russian sentiment in *Under Western Eyes* is not to reduce
the entire novel to the level of propaganda, or in Tanner's words
to unduly "confuse Conrad the conservative essayist with
Conrad the profound novelist" (198). At the same time, Keith
Carabine's work on the novel, which persuasively demonstrates
that it is a veiled narrative of Poland,[5] combined with the
identification of Germany as the post-Russian threat in "Autocracy and War," clearly indicates that the scopic regime
delineated in *Under Western Eyes* is by far not an exclusively
Russian phenomenon. As Mark Conroy has shown, for example, the London of *The Secret Agent* is also the locus of
a panoptical regime. It is worth keeping in mind however that the
Poland about which Conrad is writing is a Russified Poland, in
which his father's revolutionary activities cost himself and
Conrad's mother their lives. By the same token, Germany in the
essay may be understood not as a spontaneous phantom, but as
the reincarnation of the Russian regime. And the nocturnal

aquarium of *The Secret Agent* is muddied by the bomb plot that is initiated by Vladimir – whose Russian-sounding name numerous critics have noted – in an effort to allow the repressive practices of the European regimes to jump the channel into relatively liberal Britain. This plot culminates in the explosion at Greenwich and Winnie Verloc's fears of being hanged, elements that have, in the words, of the teacher of languages, "the associations of bomb and gallows – a lurid Russian colouring" (*UWE*, 112). It is safe to say that Conrad's association of autocracy with Russia in *Under Western Eyes* was not to limit it to Russia. It was, however, to suggest the scopic regime by which Russian autocracy maintained itself as a mechanism by which an entire national character as Conrad saw it could be turned monstrous; to suggest the strategies of deceit necessitated by existence under such conditions of perpetual scrutiny; and to worry about the spread of that spectral surveillance, and the autocracy it reinforced, far beyond the boundaries of Russia itself.

NOTES

1. A predominance of visual metaphors is just one aspect of ocularcentrism, a term which Jay applies to the more general claim that "certain cultures or ages have been...'dominated' by vision" (Jay, 3). This domination, he argues, is not attributable solely to physiology or evolution but is "best understood in historical terms" (3).

2. Jay uses this term to denote what might be called the "ideology of seeing" specific to a given society or age. The term "regime" suggests the more specific sense of centralized surveillance that I develop in this essay.

3. In his essay on "The 'Uncanny'" (1919), Freud observes that both deriving the etymology of the word "uncanny" in various languages and "collect[ing] all those properties of persons, things, sensations, experiences and situations which arouse in us the feeling of uncanniness...lead to the same result: the 'uncanny' is that class of the terrifying which leads us back to something long known to us, once very familiar" (Freud, 369-70).

4. The essay which eventually became the *Discourse on the Sciences and Arts* was written for an essay prize offered by the Academy of Dijon in 1749 on the question "Has the progress of the sciences and arts done more to corrupt morals or improve them?" Rousseau's description of his inspiration for the essay, which occurred on the road to Vincennes where he

was on his way to visit the imprisoned Diderot, are worth noting here in that they recall the mysticism associated with revolutionary fervor in *Under Western Eyes*: upon reading the question in a copy of the *Mercure de France*, Rousseau writes in *The Confessions*, "I beheld another universe and became another man....I was in a state of agitation bordering on delirium" (Rousseau, *The Confessions*, 326-7).

5. Carabine argues that "Both Razumov's 'record' and *Under Western Eyes* can be traced to Conrad's own 'fatal memories' of his 'unforgettable' Polish past, and to his deeply ambivalent attitude to and reassessment of his 'race and family'" (Carabine, 18).

WORKS CITED

Carabine Keith. "'The Figure Behind the Veil:' Conrad and Razumov in *Under Western Eyes*," in *Joseph Conrad's "Under Western Eyes:" Beginnings, Revisions, Final Forms*, ed. David R. Smith. Hamden: Archon Books, 1991, 1-37.

Conroy Mark. *Modernism and Authority: Strategies of Legitimation in Flaubert and Conrad*. Baltimore: Johns Hopkins U.P., 1985.

Crankshaw Edward. "Conrad and Russia," in *Joseph Conrad: A Commemoration*, ed. Norman Sherry. London: Macmillan, 1976, 91-104.

Fleishman Avrom. *Conrad's Politics: Community and Anarchy in the Fiction of Joseph Conrad*. Baltimore: Johns Hopkins U.P., 1967.

Foucault Michel. *Discipline and Punish: The Birth of the Prison*, trans. Alan Sheridan. New York: Vintage, 1979.

Foucault Michel. *The History of Sexuality: An Introduction*, trans. Robert Hurley. New York: Vintage, 1990.

Freud Sigmund. "The 'Uncanny'," trans. Alex Strachey, in Freud Sigmund. *Collected Papers*, vol. 4. New York: Basic Books, 1959.

Jay Martin. *Downcast Eyes: The Denigration of Vision in Twentieth-Century French Thought*. Berkeley: U. of California P., 1994.

Najder Zdzisław. "Conrad and Rousseau: Concepts of Man and Society," in *Joseph Conrad: A Commemoration*, ed. Norman Sherry, London: Macmillan, 1976.

Plato. *The Republic*, revised ed., trans. and Introduction Desmond Lee. Harmondsworth: Penguin, 1955.

Rousseau Jean-Jacques. *The Confessions*, trans. and Introduction J. M. Cohen. Harmondsworth: Penguin, 1953.

Rousseau Jean-Jacques. *Discourse on the Sciences and Arts. Collected Writings*, vol. 2, eds. Roger D. Masters and Christopher Kelly, trans. Judith R. Bush, Roger D. Masters, and Christopher Kelly. Hanover: University Press of New England, 1992.

Said Edward. *The World, the Text and the Critic*. Cambridge, MA: Harvard U.P., 1983.

Starobinski Jean. *Jean-Jacques Rousseau: Transparency and Obstruction*, trans. Arthur Goldhammer, Introduction Robert J. Morrissey. Chicago: U. of Chicago P., 1988.

Tanner Tony. "Nightmare and Complacency: Razumov and the Western Eye," *Critical Quarterly* 4:3 (1962), 197-214.

Wollaeger Mark A. *Joseph Conrad and the Fictions of Skepticism*. Stanford: Stanford U.P., 1990.

Carola M. Kaplan,
California State Polytechnic University,
Pomona, USA

Conrad the Pole: Definitively not "One of Us"

For Ricki

Józef Teodor Konrad Korzeniowski – an English writer? Obviously not. Joseph Conrad – a Polish author writing in English? Equally inconceivable. Somewhere between these two impossible literary positions resides the work of Conrad the novelist. No one understood better the anomaly of his place in letters than Conrad himself. To his French translator, Conrad explained the unique perspective of his work: "Do not forget that it is written for the English – from the point of view of the effect it will have on an English reader" (*CL*, IV, 28). Distinguishing himself from a "national writer like Kipling" who "talks about his compatriots," Conrad went on to say that his writing is "for them" (29). To a Polish correspondent, he lamented, "It is thus, with poignant grief in my heart, that I write novels to amuse the English!" (Najder, 225; *CL*, II, 55). In these statements, Conrad reveals how clearly he sees himself as an outsider to English culture, one whose approach to his readers is calculated.[1]

Particularly in the early part of his career, Conrad saw himself as a subaltern within the shadow of the dominant English culture, colonized by his adopted language: "In writing I wrestle painfully with that language which I feel I do not possess but which possesses me" (*CL*, IV, 409). Worried that, "in the case of a writer such as I am, of unconventional origin, literary achievement – as well as personal character...will be...scrutinised with no friendly eye" (*CL*, III, 260), he determined "to make such originality as I possess *acceptable* to the public" (121). For these reasons, throughout his career, but particularly early on, Conrad wrote only obliquely of his Polish background.

The question arises, how did Conrad manage to express his Polishness in his early work? Using the examples of *Lord Jim* (1900) and "Amy Foster" (1901), I will argue that Conrad does so in two crucial ways: in *Lord Jim,* he adopts an ironic mask of approval to expose the fatuousness of English self-regard; in "Amy Foster," he condemns the xenophobic intolerance that underlies this self-approbation. Through the English persona of Charlie Marlow in *Lord Jim,* who mistakenly believes that a code of honor can sustain the Englishman who is "one of us," Conrad reveals the inadequacy of any code to protect the individual from failure or to steel him against cowardice. Further, by having Jim reenact his initial failure, Conrad demonstrates that this failure is not gratuitous, that Jim is indeed "one of us" – neither better nor worse than other members of the human community, whether English, French, African, or Polish. Thus Conrad exposes the British sense of cultural superiority as a sham and a delusion. In "Amy Foster," Conrad reveals the cruel underside of this unwarranted national pride in the xenophobia that destroys the "emigrant from Central Europe" cast up on an English shore. For Conrad, the skeptical Polish outsider, the false reassurance of community and unwarranted pride in national identity obscure an essential truth of the human condition, that "We live, as we dream – alone."

Through Charlie Marlow, the self-interested interpreter of Jim, who in the face of contradictory evidence clings to "the sovereign power enthroned in a fixed standard of conduct" (*LJ,* 50), Conrad enlists the hegemonic discourse of imperialism only to subvert it. Speaking from the perspective of a socially and politically conservative British gentleman-seaman, Marlow, in his disavowal, complicity, and cultural bias, proves as "misleading" as Jim, whose story proves to be inseparable from his own. Marlow's duplicity and self-deception serve to buttress his shaky belief in the superiority of those in command, not only at sea, but in British society at large and in the colonial enterprise. In his attempt to justify the ascendancy of the European Self over the subaltern Other, Marlow reveals, in Gayatri Chakravorty Spivak's words, "the problem of the European Subject, which seeks to produce an Other that would consolidate an inside, its own subject status" (Spivak, 293).

Marlow clings to his identity as "a member of an obscure body of men held together by a community of inglorious toil and by fidelity to a certain standard of conduct" (*LJ*, 50). Yet this assertion of a community based upon shared values is undermined rather than confirmed throughout the text. The behavior of men at sea is individual, personal, and unpredictable, as the book's multiple and conflicting perspectives confirm. Demonstrating that good training and impeccable credentials are no guarantee of honorable conduct, Jim's cowardice raises an essential doubt in Marlow's mind: "He had no business to look so sound, I thought to myself – well, if this sort can go wrong like that" (40). Tellingly, Marlow never finishes his thought, which must end in the realization: "then anyone can." This realization would mean relinquishing the notion of an exclusive community bound by a shared code of values, whose moral superiority authorizes it to govern others. Despite Marlow's avoidance of this conclusion, his repeated designation "one of us" slides in the course of the narrative from an exclusive to an inclusive signifier, one that encompasses all human beings in their common fallibility. Marlow's groundless conviction of superiority is echoed in the text by the unfounded but pervasive self-assurance of the British: in the second engineer who maintains, "I am one of them fearless fellows" (26); in Brierly, "one of those lucky fellows who know nothing of indecision, much less of self-mistrust" (57); in Jim, who has "an unbounded confidence in himself" (20); in Jim's clergyman father, who "possessed such certain knowledge of the Unknowable" (5). These instances expose "the great fact of national self-righteousness" which Conrad elsewhere ironically remarks "is great and praiseworthy and very English" (*CL*, III, 489).

Despite Marlow's protestations, the text reveals that the only seamen who live up to the standard of conduct he invokes are not the officers but the Malay helmsmen who continue to steer throughout the *Patna* crisis. Governed by the code of behavior they have been taught as subordinates, they never doubt that

                                      Carola M. Kaplan

their commanding officers are bound by the same strictures. When questioned, one of the helmsmen testifies that "it never came into his mind then that the white men were about to leave the ship through fear of death. He did not believe it now. There might have been secret reasons" (*LJ*, 98). Although the power structure in which the Malay helmsmen are subordinate prevents them from questioning the behavior of their superiors, their bravery and adherence to duty as well as their trust and vulnerability comment damningly on the moral authority of whites to govern.

The only real community that exists in the first half of *Lord Jim* is not a community of seamen, but the community of pilgrims on board the *Patna* the "eight hundred men and women" (14), who are "unconscious pilgrims of an exacting belief" (15). Unable to speak within the European hegemonic context of the novel, the pilgrims enter "without a word, a murmur, or a look back" (14). As Spivak points out, the subaltern cannot speak (Spivak, 289): the western literary text can articulate only the colonialist position. Further, any attempt by a first-world writer to give voice to the subaltern position is necessarily an assimilation, "an appropriation and reinscription of the Third World as an Other" (289).

Conrad avoids this pitfall by acknowledging his ignorance. His manner of describing the pilgrims suggests his difficulty in giving any coherent interpretation of them: he presents the pilgrims as a mélange of body parts that do not cohere into a complete picture: "a chin upturned, two closed eyelids, a dark hand with silver rings, a meagre limb draped in a torn covering, a head bent back, a naked foot, a throat bared and stretched as if offering itself to the knife" (*LJ*, 18). This fragmented, literally disjointed representation suggests the indescribability of a community that is incomprehensible to a western perspective.

Aware of the violence that can befall these third-world pilgrims in giving themselves into the questionable safekeeping of the West, even foreshadowing their victimization ("a throat bared and stretched as if offering itself to the knife"), Conrad as a self-conscious "first-world subject of Knowledge" avoids the epistemic violence of "recognition" of the Third World through "assimilation" (Spivak, 292). At the same time, through his own peculiar version of synecdoche, he uses the image of body fragments to suggest a whole entity or community that is unrepresentable within the text.

As Pierre Macherey reminds us, "What the work *cannot say* is important, because there the elaboration of the utterance is acted out, in a sort of journey to silence" (Macherey, 87): "It is this silence...which informs us of the precise conditions for the appearance of an utterance, and thus its limits, giving its real significance, without, for all that, speaking in its place" (86). The silence of the pilgrims, which points up their passivity and vulnerability, is in fact a plea: it urges "a special regard for the rights of the unprivileged of the earth," which Conrad considered the constitutive feature of a Polish identity (*PR*, vii). Their silence also testifies eloquently to the gravity of Jim's dereliction of duty in his betrayal of their helplessness and trust: "The ship of iron, the men with white faces, all the sights, all the sounds, everything on board to that ignorant and pious multitude was strange alike, and as trustworthy as it would for ever remain incomprehensible" (*LJ*, 85-6).[2]

The community of believers on board the *Patna* – alien, unknowable, without individuation, voiceless – is linked metonymically to the community of Polish nationalists of Conrad's childhood. Emissaries of a foreign culture that cannot be represented in the text, they recall Conrad's professed "fidelity to an absolutely lost cause" (*CL*, II, 161) and his two-tiered identity as "homo duplex" (*CL*, III, 491), of which he wrote, "I...have a double life one of them peopled only by shadows growing more precious as the years pass" (491).[3] In psychoanalytic terms, the community of believers below deck suggests the hidden but unsinkable store of memories of another culture that impinge upon the conscious life of the writer and on the culture presented on the surface of the text. Only the pilgrims have "a faith invulnerable to the strength of facts" (*LJ*, 43), which Marlow stipulates is necessary for heroic action. Compared to their transcendent belief, any standard of conduct without divine authority, is, as J. Hillis Miller observes in his discussion of *Lord Jim,* "without validity...an arbitrary code of behavior....Nothing matters, and anything is possible, as in that condition of spiritual anarchy which takes over on the ship's boat after Jim and the other officers have deserted the *Patna* and left her to sink with eight hundred men, women, and children" (217).

In light of this awareness, the narrative of *Lord Jim* expresses a nostalgic longing for a lost community of belief rather than confirms the existence of a modern value-based community within the British Empire. As Fredric Jameson points out, the question of value – of "the reason for pursuing this or that life task, in this or that fashion" (Jameson, 249) – arises in western culture only after "the secularization of life under capitalism and the breaking up...of the older tradition-oriented systems of castes and inherited professions" (249). The moral crisis of the individual, as exemplified by Jim's story, arises from the loss of traditional patterns and communal belief systems in the modern world. Thus, value "becomes visible as...a strange afterimage on the retina" (250). Paradoxically, then, "the very idea of value comes into being at the moment of its own disappearance" (251). In applauding value as an abstraction, *Lord Jim* confirms its loss and yearns for an un-self-conscious communal system of belief, such as that of the pilgrims, to which the modern industrial nation-state can no longer subscribe.

Thus, if we reverse the displacement in the text, the locus of meaning shifts from the ruling class of the British Empire to the subalterns they govern. Communal responsibility and courageous action are exemplified not by the officers but by the Malay seamen; not by the colonizers but by the Bugis tribesmen. Analogously, the community based on faith and sacrifice is not that of British seamen but that of the pilgrims bound for Mecca.

If the value-based community that Marlow posits does not exist, his narrative suggests that British colonial power is arbitrary and that Jim's use of Patusan as a site for personal redemption in an unwarranted appropriation of another culture that necessarily ends in betrayal and social destruction. The underlying justification for Jim's course of action, the text reveals, is not a communal code but the unconscious assumption of racial and cultural superiority. This assumption suffuses Marlow's language of binary oppositions: in his distinctions between "one of us" and "one of them," between "the right sort" and "no-account chaps," between good traders like Stein and exploitative colonizers like Chester.

Upon examination, however, these distinctions break down. The label "one of us" proves to be no greater a mark of distinction than the labels that adorn the trunks of the white travellers who remain ignorant throughout their around-the--world tour: "Henceforth they would be labelled as having passed through this and that place, and so would be their luggage. They would cherish this distinction...and preserve the gummed tickets on their portmanteaux...as the only permanent trace of their improving enterprise" (*LJ,* 77). In this context, as on the *Patna,* only the natives, in their jobs as waiters, know why they are there and behave creditably: "The dark-faced servants tripped without noise over the vast and polished floor" (77). Although Marlow and Jim maintain that Jim is "altogether of another sort" (80) from that "hound" the German captain of the *Patna,* Jim thinks he overhears himself called a "wretched cur" (70) because he unconsciously equates himself with the cowardly captain. Finally, the apparently benevolent Stein, in his habit of collecting butterflies and beetles, shows himself as ruthless as Chester in acquiring native materials for personal gain: "Stein never failed to annex on his own account every butterfly or beetle he could lay hands on" (206). Never does Stein consider returning his specimens to the places from which he seized them: "To my small native town this my collection I shall bequeath. Something of me. The best" (205). Thus, in his own words, Stein equates his sense of himself with the appropriation of the Other.

Although Marlow's false binary oppositions do not survive scrutiny, they suffuse his discourse as justification of the right of "one of us" to govern, both at home and abroad. This justification is based on what Abdul R. JanMohamed terms "the manichean allegory...a field of diverse yet interchangeable oppositions between white and black, good and evil, superiority and inferiority...self and Other, subject and object" (JanMohamed, 82). While the value accorded each of the oppositional terms is arbitrary, the meaning of the opposition of black and white never shifts. Within the colonial construct, white is always superior and therefore necessarily ascendant over black. Revealingly, the attractive physical attributes Marlow most repeatedly cites as evidence that Jim is "one of us" are his distinctively white features: his blue eyes, fair skin, and fair hair.

Just as Stein considers any buttefly he finds in a colonial outpost his for the taking, Patusan exists for Jim solely as an "opportunity" that "sat veiled by his side like an Eastern bride waiting to be uncovered by the hand of the master" (*LJ*, 243-4). Jim's entry into Patusan is authorized by the colonialist assumption that it is a place without worth, culture, or history, except for those that white men confer upon it. As Marlow avers, "This was, indeed, one of the lost, forgotten, unknown places of the earth" (323), "of no earthly importance to anybody" (218). Clearly, the Bugis who live there are not "anybody" in Marlow's terms. They are but the shadow projections of British narcissism. Both Marlow and Jim see Patusan as existing apart from "the world where events move, men change, light flickers" (330). To them, only the western world contains events that move and men who matter. Finally, Patusan, for Marlow and Jim, is merely an imaginary place: "a picture created by fancy on a canvas" (330); and "like something you read of in books" (233-4). This interpretation of Patusan exemplifies what Edward Said terms "a textual attitude" (Said, 295), in which the visitor finds in a culture only that which he already knows, what he has seen in paintings or read in books. Never does the outsider then have to learn the distinct features of a culture he is ignorant of nor respond to the human claims of its inhabitants. Like a painting or a book, the colony – in this instance, Patusan – functions as a commodity to enrich the life of the colonizer.

According to this view, the people of Patusan are also commodites. Not surprisingly, Jim's beloved, Jewel, becomes conflated with the precious gem her name suggests. Thus, Jim's relationship with Jewel gets transposed into a rumor that a mysterious white man in Patusan has obtained an enormous, priceless emerald and that, since "such a jewel...is best preserved by being concealed about the person of a woman," " a tall girl, whom the white man treated with great respect and care...wore the white man's jewel concealed upon her bosom" (*LJ*, 280-1). Since within a colonial context, Jewel is necessarily commodified, Jim's devotion to her can be understood only as a protection of his material interests.

Indeed, the text suggests that Jim does view Jewel as his most prized possession. Since Jim's love is inextricably interwoven with his egotism, he never sees Jewel as a separate and distinct person. Accordingly, he ignores her assertion that she can defend herself and that only pity prevents her form killing Cornelius; and he insists upon "rescuing" her. In their time together, he does not respond to her anxieties, to her advice, or even to her desperate pleas. Jewel exists for Jim only as an extension of self, as a flattering specular image. As Spivak notes, "Within the effaced itinerary of the subaltern subject, the tract of sexual difference is doubly effaced....If, in the context of colonial production, the subaltern has no history and cannot speak, the subaltern as female is even more deeply in shadow" (Spivak, 289).

Within this conceptual framework, a mutual or syncretic relationship between colonizer and colonized is impossible. In Lacanian terms, the Bugis community exists for Marlow and Jim only within the imaginary order.[4] Thus, the natives serve as a projection of displaced elements of the imperialist self. This specular image is characterized by disorder, childlike dependency, and unfocused aggression. The imaginary construction of the Other confirms the identity of the European subject as powerful, all-knowing, and necessary for the natives' survival. In the course of the narrative, this imaginary construction undermines both the colonizers and the colonized in several crucial ways.

First, the natives internalize the colonizers' inflated sense of self-worth. Thus they get into "the habit of taking [Jim's] word for anything and everything" (*LJ*, 268) and consider Jim's pledge "the one truth of every passing day" (272). As a result, Jim becomes "the virtual ruler of the land" (273), esteemed above Doramin, their own elected leader. Unable to understand Jim and therefore unable to appraise him, they turn Jim into myth, ascribing to him "supernatural powers" (266). Their veneration in turn intensifies Jim's grandiose narcissism; and Jim loses all ability to assess himself or to acknowledge his limitations. Symptomatically, Jim invites Marlow to appreciate the "wonderful effect" of the moon over Patusan, "as though he had had a hand in regulating that unique spectacle" (221).

Second, in overvaluing themselves, Marlow and Jim necessarily undervalue the natives. More than either can acknowledge, Marlow and Jim act out of racist assumptions. Marlow values Dain Waris only in relation to Jim, although he is more courageous, intelligent, and trustworthy than his friend. For his part, Jim is swayed by Brown's appeal to his residual racism: "You have been white once, for all your tall talk of this being your own people and you being one with them. Are you?" (381). On the assumption of their racial and cultural superiority, Jim "did not distrust Brown" (394) and defends Brown to the Bugis, explaining, "Their chief had spoken to him in the language of his own people, making clear many things difficult to explain in any other speech" (391).

In response, the Bugis internalize the colonizers' depreciation of native culture. Esteeming themselves insufficiently, they ignore the sound advice of Dain Waris, their own leader, who urges them to fight Brown; and instead follow Jim's advice, even though it makes no sense to them. Dain Waris, "that brave and intelligent youth...had not Jim's racial prestige and the reputation of invincible, supernatural power....Beloved, trusted, and admired as he was, he was still one of *them,* while Jim was one of *us*" (220). In this statement, Marlow exposes the malignant underside of the "one of us – one of them" distinction, which robs a people of their power and of their belief in themselves. As JanMohamed points out, the colonialist, "exercising his assumed superiority...destroys without any significant qualms the effectiveness of indigenous economic, social, political, legal, and moral systems and imposes his own versions of these structures on the Other" (JanMohamed, 85).

In short, *Lord Jim* uses the conventions of the colonialist adventure tale to question imperialist ideology and cultural hegemony.[5] Calling upon his own experience of marginality and oppression, Conrad employs the discourse of domination only to reveal its self-deceptions, its blindnesses, and its tyranny. The novel exemplifies what Homi K. Bhabha terms "hybridity:" a discourse that apparently repeats the "discriminatory identity effects" of colonialism, only to reimplicate these effects in "strategies of subversion that turn the gaze of the discriminated back upon the eye of power" (Bhabha, 173).

Reworking the same material from a different perspective, Conrad in "Amy Foster" offers something akin to a mathematical proof of the voicelessness and unrepresentability of the Other. Although apparently "taken in" by English villagers, Yanko, the castaway from central Europe who is the focus of the narrative, remains an outsider: his native language is considered gibberish; his behavior, madness; his faith, heathenism. Even the woman who loves him turns against him and leaves him to die of thirst and exposure. Despite his intense efforts to make himself known, he dies without anyone learning his real name.[6]

Like the pilgrims, the Malay helmsmen, and the Bugis community, Yanko is in many ways superior to the English – imaginative, graceful, sensitive, loyal, "innocent of heart, and full of good will" (*TS,* 132) – yet the English see him as inferior simply because he is different from them; and, in effect, they render him speechless. Consequently, he does not tell his own story, for, like the pilgrims, he cannot: his tale is told only after his death by a well-intentioned but culturally short-sighted confidant, who evinces much the same limited perspective as Marlow. Although Conrad originally intended to name the story either "A Husband" or "A Castaway," his final title, "Amy Foster," emphasizes that the Other is necessarily effaced by a culture that cannot understand him.

Analogously, the eponymous heroine, who also never speaks for herself, is effaced from the text in much the same way as her foreign husband. This double erasure suggests that women, even within their own culture, are viewed as the Other; and therefore remain unknowable from a male perspective. The apparently well-meaning Dr. Kennedy, in telling Amy's story, eerily echoes the obtuseness and silencing of the English in their treatment of Yanko. Thus, Kennedy describes "the inertness of her mind" (107), the "curious want of definiteness" in her face (108), "her dumb eyes" (138), and her "dull nature" (138). He cannot fathom how a woman with such a "dull brain" (142) could command the imagination to fall in love with Yanko; and he speculates without evidence that after Yanko's death she forgets all about him (142).

Kennedy seems as determined to see Amy in terms of his preconceptions about her as the English are determined to overlook Yanko's good qualities in favor of their deep-seated prejudices. In a story devoted to showing that the Other is unknowable and that people see only what they want to see, the doctor, a distanced diagnostician, demonstrates the unreliability of a narration in which one who holds power attempts to represent the subaltern position. As in many of his other fictions, Conrad supplements his primary story in "Amy Foster" with an analogous secondary narrative that underscores his central theme.

In "Amy Foster," Conrad's central concern is to reconstruct – if only posthumously and at one remove – the overlooked story of the Other. Accordingly, there is a close intertextual relationship between Yanko's experiences on board the ship during its crisis and the experiences of the pilgrims in *Lord Jim* on board the *Patna*. Relating the story in "Amy Foster" from the vantage point of the victim below deck, Conrad in effect retells the *Patna* incident from the standpoint of one of the pilgrims:

> He [Yanko] had been hustled together with many others on board an emigrant ship...too bewildered to take note of his surroundings, too weary to see anything, too anxious to care. They were driven below into the 'tween-deck and battened down....It was very large, very cold, damp, and sombre....People groaned, children cried, water dripped, the lights went out, the walls of the place creaked, and everything was

> being shaken....An awful sickness overcame him...one could not tell whether it was morning or evening. It seemed always to be night in that place. (*TS*, 115-16)

The effect of reading Yanko's and the pilgrims' experiences intertextually is to condemn outright Jim's abandonment of eight hundred human beings such as Yanko.

Further, the reader is made to participate in Yanko's bewilderment, discomfort, and disorientation through Conrad's use of a narrative device that Victor Shklovsky terms "defamiliarization" (Shklovsky, 792), a technique that describes ordinary objects and events in terms of discrete details and sensations as experienced by someone who has never encountered them before and who is therefore unable to interpret them. Thus Yanko, who has never before seen a ship, describes the mast as "bare trees in the shape of crosses, extremely high" (*TS*, 115); he describes his first railway ride as "travelling a long, long time on the iron track" (114); and a railway terminal as "large and lofty and full of noise and smoke and gloom" where "they rang a bell, and another steam-machine came in" (115). Through this technique of defamiliarization, the reader experiences the difficulties of entering into a new culture and attempting to make sense of it.

As an inexperienced interpreter of his new world, England, Yanko is prone to make errors in cultural interpretation similar to those made by colonizers in entering another culture. For a long time he thinks that the "undiscovered country" (112) of England is America (129) where "he might have expected to find wild beasts or wild men" (112); he is puzzled to find that ships have names "like Christian people;" he speaks of the American head of state as alternately "the Emperor or America" and "the American Kaiser" (116); he takes the servant girl Amy Foster for a "gracious lady" (124); and he considers people of modest means wealthy. At times, Yanko's naive observations function as criticism of the culture he has entered: surprised at the bareness of churches in a country of such wealth, he cannot understand why they are locked on weekdays: "There was nothing to steal in them. Was it to keep people from praying too often?" (131). In following Yanko's errors, the reader becomes aware of the errors that necessarily result from entrance into a culture different from one's own. Perhaps Conrad's awareness of the errors of cultural interpretation helps to explain his own reluctance, beyond superficial description, to represent cultures he knows little about.

By reading this story from Yanko's perspective, the reader in effect experiences the English through the eyes of the colonized. The most appalling feature of the villagers' treatment of Yanko is their failure to acknowledge him as a fellow human being. They refer to him as "something" (125), "the creature" (120), and "outlandish" (127). Although, as Kennedy observes, he is "very good-looking, and most graceful in his bearing" (134), the villagers continue to find him "odious" (134). All his graces and virtues – his "voice light and soaring – like a lark's" (132); his nimble dancing (132); his "quick, fervent utterance" (132) – they consider "peculiarities" (132) or even "insanity" (120). And although "people became used to see him," "they never became used to him" (132). In reality, they never really see him at all.

In all these cruel details of Yanko's life as an exile, Conrad reveals the utter loneliness of being viewed as the Other. "We feel profoundly our own strangeness – the strangeness of creatures thrown...upon the mercy of another race...whose tongue, thoughts, manners are a complete and momentous mystery."[7] Further, Conrad's portrait of the English is of a remarkably cruel, suspicious, and mean-spirited people, utterly unable to sympathize with anyone from another culture. In his outcast state, Yanko's cruelest suffering is not physical but psychological: "He remembered the pain of his wretchedness and misery, his heartbroken astonishment that it was neither seen nor understood, his dismay at finding all the men angry and all the women fierce" (124). Although he lives in England for the rest of his life, he remains a stranger. In Yanko's "dismal story" (*CL*, II, 401), "arising from irreconcilable differences and from that fear of the Incomprehensible that hangs over all our heads" (*TS*, 108), Conrad dramatizes the reasons for his reluctance to speak about his Polish background to his English readers.

Viewed together, these two early works by Conrad problematize the construction of self and Other and demonstrate that if syncretism is not possible within the power structure of colonialism, then neither is the appropriation of the Other its necessary alternative. By interrogating the hegemonic outlook that conceives of the subaltern only as a narcissistic extension of the western subject, Conrad's symbolic fictions stage their own resistance to colonialism from within the apparent confines of European ethnocentrism. Occupying an uneasy space between two cultures, resonating to the suffering of the dispossessed yet acknowledging the impossibility of speaking for the traditional cultures that have suffered western intrusion, Conrad's early writings reveal the abuses of imperial power, expose the vacuous claim of western cultural superiority, and lament the cost for both colonizer and colonized of arbitrary divisions among human beings. Thus in these seminal works, Conrad's writing practice prepares the way for an even more radical discourse in which writers will no longer attempt to interpret the Other but rather will help us to listen to the voice of the *tout-autre,* the "quite-other" (Derrida quoted by Spivak, 294), within ourselves.

NOTES

1. Conrad's complex response to his uneasy position as a writer in English is abundantly documented in his correspondence. At times, he sees his anomaly as his greatest strength, the source of his originality, as when he declares, "One may read everybody and yet in the end want to read me....For I don't resemble anybody....There is nothing in me but a turn of mind which whether valuable or worthless can not be imitated" (*CL,* III, 460). At other times, he feels persecuted and misunderstood: In reaction to a critic who has assailed him as a man "without country and language," he declares: "The answer that could be made would be incomprehensible to nine tenths of the hearers who would not have imagination enough to believe that a complex sentiment can be true. I wonder in what language the Nigger, Youth or the Mirror *could* have been written?" (*CL,* IV, 110). Often, he reveals the distance he feels from his English audience: "I have some feeling for far-off things and a taste for the analysis of simple feelings with a turn of phrase which impresses – the English. Note well that I do not say which pleases. I believe that I please nobody here" (34). Throughout, he

clearly distinguishes himself from his writing persona: for example, he describes *Nostromo* as "a very genuine Conrad" (*CL,* III, 55); and he proposes a volume of combined literary papers on the basis of "the very originality of it – the whole Conrad as it were between the covers" (229).

2. Conrad's characteristically odd phrasing in the oxymoron "strange alike" reflects in its verbal incongruity the displacement of the pilgrims and exemplifies linguistically the "strange alikeness" of Conrad's own writing, at once alien and familiar, both native and foreign to English prose style.

3. Conrad makes clear in his letters the extent to which he continued to regard himself as a Pole and therefore was unable to express in his writing a central part of his identity and of his background of experience. Describing himself as "a Polish nobleman, cased in British tar!" (*CL,* I, 52) and as "a Slav" (*CL,* III, 503), he declares at one point, "The Malays say: 'The tiger cannot change his stripes' – and I – my ultra-Slav nature" (*CL,* I, 230). To a Polish correspondent, he affirms, "During the course of all my travels round the world I never, in mind or heart, separated myself from my country;" and he expresses the hope, "then I may surely be accepted there as a compatriot, in spite of my writing in English" (*CL,* III, 78).

4. "The imaginary," according to Lacan, dates from the mirror stage of infant life, in which the child of six to eighteen months jubilantly identifies itself with its mirror image, whose wholeness and integrity belie the internal flux and fragmentation the child experiences (Lacan, 4). Because of the unbridgeable distance of the specular image with which the child identifies, the child situates within it rivalry, opposition, and aggressivity. The relation between the self and its image, which Lacan terms "the imaginary," is one in which mirroring forestalls intersubjectivity.

After the child becomes convinced of its wholeness and integrity, it is ready to enter the "symbolic order," in which it is able to recognize and identify with an imago or subject-image as a counterpart; and is then able to enter into a dialectic that links the self or I "with socially elaborated situations" (5). An equivalent stage in culture would make possible a dialectic encounter between self and Other, in which the dominant culture is able to bracket its own values and thus radically to question its basis for cultural inference and interpretation. Such a dialectic or exchange would aim at resolving cultural oppositions through syncretic solutions.

5. For a fuller discussion of Conrad's use of and departure from the conventions of the imperialist adventure tale, see White. Also consult McGee and Bongie on the colonialist and exoticist aspects, respectively, of Conrad's work.

6. Conrad's letters reveal his sensitivity about the difficulties the English had in pronouncing Slavic names. In naming his first-born son Borys, he explained to Aniela Zagórska: "I wanted to have a purely Slavonic name, but one which could not be distorted either in speech or in writing – and at the same time one which was not too difficult for foreigners (non--Slavonic)" (*CL,* II, 24). Significantly, the dilemma Conrad reported in his

choice of a name for his son mirrors his dilemma as a writer: how to present his Polish viewpoint and experiences in a manner comprehensible and acceptable to his English readers.

7. This intensely personal and emotional description appears in the manuscript. See Kirschner 299n. In the published version, the description is more subdued and impersonal: "It is indeed hard upon a man to find himself a lost stranger, helpless, incomprehensible, and of a mysterious origin, in some obscure corner of the earth" (113).

WORKS CITED

Bhabha Homi K. "Signs Taken for Wonders: Questions of Ambivalence and Authority and under a Tree Outside Delhi, May 1817," in *"Race," Writing, and Difference,* ed. Henry Louis Gates, Jr. Chicago: U. of Chicago P., 1986, 163-84.

Bongie Chris. *Exotic Memories: Literature, Colonialism, and the Fin de Siècle.* Stanford: Stanford U.P., 1991.

Jameson Fredric. *The Political Unconscious: Narrative as a Socially Symbolic Act.* Ithaca: Cornell U.P., 1981.

JanMohamed Abdul R. "The Economy of Manichean Allegory: The Function of Racial Difference in Colonial Literature," in *"Race," Writing, and Difference,* ed. Henry Louis Gates, Jr. Chicago: Chicago U.P., 1986, 78-106.

Lacan Jacques. *Écrits: A Selection,* trans. Alan Sheridan. New York: Norton, 1977.

Macherey Pierre. *A Theory of Literary Production.* London: Routledge, 1978.

McGee Patrick. *Telling the Other: The Question of Value in Modern and Postcolonial Writing.* Ithaca: Cornel U.P., 1992.

Miller J. Hillis. "The Interpretation of *Lord Jim,*" in *The Interpretation of Narrative: Theory and Practice,* ed. Morton W. Bloomfield. Cambridge, MA: Harvard U.P., 1970, 211-28.

Najder Zdzisław, ed. *Conrad's Polish Background: Letters to and from Polish Friends,* trans. Halina Carroll. London: Oxford U.P., 1964.

Said Edward. *Orientalism.* New York: Vintage, 1979.

Shklovsky Victor. "Art as Technique," in *The Critical Tradition: Classic Texts and Contemporary Trends,* ed. David H. Richter. New York: St. Martin's, 1989.

Spivak Gayatri Chakravorty. "Can the Subaltern Speak?," in *Marxism and the Interpretation of Culture,* ed. Gary Nelson and Lawrence Grossberg. Urbana: U. of Illinois P., 1988, 271-313.

White Andrea. *Joseph Conrad and the Adventure Tradition: Constructing and Deconstructing the Imperial Subject.* New York: Cambridge U.P., 1993.

Mary Morzinski,
Berry College,
Mount Berry, USA

Polish Influence on Conrad's Style

Because Joseph Conrad is known as one of the great writers of British literature, most readers are quite surprised to learn that his nationality was Polish and that he did not begin to learn English until he was nearly twenty years old. Some critics, however, in particular those with knowledge of Polish, have noticed certain peculiarities about his style, generally referred to as "foreign flavor," which might be attributable to influence from his native language.[1] One primary source of influence is the difference between the English and Polish verbal systems. Whereas the salient feature of Polish verbs is their aspect, distinctions in tense are of major concern in English. The most noticeable effects of this difference is Conrad's unusual placement of adverbs and the occasional misuse of verb forms. Less noticeable, however, is another effect which contributes to what critics describe as impressionistic writing. This feature, which distinguishes Conrad's writing from that of his nineteenth- and twentieth-century counterparts, is the unusually frequent use of intransitive verbs, and it can be traced to Polish reflexive voice. A third area of influence on Conrad's style comes from the fact that Polish is a highly inflected language. Case endings on individual words indicate their grammatical function in the sentence, thus giving word order secondary importance to the pragmatic relationship of ideas in the sentence. The result in Conrad's style is looser word order than is normally found in English.

Although exact details of how Conrad learned English are hazy, it most probably occurred in natural environments: British sailing ships, daily life in England, and English literary social circles. Thus, his awareness of syntactic patterns in English developed as a result of listening to and assimilating actual utterances rather than intellectualizing abstract rules. Perhaps it is for this reason that in those areas where there is no one-to-one correspondence between the syntactic-semantic relationships in English and Polish, his reliance on the Polish relationship shows through.

Aspect

Aspect is one of the main features of the Slavic verbal system which distinguishes it from other Indo-European languages. Most scholars agree that, in Proto-Indo-European, tense probably developed later than aspect and that one of the distinguishing marks of its daughters was the evolution of their verbal systems. Whereas tense developed more in some language groups, such as Germanic, aspect retained its semantic significance in the Slavic languages. In modern Polish temporal semantics are morphologically built into a verb by virtue of its aspect.

This characteristic of Polish influenced Conrad's English in two areas: his choice of verb forms and his placement of adverbs. In English, the primary specification of verbal action is through the obligatory grammatical category of tense. The tense of an English verb group is either past or nonpast, and a finite clause in English must be marked for one or the other. Thus the time of the action indicated by the verb must be marked as either past or nonpast, that is, present or future. A secondary and subordinate marking of the action indicated by the verb in English is aspectual – whether the action is "perfected" (perfect aspect) or "ongoing" (progressive aspect). In contrast, the primary specification of verbal action in Polish is through the grammatical category of aspect, i.e., either perfective of imperfective. In a simplified version, the aspectual marking of a Polish verb indicates whether an action is complete or incomplete. Secondary and subordinate to its aspectual nature is the time of a verbal action in Polish. Whether the action took place in the past, is taking place at present, or will take place in the future is signalled by the appropriate inflection for tense.

On a time line, English verb groups can denote action occurring at any moment or length of time in the past; action occurring before another moment or length of time in the past; action occurring in the past and including or excluding the present moment; action occurring only now; and action occurring in the future. Structurally, English can combine past or present tense markers with one or both of the primary auxiliaries (have, be) to form multiple referents to the time and nature of verbal action. To the native speaker of Polish, on the other hand, denoting exactly when a certain action occurred is of less concern. Of primary importance is whether the action was completed, whether it occurred habitually, or whether it produced an expected result. Also, the Polish temporal distinctions are less complex. An action is either before now, now, or after now. The perfective forms have present and past tense markers, and the imperfective forms have past, present, and future. Therefore, for a Pole, choosing the appropriate aspectual form of the verb is critical to expression of semantic intent, but choice of tense markers is relatively simple. Conrad's occasional inconsistencies with proper verb forms in English indicate that this is an area of the language which is susceptible to influence from Polish.

> (1) It looked to him at first like a strip of red cloth. The next moment Mahmat *had* made it out and raised a shout. (*Almayer's Folly, AF,* 92)
>
> (2) and I dragged him by the feet; in through the mud I *have* dragged him....(*AF,* 96)
>
> (3) He *has been* dead once before, and came to life to die again now. (109)
>
> (4) they live in a world of their own, and there *had* never been anything like it, and never can be. ("Heart of Darkness," *YS,* 149)

Some of these errors are quite obvious while others are more easily recognized in their broader contexts of meaning. In sentence (1) "the next moment" requires a simple past tense verb, but Conrad has used past perfect "had made." Mixing simple past "dragged" with present perfect "have dragged" in sentence (2) has no semantic justification in English and seems non-native, if not ungrammatical. Since Conrad frequently uses repetition for emphasis, this may be an instance where he wanted to stress the completion of the action (rendered by perfective aspect in Polish) and added the present perfect "have" in his attempt. In sentence (3) the adverbial phrase "once before" would allow either "was" or "had been" in the verb, but it definitely precludes using the present perfect "has been" as Conrad has done. In (4) the past perfect auxiliary "had" has been incorrectly used among a sequence of present tense forms. In all of these cases, Conrad was describing a completed action, which would be rendered in Polish by the perfective aspect of the verb. It is quite likely that, for Conrad, the English notion of action having ended at a definite time in the past most closely approximated the semantic value of Polish aspect, thus accounting for his choice of the perfect form rather than simple past.

Another consequence of this aspect/tense difference between the Polish and English verbal systems is that more explicit meaning can be expressed in one Polish verb by virtue of its aspect than can be expressed in a comparable English lexical item. For example, if the question "What did you do last night?" were asked and the answer in English were "I read a book," it is not clear whether the person read an entire book or whether he simply spent some time reading. The same answer in Polish, however, could express either meaning, depending on the choice of verbs: "*Ja czytałam książkę*" would mean "I read a book (but did not finish it)" whereas "*Ja przeczytałam książkę*" would mean that the reader finished the book. Besides the notion of completion, other more subtle connotations, such as intention, complexity, and fulfillment of promise, can be expressed by Polish simple verbs. These implications of meaning could only be rendered in English through adverbial constructions denoting frequency, duration, manner, or completion. Thus the absence of morphological aspect in English is evident in Conrad's awkward placement of adverbs of frequency, such as "sometimes," "often," "already," "periodically," "still," "just," "only," or "once."

"Has she been *long* ill?" ("The Lagoon," *TU*, 41)
Several had *still* their staves in their hands. ("Heart of Darkness,"
YS, 120)
I felt *often* its mysterious stillness watching....(183-4)
I knew *once* a Scotch sailmaker....(171-2)

For the most part, Conrad's use of adverbs sounds natural to native speakers of English. But often when they are placed awkwardly, the reason seems to be that he is using English adverbs which in Polish would be unnecessary because the verb itself would carry its aspectual meaning.

The evidence here suggests that the most important thing to have been preserved from Conrad's native language is semantic intent. When he uses incorrect verb forms, it is because their semantic equivalence to the intricate time relationships known to a native speaker of English are not integral to his concept of verbal expression. Conversely, when Conrad wants to express certain semantic features of Polish aspect in a language with no morphological or syntactic equivalence, he presses the adverbial lexical items which come closest to simulating his intended semantic significance into sentences, causing his otherwise native-like fluency to take on the non-native characteristic recognized by some as foreign flavor in his style.

Reflexive Voice

Just as the salience of aspect in the Polish verbal system can account for Conrad's sometimes unusual verbal periphrasis in English, so can the presence of reflexive voice in Polish be seen to influence his choice of verb forms. The types of grammatical categories that grammarians refer to as active and passive voice are similar in English and Polish, that is equivalent translation is possible. In active voice the agent of the action is the subject, and if there is a direct object the verb is transitive. In passive voice the subject is not the agent, and since there is no direct object the verb is intransitive. In Polish, however, there is a third voice, called reflexive, which does not have equivalent translation in

English and which accounts for another distinctive feature of
Conrad's style. The reflexive particle *się* is used very frequently
in Polish and, among its other functions, renders a sentence
intransitive. When translated into English, Polish sentences with
the reflexive particle *się* generally become intransitive. This
propensity for intransitivity in Polish carries over into Conrad's
English, and what we see is an inordinate number of intransitive
verbs in his writing.[2]

The thematic effect created by this linguistic feature of
Conrad's style manifests itself in his characters' submission to
fate or to natural elements. The opening lines of "Heart of
Darkenss" convey the impression of powerlessness which pervades the entire story.

> The *Nellie,* a cruising yawl, swung to her anchor without a flutter of
> the sails, and was at rest. The flood had made, the wind was nearly
> calm, and being bound down the river, the only thing for it was to
> come to and wait for the turn of the tide.

The fate of the ship seems to lie at the mercy of nature. This is
largely because there are no people in the description, no
potiential agents of power. A closer look at Conrad's syntactic
choices, particularly active or stative verb forms, suggests
linguistic reasons for this effect on the reader.

The following explication juxtaposes Conrad's text, then
Aniela Zagórska's Polish version and, finally, a word-by-word
English translation of Zagórska's Polish version, with appro-
priate indications of verbal morphology, back into English.

The *Nellie,* a cruising yawl, swung to her anchor
Jol krążowniczy "Nellie" obrócił się na kotwicy
yawl cruising *Nellie* swung around on anchor

without a flutter of the sails, and was at rest.
bez trzepotu żagli i stanął nieruchomo.
without flutter of sails and stayed unmovingly

The flood had made,
Przypływ się skończył,
flow of the tide finished itself

the wind was nearly calm
wiatr ucichł prawie zupełnie
wind quieted down nearly completely

and being bound down the river
a że jacht kierował się w dół rzeki,
and that yacht went downstream

the only thing for it was to come to
nie pozostawało nic innego, tylko zatrzymać się
not was left nothing other only to come to a standstill

and wait for the turn of the tide.
i czekać odpływu
and to wait for ebb-tide

It is important to notice that the English version has no transitive verbs. The skeletal structures of the finite clauses follow:

Nellie swung – *jol obrócił się*
(*Nellie*) was – *stanął*
flood had made – *przypływ się skończył*
wind was – *wiatr ucichł*
thing was – *nie pozostawało nic innego*

In these clauses, all the verbs in both languages are nontransitive. That there is a direct correspondence in this case between the English copulars (forms of "to be") and Polish nonreflexives is purely coincidental. The nonfinite English verbs are intransitive as well, but the passive participle in English is translated as a finite intransitive verb in Polish.

being bound – (*jacht*) *kierował się*
to come to – *zatrzymać się*
(to) wait – *czekać*

The fact that there are no transitive verbs in this paragraph is stylistically noticeable. This creates an atmosphere in which circumstances seem to be left to the elements, or fate, or some unseen power beyond human control. Some writers may exhibit this kind of mood-setting style only in the opening paragraphs. Conrad, however, characteristically makes use of it throughout his writing.

Here is another impressionistic passage from "Heart of Darkness," the setting for Marlow's arrival at his station in the Congo.

> Black shapes crouched, lay, sat between the trees, leaning against the trunks, clinging to the earth half coming out, half effaced within the dim light in all the attitudes of pain, abandonment, and despair. Another mine on the cliff went off, followed by a slight shudder of the soil under my feet. (*YS*, 17)

Although part of the effect of this description is achieved by means of the collocations of phrases such as "dim light" and "pain, abandonment, and despair," nonagentive subjects and nontransitive verbs also create an underlying impression of ineffectualness.

Black shapes crouched, lay,
Czarne kształty czołgały się, leżały,
black shapes crawled/crept lay

sat between the trees,
siedziały między drzewami,
sat between trees

leaning against the trunks, clinging to the earth
opierając się o pnie, tuliły się do ziemi
leaning against trunks clinging to earth

half coming out, half effaced within the dim light
to widzialne, to przesłonięte mętnym półmrokiem –
first seen then veiled by dim half-light

in all the attitudes of pain,
we wszelkich możliwych postawach bólu,
in all possible poses of pain

abandonment, and despair.
zgnębienia, i rozpaczy.
abandonment and despair

Another mine on the cliff went off,
Rozległ się znowu wybuch miny w skale
burst upon the ear again explosion of mine on cliff

followed by a slight shudder of the soil under my feet.
i ziemia wzdrygnęła się pod mymi nogami.
and earth shuddered under my feet

In English this passage contains eight intransitive verb forms, half of them finite, and one passive construction. The Polish translation has seven verb forms, all intransitive and all but one finite.

English	Polish
crouched (f)	*czołgały się* (f)
lay (f)	*leżały* (f)
sat (f)	*siedziały* (f)
leaning (nf)	*opierając się* (nf)
clinging (nf)	*tuliły się* (f)
coming (nf)	*widzialne* (adj. form)
effaced (nf)	*przesłonięte* (adj. form)
went off (f)	*rozlegl się* (f)
followed (part.)	no equivalent
noun form	*wzdrygnęła się* (f)

It is not only the verb forms which create an impression of powerlessness. The synecdochal reference to the only possible human agents, "black shapes," underscores their ineffectuality as none of the verbs associated with them transfer action to a goal or affect a patient. Another passage, which appears near the beginning of the story when Marlow meets his future employer, demonstrates how the lack of directly expressed agency contributes to Conrad's style.

> A door opened, a white-haired secretarial head, but wearing a compassionate expression, appeared, and a skinny forefinger beckoned me into the sanctuary. Its light was dim, and a heavy writing-desk squatted in the middle. From behind that structure came out an impression of pale plumpness in a frockcoat. The great man himself. (10)

The use of intransitive verbs along with synecdochal subjects suggests that there are human beings in the scene, but none function as agents. And the verb most likely to have a human subject, I "squatted," has an inanimate one. The only transitive verbs, "beckoned" and "wearing," are intranstivie in the Polish translation.

A door opened, a white-haired secretarial head,
Otworzyły się drzwi, ukazała się białowłosa głowa sekretarza
opened door appeared white-haired head of secretary

but wearing a compassionate expression, appeared,
o współczującym wyrazie twarzy
with sympathizing expression facial

and a skinny forefinger beckoned me
i kościsty palec kiwnął na mnie.
and bony finger beckoned to me

into the sanctuary. Its light was dim,
Wszedłem do sanktuarium. Światło to było przyćmione,
I walked into sanctuary. Light was dimmed

and a heavy writing-desk squatted in the middle.
a ciężkie biurko przykucnęło w środku pokoju.
and heavy desk squatted in middle of room

From behind that structure came out
Zza owego gmachu wynurzyła się
out from behind the said structure came into view

an impression of pale plumpness in a frockcoat.
blada otyła zjawa w surducie.
pallid corpulent specter in frockcoat

The great man himself.
Był to ów wielki człowiek we własnej osobie.
(it was) the said great man [in person]

In this passage, five of the seven English verbs are intransitive, which exactly represents the average ratio – two to five – of transitive to intransitive verbs in Conrad's writing. In the Polish version, all seven of the verbs are intransitive, and the one copular + adjective construction in English ("was dim") becomes a past participle (*było przyćmione*). The last sentence, which is subjectless in English, is an impersonal construction in Polish. Thus, this inordinately large number of intransitive verbs, which typically have nonagentive subjects, usually describe states rather than actions, leaving the reader to invent in her own mind the actual event which caused or resulted from that state.

The following passage occurs at a point in the story when the boat in Marlow's charge gets snagged near the bank of the river and suffers an attack from natives on shore.

> the bush was swarming with human limbs in movement, glistening, of bronze colour. The twigs shook, swayed, and rustled, the arrows flew out of them, and then the shutter came to. "Steer her straight," I said to the helmsman. He held his head rigid, face forward; but his eyes rolled, he kept on lifting and setting down his feet gently, his mouth foamed a little. (46)

zarośla zaroiły się od ludzkich członków w ruchu,
bushes swarmed from people's limbs in motion

połyskujących, brązowych. Gałązki trzęsły się,
glistening bronze twigs shook

(się) chwiały, szeleściły, strzały sypały się
tossed about rustled arrows poured

spośród nich i okiennica zamknęla się wreszcie.
from the midst of them and shutter closed completely

– Steruj na wprost – powiedziałem do sternika.
"Steer straight" I said to steerer

Trzymał sztywno głowę zwróconą twarzą ku przodowi,
he held rigidly head (with) turned face toward front

ale przewracał oczami, jego nogi wciąż
but he inverted eyes his legs continually

się z wolna podnosiły i opuszczały,
with freedom were lifted and set down

na ustach pokazało się trochę piany.
from mouth (it was) shown a little foam

Of the fourteen verbs in this passage, only "steer," "held," "lifting" and "setting" are transitive in English. In the Polish version only two – "*trzymał*" ("held") and "*przewracał*" ("turn over, invert") – are transitive. Of the remaining twelve, five are reflexive, and one, "*pokazało się*" ("[it] was shown"), is impersonal. The other six are intransitive by nature. Those verbs which are inherently intransitive in both English and Polish suggest that Conrad's higher than average use of them may be a Polish linguistic habit that has become part of his English style. But the verbs that are reflexive or impersonal in Polish and intransitive in English much more strongly indicate that Conrad tried to retain their Polish syntactic/semantic relationship in his English. In Polish there is a slight semantic difference between an intransitive verb and a reflexive one, which involves the element of agency. But in English, when possible, both verb forms are rendered intransitive. It appears that when an equivalent intransitive verb was unavailable in English, Conrad preferred a transitive construction to formal passive. Notice that in the example above, the English "he kept on lifting and letting down his feet gently" becomes "*jego nogi wciąż się z wolna podnosiły i opuszczały*" (the reflexive particle *się* need not appear right with the verb, and it is not repeated with compound verbs) in Polish. At this point in the narrative, the reason for the helmsman's behavior is not yet clear, but on the next page, after the boat is free of the snag and is once again moving up river, the reader learns that the steersman was stabbed by one of the natives on shore. Actually, then the helmsman was lifting and setting his feet down involuntarily in the moments before he died. Thus, the reflexive verb forms in Polish, *podnosiły się* and *opuszczały się* are slightly more appropriate than the transitive ones in English. The passive forms in English, "were lifted and set down," would have been totally misleading, however, so Conrad chose a transitive construction instead.

Without an authoritative Polish translation, it is slightly more difficult to see how Conrad's choice of subjects and verbs may be related to Polish reflexive voice and passive constructions. Nevertheless, the following impressionistic passages can easily be recognized as lacking human agency in the subjects and the presence of passive, copular or intransitive verbs. Countless numbers of similar passages can be found in Conrad's work.

> He was not asked to sit down. Half an hour later they appeared in the hall together. The lackeys stood up, and the Prince, moving with difficulty on his gouty feet, was helped into his furs. The carriage had been ordered before. When the great double door was flung open with a crash, Razumov, who had been standing silent with a lost gaze but with every faculty intensely on the alert, heard the Prince's voice. (*Under Western Eyes, UWE,* 41)
> A moment after I heard the click of the gate-latch and then in an ecstasy of barking from his demonstrative dog his serious head went past my window on the other side of the hedge, its troubled gaze fixed forward, and the mind inside obviously employed in earnest speculation of an intricate nature. (*Chance, Ch,* 135)

Conrad's native language affords a variety of verbal constructions – formal passives, reflexive passives, and impersonals – which in English are expressed as either copular or intransitive constructions. His frequency of intransitive verb forms in English is nearly double that of his contemporaries. Juxtaposing these two facts suggests a type of transfer from Polish to English. Conrad may have thought in Polish and translated into English; or his propensity for using non-transitive verb forms may simply have been ingrained, a native linguistic habit which influenced his perspective on the world and consequently the style in which he expressed that perspective.

Word Order

Conrad's word order at times may seem unnatural to the native English reader. Word order phenomena, depending on the typological basis for study, may be seen as determined by grammatical rules – which explain the freedom and restrictions of syntactic elements – or as the result of discourse rules, which explain the various ways in which encoded information is combined to make up an intelligible utterance. Usually languages which have relatively fixed word order, such as English, are analyzed in grammatical terms whereas languges such as Polish, whose word order is relatively free, tend to be studied in discourse contexts. Although it would be impossible to draw a direct correspondence between Conrad's word order patterns and those of Polish, there is nevertheless evidence that his English does in many ways reflect Polish syntax.

Since Polish is a highly inflected language – that is, one in which a word's functional relationship to other words in the sentence is dependent not upon its position in the sentence but rather on its case ending – a variety of different word orders will render the same meaning. The word order of English, on the other hand, is much more restrictive. Some configurations actually violate grammatical rules, some cause semantic confusion or ambiguity, and others simply disturb fluency. It is difficult to draw a distinct line between a disturbance in fluency and semantic ambiguity because so much depends upon the individual reader's logical ability to resolve grammatical or semantic ambiguity. Because different readers will judge the level of fluency or ambiguity differently, the concern here is not with degree. Instead we will look at the different types of grammatical configurations in Conrad's writing which, to any native reader of English, noticeably breach normal English sentence patterns.

The canonical word order for both English and Polish is Subject-Verb-Object; however, the level of flexibility between the two languages differs. Polish inflections allow lexical items with the most semantic significance to be syntactically foregrounded by simply arranging the word order of a sentence. Thus in Conrad's English, inverted word order is not uncommon. The following examples are from four pages of the short story "Falk:"

> Hermann I would find in his shirt-sleeves. (*TS*, 113)
> Their teeth, I should judge, they cut on the ends of her running gear. (110)
> Mrs. Hermann, who always let off one speech at least at me in an hospitable, cordial tone (and in *Platt-Deutsch,* I suppose) I could not understand. (112)

Although these OSV sentences are stylistically marked in English, the same word order would be easily understood in Polish, where, regardless of their sentence position, the accusative case ending distinguishes the object. In English, on the other hand, the further the object is from the verb, the more difficult the sentence is to understand. Here are other examples of main sentence element inversion from other Conrad works:

> The young man Leonard he had met in town. (*An Outcast of the Islands, OI,* 34)
> a sort of interpreter he would be. Bun Hin's clerk he was, and wanted to have a look at the space....("Typhoon," *TS*, 13)
> But the resources of sagacity I did not review....(*Chance, Ch,* 136)
> Your Landfall, be it a peculiarly shaped mountain, a rocky headland,

or a stretch of sand-dunes, you meet at first with a single glance....(*The Mirror of the Sea, MS,* 3)
That Mrs. Fyne found means to comfort the child I doubt very much....(*Chance, Ch,* 138)

Another inversion of main sentence elements which is noticeable in Conrad's writing is the VS pattern. The following examples are from *Almayer's Folly,* with the verb and subject in italics:

(5) not far from a little green painted door, by which always *stood* a *Malay* in a red sash and turban, and whose hand, holding a small string dangling from above, moved up and down with the regularity of a machine....(*AF,* 6)
(6) It was the point in the islands where *tended* all those bold *spirits* who, fitting out schooners on the Australian coast, invaded the Malay Archipelago in search of money and adventure. (6)
(7) like a flash of lightning *came* to her the *reminiscence* of that despised and almost forgotten civilization she had only glanced at in her days of restraint, of sorrow, and of anger....(72)
(8) "And Captain Lingard has lots of money," *would say Mr. Vinck* solemnly, with his head on one side, "lots of money; more than Hudig!" (7)
(9) in the far future *gleamed* like a fairy palace the big *mansion* in Amsterdam, that earthly paradise of his dreams, where made king amongst men by old Lingard's money, he would pass the evening of his days in inexpressible splendour....(10)
(10) while above, away up in the broad of day, *flamed* immense red *blossoms* sending down on their heads a shower of great dew-sparkling petals....(71)

Although VS sentences do occur in English, particularly with expletives and sentence initial adverbs (there was no food on the table; then came the rains), there is something particular about each of these examples which disturbs their fluency. In (5) and (6), it appears that Conrad may have placed the subject after the verb in order to keep the post subject position open for the lengthy noun modifiers which appear there. But in normal English sentences, VS patterns do not occur in subordinate clauses. The prepositional phrase "like a flash of lightning," at the beginning of sentence (7), does not seem out of place until the reader encounters a verb rather than the subject immediately following it. The pattern in sentence (8) is quite similar to one used in fairy tales: "Not I," said the little red hen. But it is apparent that "would say" cannot replace "said" and retain the same level of fluency. In (9), the separation of verb and subject by a prepositional phrase prolongs the reader's expectation. The VS disturbance in (10) is augmented not only because the reader does not expect "flamed" to be a participial verb but also because normally a verb form in prenominal position would be adjectival. Thus Conrad's VS patterns violate a variety of reader expectations which normally account for fluency.

Although it appears from these examples that Conrad was concerned with keeping adjectival and adverbial complements close to their heads (the words they modify), a very large number of sentences disprove this assumption. Here are further examples:

> neither *ran he* much risk of being suddenly lassoed on the road by a recruiting party of lanceros....(*Nostromo, N,* 97)
> The street door had swung open, and bursting out, *appeared* the odious young *man*. (*Chance, Ch,* 23-4)
> From under the house, where there were bathrooms and a tool closet, *appeared Leonard,* a rusty iron bar in his hand. (*An Outcast of the Islands, OI,* 28)
> And yet upon them *will depend,* more than once, the very *life* of the ship. (*The Mirror of the Sea, MS,* 13)
> And then *came* vividly into his recollection the *morning* when he met again that fellow coming out of Hudig's office. (*An Outcast of the Islands, OI,* 35)
> Over the white rims of berths *stuck out heads* with blinking eyes. (*The Nigger of the "Narcissus," NN,* 8)
> Her intention was arrested by the sight of that awful, sombrely glistening door, swinging back suddenly on the yawning darkness of the hall, out of which literally *flew,* right out on the pavement, almost without touching the white steps, a little *figure* swathed in a holland pinafore. (*Chance, Ch,* 124)
> *Remained* the *steward,* but he was not likely to wake up before he was called. ("The Secret Sharer," 252)

These sentences illustrate a variety of sentence structures, but they all have inverted Subject-Verb word order and strike the native speaker of English as somewhat awkward.

Even more common than the inversion of main sentence elements in Conrad's writing is the separation of prepositional phrases from the words they modify. In the following excerpts, the grammatical elements to be observed are in italics.

> *of the divine frivolity of laughter* he was only *capable* over a chess-
> -board....(*Chance, Ch,* 42)
> *From that danger* Niclaus felt certain he *defend* himself....("Because of
> the Dollars," *WT,* 288)
> *For Mrs. Almayer's mature wisdom,* and for the easy aptitude in
> intrigue that comes with years to the feminine mind, he felt the most
> sincere *respect....*(*Almayer's Folly, AF,* 133)
> *of a fiddle,* however, the only *trace* on board was the case, its empty
> husk as it were;....("Falk," *TS,* 114)
> *By his feet* I *dragged* him out....(*Almayer's Folly, AF,* 105)
> *To a telegram* in guarded terms dispatched to de Barral no *answer* was
> received for more than twenty-four hours....(*Chance, Ch,* 128)

Whereas English requires that prepositional phrases remain near their heads, Polish prepositional phrases have the freedom to appear anywhere in the sentence, very often initially. The sentences above, though understandable after some consideration, lack the fluency of normal English patterns because, although prepositional phrase fronting is not unknown in English, it is nevertheless stylistically marked. These sentences do, however, reflect a sentence pattern which would not be at all unusual in Polish.

In addition to appearing at the beginning of sentences, regardless of the position of their heads, Conrad's prepositional phrases also often separate verbs from their objects. In the following examples, all from *Almayer's Folly,* the interrupting phrases are in italics:

(11) And he was going forth to speak *to that man* words of cold and
     worldly wisdom....(*AF,* 132)
(12) they could hear *from time to time* Almayer's voice....(135)
(13) Nina approached her mother and touched lightly *with her lips* the
     wrinkled forehead. (152)
(14) As he skirted *in his weary march* the edge of the forest he glanced
     now and then into its dark shade....(166-7)

(15) We have had orders *secretly and in the night* to take *off from this islet* a man and a woman....(193)

(16) the sea-breeze sprang up from the northward and shivered *with its breath* the glassy surface of the water....(194)

Of these excerpts, a few seem particularly awkward. In (15), for example, "secretly and in the night" is not only a nonparallel compound construction, but it precedes the verb that it is supposed to complement – "to take." Because of its position, however, the reader expects "secretly and in the night" to complement "have had." After this mental correction has been made, the juxtaposition of "take" and "off" leads to another misreading: that the order given was for the speaker, "we," to "take off," or flee from the islet. Not until the object, "a man and a woman," ends the sentence does Conrad's intended meaning become apparent. Contributing to the confusion created by the interrupting phrase in (16) is Conrad's use of "shivered" as a transitive verb. Since the reader does not expect this verb to have an object in the first place, its further separation by a prepositional phrase compounds the ambiguity of the sentence. Numerous examples of interrupting prepositional phrases can be found in Conrad's writing:

> Trunks without heads waved *at you* arms without hands....("Falk," *TS*, 109)
>
> Hermann walked in first, starting *in the very doorway* to pull off his coat....(119)
>
> he seemed now to hold *on the wall with his fixed stare* the vision of that city office....("The Partner," *WT*, 319)
>
> Davidson was known to visit *in her* places that no one else could find. ("Because of the Dollars," *WT*, 273)
>
> she appeared to be dragging *with her for a penance* the burden of that infirm bulk....("To-morrow," *TS*, 140)

The lack of fluency in these examples is quite noticeable, especially when the phrase which separates the verb from its object is particularly long or when there are two such phrases. But in many other cases, just the misplacement of a single adverb is enough to disturb the flow of the sentence.

Placement of adverbs in English is more restrictive than in Polish. For example, in many other languages adverbs of manner do not precede auxiliaries, but they do precede transitive verbs. Thus, "the thief *silently left* the house" and "the thief *is silently leaving* the house" are preferable to "the thief *silently is leaving* the house." The following examples would probably be judged by most native speakers of English as not just awkward but ungrammatical.

> where the tepid wind entering through the sashless windows whirled *gently* the dried leaves and the dust of many days of neglect....(*Almayer's Folly, AF,* 35)
> And the two would separate, the Arab cursing *inwardly* the wily dog....(58)
> Almayer, strolling along the muddy beach between his houses, watched *uneasily* the river rising inch by inch, creeping slowly nearer to the boats. (73)
> So Dain felt tolerably secure as he sat meditating *quietly* his answer to the Rajah's blood-thirsty speech. (83)
> For that I bore *patiently* the burden of work. (101)
> He lingered by his uncle, pulling *thoughtfully* his neatly trimmed beard. (109)
> and lifting *cautiously* the red curtain....(157)
> he went away, thumping *slowly* the plank floor as if his feet had been shod with iron....("Falk," *TS,* 168)
> while the way of the tug carried *slowly* past her the lingering and profound homage of the man....("Falk," *TS,* 169)
> He had *naturally* the chart of his voyages in his head. ("Beacuse of the Dollars," *WT,* 273)
> He refused *steadily* all medicine....(*The Nigger of the "Narcissus," NN,* 45)
> but his letters – unless those expressing *formally* his dutiful affection – were seldom entrusted to the Costaguana Post Office....(*Nostromo, N,* 93)
> The universal aspiration with all its profound and melancholy meaning assailed *heavily* Razumov....(*Under Western Eyes, UWE,* 39)

In these examples, each adverb in italics would appear either before the verb or after the direct object in normal English word order. The inflexibility of word order creates expectations for the English reader which, when violated, cause a disturbance in fluency. In English, an intransitive verb, that is one without a direct object, is quite often followed by an adverb of manner, but the object of a transitive verb is usually the next constituent to follow. In fact, since a verb's transitivity depends in English by definition upon its object, until that object appears, the reader is held in suspense of the verb's function, particularly in the case of those which can be used both transitively and intransitively. In Polish, however, transitivity versus intransitivity is often indicated morphologically by use of the particle *się*. Thus, even when an object is separated from its verb by strings of complements – and this is a common occurrence – the reader of Polish can interpret the verb as transitive or intransitive because of its form. Because the Polish object has no syntactic responsibility to clarify semantics for the verb, it is quite usual for an instrumental prepositional phrase, which often translates as an adverb of manner in English (with silence = silently), to follow a transitive verb immediately.

The following examples from *Wierna rzeka,* by Stefan Żeromski, further illustrate that this word order is natural in Polish. The verb and its adverb are in boldface type:

> *Panna Salomea **sypiała początkowo** w zimnym salonie przytykającym do jej dawnej alkowy....*(Żeromski, *Wierna rzeka,* 46)
> Miss Salomea slept initially in the cold rooms reminiscent of her former alcove
> ***wynalazł omackiem** zapadnię nakrytą drzewianym wiekiem....*(47)
> he grasped gropingly the trap door covering with the wooden cover
> *i **począł ostrożnie** spuszczać rannego w ciemny otwór....*(47)
> and he began carefully to lower the sick one into the dark opening

In these examples from Polish, all of which were easily found within the space of one page, the verb precedes the adverb, the same pattern of word order in the previous examples from Conrad's prose.

The English reader will also notice Conrad's unusual placement of adverbs which denote aspectual semantics, such as duration and frequency. In English, these adverbs are usually placed before the main verb or after the main verb's complement, but never immediately following it. Polish, on the other hand, has no such restrictions. Despite the relative "freedom" of word order in Polish, there are nevertheless stylistic norms, and adverbs of frequency and duration are often found immediately following the main verb. Thus, it is not surprising that we very often find this configuration in Conrad's English.

Of all the types of shuffled word order in Conrad's writing, instances of the awkward placement of adverbs are the most copious. Of the following examples, individual readers will find some more awkward, others less.

> who seem *so often* unaware....("Heart of Darkness," *YS*, 141)
> one gets *sometimes* such a flash of inspiration, you know. (233)
> After work hours he used *sometimes* to come over....(175)
> For a long time *already* he, sitting apart, had been no more to us than a voice. (173)
> I had been *very long* on the road. (164)
> but he had been a couple of years *already* out there engaged....(144)
> Almayer had *now* a friend. (*Almayer's Folly, AF*, 49)
> swinging *regularly* his long ebony staff....(94)
> he fancied *suddenly* he heard his wife's voice in the thickest of the throng....(94)
> shaking *from time to time* her dishevelled grey locks....(98)
> and no remorse at leaving *suddenly* that man....(151)
> After listening *for a while* intently on her knees....(154)
> I have *many times* observed the baby Hermann (Nicholas) engaged in gnawing the whipping of the fore-royal brace. ("Falk," *TS*, 179)
> Hermann kept on running *frequently* against the corners of the table. (179)
> I caught *several times* the word "Mensch," man....(181)
> He advertised *still* in the Sunday papers for Harry Hagberd ("To--morrow," *TS*, 140)
> He had been *many times* in charge of royal yachts in and out of Port Victoria. ("The Brute," *SS*, 100)
> he recognized *at once* Razumov....(*Under Western Eyes, UWE*, 41)
> Inwardly he wept and trembled *already*. (40)
> I was told that Mrs. Fyne was *very little* at the cottage at the time....(*Chance, Ch*, 155)
> The dog became *at once* wildly demonstrative....(142)
> She actually seemed to have...formed a plot *already* to marry *eventually* her charge to an impecunious relation of her own....(90)
> This old rice-clearing, which had been *several years* lying fallow....(*An Outcast of the Islands, OI*, 49)

> When the fact broke through the incognito he would leave *suddenly* the seaport where he happened to be at the time....(*Lord Jim, LJ*, 4)

There is widespread occurrence of Conrad's odd placement of English adverbs which denote Polish aspectual semantics. Not only are the instances numerous in any one work, but they are prevalent in all his writings. It may be noted that in each of these examples, Conrad has placed the adverb immediately after the verb. In Polish, the verbs themselves would be morphologically marked with imperfective or perfective aspect, in many cases qualifying the frequency of action. Given Conrad's concern for expressing semantics precisely, it may be that this verb-adverb word order in English reflects the mental association of action and qualifier inherent in the aspect of equivalent Polish verbs as well as stylistic word order patterns in Polish.

The flexibility of Polish word order afforded by case inflections is reflected in Conrad's frequent inversion of English SVO word order, the interruption of main sentence elements by phrasal complements, and the misplacement of adverbs of manner. Adverbs of frequency and duration, which express aspectual semantics, are also placed awkwardly, indicating that Conrad may have encountered problems dealing with the lack of morphologically marked aspectual distinctions in English verbs. What readers recognize, then, as loose syntax in Conrad's writing can be attributed to morphological and semantic influence from his native Polish language.

Conclusion

Casual readers may notice an exotic quality in Joseph Conrad's style regardless of their knowledge about his native language. At another level of examination, literary critics have characterized his writing by identifying such elements as idiomatic expressions and rhetorical devices typical of Polish writing. Looking even more closely reveals influences which lie beneath the surface, at the syntactic-semantic infrastructure of the Polish language.

Three of these properties – verbal aspects, reflexive voice, and nominal inflection – account for the author's occasional misuse of verb forms, awkward placement of adverbs, and preponderance of intransitive verbs, which contributes to the impressionistic effect of Conrad's writing. Together these characteristics form the inimitable style for which he is known.

NOTES

1. Whereas Gustav Morf confined remarks about the influence of Polish on Conrad's English to "the speech of his Polish characters" (Morf, 215), A. P. Coleman focused on *Chance* as exemplifying the influence of "Polish idiom" in more than just his foreign characters' dialogue. His initial remarks describe Conrad's *Chance* as having a "richly colorful style," "lavish use of similes," and "that Slavonic defeatism with which all his writing is permeated" (Coleman, 463). Coleman's article goes on to illustrate "Polonisms" which are traceable to differences between the English and Polish languages, giving examples of Conrad's odd use of prepositions, articles, and the expletives "there" and "it." Zdzisław Najder recognized loose structure as resembling Polish style, and Stefan Żeromski calls it the "music" of Conrad's phrases that come from Polish (Najder, *Joseph Conrad: A Chronicle*, 474). I. M. Pulc, who attributes the Polish tonality of Conrad's writing to asyndeton (omission of conjunctions), anaphora (pronominal reference) and parallelism (repetition of grammatical constructions), and postpositioning of adjectives, claims that Conrad's rhythm resembles that of other Polish writers with whom these same rhetorical devices are popular. Similar to Pulc, Adam Gillon likens Conrad's rhetorical devices to nineteenth/twentieth-century Polish prose and to the diction of Polish romantic poetry.

2. A comparative frequency study of 19th/20th-century English and Polish writing shows that the occurrence of intransitive verbs is significantly higher in Conrad's writing than in that of his contemporaries. Of 1000 consecutive verbs, 286 were transitive and 426 were intransitive for Conrad, compared to 380 transitive and 190 intransitive for Ford Madox Ford, 390 transitive and 296 intransitive for John Galsworthy, 393 transitive and 227 intransitive for Henry James, and 383 transitive and 265 intransitive for H. G. Wells. Whereas Conrad's intransitive verbs far outnumber transitive verbs, the opposite tendency occurs with Ford, Galsworthy, James and Wells. For a complete account of this frequency study, see Mary Morzinski, *Linguistic Influence of Polish on Joseph Conrad's Style*, New York–Boulder–Lublin: Columbia U.P. – East European Monographs – Maria Curie-Skłodowska University, 1994; *Conrad: Eastern and Western Perspectives,* ed. Wiesław Krajka, vol. III.

WORKS CITED

Coleman Arthur P. "Polonisms in Conrad's *Chance*," *Modern Language Notes*, 46 (1931), 463-8.

Conrad Joseph. "Jądro ciemności" ["Heart of Darkness"], trans. Aniela Zagórska. *Dzieła wybrane Josepha Conrada* [Selected Works by Joseph Conrad]. Warszawa: Państwowy Instytut Wydawniczy, 1987.

Ford Ford Maddox. *Joseph Conrad: A Personal Remembrance.* New York: Octagon Books, 1965.

Gillon Adam. "Shakespearean and Polish Tonalities in Conrad's 'The Lagoon'," *Conradiana* 8:2 (1976), 127-36.

Jean-Aubry Georges. *Joseph Conrad: Life and Letters,* 2 vols. Garden City: Doubleday, 1927.

Morf Gustav. *The Polish Heritage of Joseph Conrad.* London: Oxford U.P., 1930.

Morzinski Mary. *Linguistic Influence of Polish on Joseph Conrad's Style.* New York–Boulder–Lublin: Columbia U.P. – East European Monographs – Maria Curie-Skłodowska University, 1994; *Conrad: Eastern and Western Perspectives,* ed. Wiesław Krajka, vol. III.

Najder Zdzisław, ed. *Conrad's Polish Background: Letters to and from Polish Friends,* trans. Halina Carroll. London: Oxford U.P., 1964.

Najder Zdzisław. *Joseph Conrad: A Chronicle.* New Brunswick, N J: Rutgers U.P., 1984.

Pulc Imogene M. "The Imprint of Polish on Conrad's Prose," in *Joseph Conrad: Theory and World Fiction. Proceedings of the Comparative Literature Symposium,* January 23-25, 1974, eds. Wendell M. Aycock and Wołodymyr T. Żyła. Lubbock: Texas Tech U. 1974, 117-39.

Tarnawski Wit M. *Conrad the Man, the Writer, the Pole,* trans. R. Batchelor. London: Polish Cultural Foundation, 1984.

Żeromski Stefan. *Wierna rzeka: klechda domowa* [River of Truth]. Warszawa: Czytelnik, 1970.

Laurence Davies,
Dartmouth College,
Hanover, USA

Conrad and Potocki, a Speculation

A Pole of illustrious descent, Jan Potocki was thoroughly at home with French life and literature. An urbane yet mercurial man, subject to terrible depressions and unanticipated liftings of the spirit, he travelled widely in Africa and Asia as well as Europe and, though he never went there, by no means ignored Latin America. In the course of his life, he mingled with radicals – some of them revolutionaries – and conservatives to such an extent that scholarly opinion cannot agree upon the true direction of his sympathies. One might indeed describe him as a man of many cultures whose writings seem even more enigmatic than his life; his life and his writings, moreover, show intriguing resemblances to Conrad's own.

Potocki's literary work displays a polyglot's command of languages, a familiarity with certain aspects of Islamic culture, and a gift for dramatizing a wide variety of ideas and beliefs so that in his writing (both public and private) as in other aspects of his life one sees a notable talent for disguise. Perhaps his most constant literary identity is that of an ironist with an aptitude for gallows humor. Formally, his narratives abound with nesting narratives: stories within stories, placed in ways that both bewilder and illuminate. Thanks not only to the proliferation of story lines but also to the presence of what Cedric Watts has called "covert plots" and a manifest suspicion of what a post-modernist might call "master narratives", this author's fictions shift disconcertingly in time and space. How to explain these shifts? One should certainly acknowledge the influence of traditional Indian, Persian, and Arabian storytelling as revealed directly in the *Thousand and One Nights* and indirectly in Cervantes and his successors. One might unmask the tropes of contemporary popular fiction – tropes familiar from stories of adventure, romance, the exotic, and the uncanny made unfamiliar again as if in mockery and celebration. In the temporal and geographical shifts, one might detect an awareness that we experience history as a circular as well as linear process, coming back time and again, tragically, absurdly, comically, to where we have been before. In the geographical and temporal disruptions one might see a cosmopolitan spirit at work, a consciousness of the world's richness and complexity. Rounding off this speculative list for now, one might regard the author's perspectivism as the expression of a culture or society in transition, as the evolution of an artistic repertoire adequate to the strangeness of the times.

Like Conrad's, Potocki's stories try out ideologies and moral codes, testing them, as an engineer migth say, to destruction. All sorts of devotion, duty, and obsessiveness come under scrutiny. Sometimes deviously, sometimes directly, skepticism and romanticism, doubt and belief battle for mastery. The imperatives of honor fascinate Potocki both as guides to living decently and as sources of folly, fanaticism, or madness, both as a set of ideas that aristocrats and robbers might share alike, and as an incessant generator of illusion. Illusions, illusion, illusionism all come into play. There are the illusions of the naive or inexperienced; there is the veil of illusion, of Maya, that occludes human vision; there is the illusionism, the "delayed decoding" in Ian Watt's succinct phrase, that shows us, so to speak, illusion at work. The illusory, moreover, may concern the concrete rather than the abstract: material interest burrow away. In the author's masterpiece, *Manuscrit trouvé à Saragosse,* the very center of deception and intrigue, of false ideals and false consciousness, is a vast metalliferous mine.

A child of two families famous in Polish history, the Ossolińskis and the Potockis, Count Jan Potocki was born in Podolia in 1761.[1] In 1778, after studying in Vienna, Geneva, and Lausanne and campaigning with the Austrian army in the War of Bavarian Succession, Potocki made the first of his many journeys outside Europe. His early travels took him to North Africa (Tunisia, Egypt, and Morocco) and the Middle East (Turkey and its hinterland). The general curiosity of an Enlightenment gentle-man spurred him on, but he had already become fascinated by the early history of the Slavonic peoples. As well as the quest for unexamined archives and archaelogical clues, his research on this topic involved comparative ethnographic studies whereby, for example, his first-hand knowledge of Circassian tribal life could illuminate the tribal life of his own remote, Scythian forebears. Always writing in French, he published the first of his many travel books, *Voyage en Turquie et en Egypte* in 1788, and in 1789, the first of his equally abundant scholarly works, *Essai sur l'histoire universelle et recherches sur celle de la Sarmatie.* By then he had become a political figure as well as a genuinely original and enterprising scholar, the representative of Poznań in the Polish Parliament or *Seym,* and the publisher of the *Journal hebdomadaire de la Diète.* In 1790, this hyperactive aristocrat, so much of his time and yet so modern, having just made a celebrated balloon ascent from Warsaw, went off to Paris to consort with the Jacobins. Between then and 1802 he published some of his short plays and several more books, witnessed the quashing of Polish hopes and liberties, and made a lengthy expedition to the Caucasus. Although both the extent of the change and its motivation remain contentious,[2] his politics had moved to the right; in 1802 he became one of Tsar Alexander I's Privy Councillors and an intimate of Joseph de Maistre. It was in the service of the Russian Ministry of Foreign Affairs that he took up the post of scientific adviser to the Russian mission to China, 1805-1806, a mission that travelled across Siberia and on to Mongolia. Potocki spent his last years on family estates in Podolia where in 1815, severely afflicted by depression, he blew out his brains. According to legend, he melted down the knob of his baroque teapot to cast the silver bullet.

This remarkable list, however, does not exhaust the catalogue of Potocki's activities. From 1797 to the year of his death, he was creating the perplexing collection of stories usually known as *Manuscrit trouvé à Saragosse* or *The Saragossa Manuscript.* Nothing about this work is simple, not even the title. When in 1804 proofs of the first ten stories of "First Decameron" were

printed in Saint Petersburg, they bore no name – and indeed the
siege of Saragossa, which provides the outermost narrative
frame, had not yet taken place. Although the set of sixty six
stories was written in French, the first allegedly complete French
edition only came out in 1989 – and has been attacked as too
hasty, premature.[3] A complete version in Polish, however,
translated by Edmund Chojecki from fugitive manuscripts,
appeared in 1847. Meanwhile in France, various sections of the
whole (if whole there be[4]) had been published either under
Potocki's initials or anonymously.[5] To make matters more
confusing, the tales became a quarry for plagiarists, one of whom
was brazen enough to defend his claims to authorship in court.

Despite or even because of its elusiveness, *The Saragossa
Manuscript* had some distinguished nineteenth-century admir-
ers. They included Washington Irving (whose *The Alhambra*
shows that his admiration led him to join the plagiarists),
Pushkin, Mickiewicz, Nodier, and Nerval. While abundantly
inventive and original, the book belongs among the great
collections of stories within a frame, such as the *Thousand and
One Nights,* the *Canterbury Tales,* the *Decameron* and the
Heptameron. Polish readers may well notice a special affinity
with the *gawęda,* the often humorous and digressive oral tale
beloved of the *szlachta.*

According to the prefatory "Avertissement," we are going to
read a translation from Spanish into French of several notebooks found by a French officer at the siege of Saragossa (1809).
The notebooks tell the story of Alphonse Van Worden, a soldier
in the service of Philip V of Spain, who tries to travel from
Andalusia to Madrid, where he is to take up the commission in
the Walloon Guards. In the new French edition, he needs 630
large pages to get there. For all that time (or space) Alphonse is
trapped among the threatening and desolate mountains of the
Sierra Morena, where he meets among others ghosts, vampires,
gibbeted brigands who come to life, a hermit, a one-eyed maniac,
a pilgrim and former encyclopedist whose books have been eaten
by rats, an absent-minded mathematician, the leader of a band
of Gypsies, a female cabbalist who is betrothed to Castor and

Pollux and her no less learned brother who communicates with demiurges, Ahasuerus the Wandering Jew, and two beautiful Moorish women who claim to be Alphonse's cousins. These characters have many tales to offer, often embodying other characters who have yet more tales. Towards the end of the Thirty-fifth Day, Pandesowna the Gypsy chieftain (known at other junctures of the labyrinth as Avadoro and the Marquess of Castelli) continues the story of Lope Soarez, who continues the story of Roque Busqueros who – lest we innocently think we have reached the center of the maze of the bottom of the abyss – tells us a story told him by Frasqueta Solera. At this point, then, we have five stories nested inside each other – or six if we include the story of finding and translating the manuscript itself.

Such virtuosity recalls Shahrazad's feats of narrative layering in stories such as "The Hunchback and the Tailor." Several significant features, however, distinguish *The Saragossa Manuscript* from the *Thousand and One Nights*. In terms of epistemology and belief, Potocki's is the far more sceptical work. In *The Saragossa Manuscript,* Muslims, Jews, and Christians speak with equal narrative authority or, on occasions, equal fanaticism or absurdity. Nor does scepticism itself enjoy a special privilege: Velasquez the "geometer" might be said to speak for the Enlightenment, but he is intent on reducing passions to numbers and cannot stop falling into ditches. To speak in formal as well as credal terms, point of view fascinates Potocki. When reading him, it is a common experience to feel one's perspectives unexpectedly change because a peripheral character from an earlier story has reached the narrative centre and is now giving his or her very different version of events. At last we imagine we know what really happened – but no, other witnesses will appear and perspectives will shift again. In an idle moment at the cabbalist's castle, Alphonse picks up a volume of *Relations curieuses* by the phantom author Heppelius. These *Curious Tales* have been left open, no doubt deliberately, to one about Thibaud de la Jacquière, a profligate Frenchman. One night he picks up an innocent young woman, Orlandine, who describes from the point of view of complete inexperience an orgy she has witnessed

through a window. From what could only be called an experienced point of view, Thibaud recognises the orgy as one in which
he has just participated. He takes the young innocent to bed,
only to find that she is Beelzebub in disguise. The next morning,
sick unto death, he wakes beside a putrefying corpse.

This story is one of the few literally bookish ones, presented as
read rather than heard. It intersects, however, with Alphonse's
own experience of everyday madness and horror in the Sierra
Morena. He himself has fallen asleep in a haunted inn after
a night of love with his two Moorish cousins and woken at the
foot of a gibbet embracing a hanged thief, a fate experienced by
several other characters. The motif of sexual treesomes also
recurs throughout. Such repeated motifs are simultaneously
playful and disturbing. They create an effect of macabre comedy,
they put to flight any notions of narrative decorum, and at the
same time they imply a distressing circularity in human events.
No one ever seems to get anywhere. Characters with trium-
phalist views of history proliferate in the book: Catholics,
Freethinkers, and Muslims are all convinced that their own faith
will win, that their particular reading of truth will prevail – but
none of them does. When at the very end we learn that
Alphonse's ordeal was staged by the fabulously wealthy Gomelez family out of the proceeds of their now exhausted mine, the
explanation seems inadequate, as though there's more to come,
always more, and always the same.

Futility, ironic comedy, plurality of vision, epistemological
suspicion, the perils of fanaticism.... Conradians have been here
before. If Conrad didn't know Potocki's work, he should have.
The author of "The Duel" would, for example, have appreciated
both the Napoleonic setting of the outermost narration and the
figure of Brigadier-General Van Worden, Senior, who invites to
his wedding banquet 122 men who have duelled against him and
nearly kills his son Alphonse when the boy admits to being
frightened by a ghost story. An incident in which another
traveller overtakes the brigadier's chaise well illustrates Potocki's gift for the *reductio ad absurdum*:

> When they were alone, my father said to the other traveller: "Good sir, your chaise overtook my coach so as to reach the post house before me. This in itself is no insult, nevertheless there is something disobliging about it, for which I believe I must demand satisfaction of you."
>
> Very surprised, the colonel laid all blame on the postilions, and assured my father there was no offence on his part.
>
> "Good sir," said my father, "neither do I wish to make a serious issue of this, and I shall settle for duelling until blood is drawn." As he spoke, he drew his sword.
>
> "Just a moment," said the Frenchman. "As I see it, it was not that my postilions overtook yours, but that yours, by going more slowly, lagged behind."
>
> My father gave this some thought, then said to the colonel: "Good sir, I believe you are right, and had you pointed this out to me sooner, before I had drawn my sword, I think we should not have duelled. But surely you see that as matters stand we must have a little blood."[6]

Such is Alphonse Van Worden's inheritance: a code of absolute, almost insane rigor. Dominique Triaire[7] has pointed out the frequency of characters in Potocki who must endure and, in the interests of sanity and harmony, eventually modify paternal rules and restrictions. Although fathers in Conrad from Mr. Almayer onwards are often ineffectual or simply absent, the same pattern exists of inherited moral schemas (inherited in Conrad's case from a community as often as from a parent) that must be tested and perhaps modified under the pressure of contemporary life.

What of Conrad, then, as a putative heir of Potocki? In a little while, I shall discuss certain reasons for suspecting that the later writer knew the former's work. First, however, I must pay heed to my secret skeptic, an invaluable companion on any scholarly voyage.

An affinity is not an influence. The testing of overly rigid or overly bookish ideas in a context of modernity is the stuff of countless works of literature: one need look no further for examples than to Flaubert or Mickiewicz, authors certainly familiar to Conrad. Although familiarity does not guarantee influence, these two authors undoubtedly became shaping forces upon Conrad's work. What goes for those who came after

Potocki surely goes for those who came before. Resemblances between *The Saragossa Manuscript* and Conrad's novels and stories may stem from a common ancestry rather than from some hypothetical grafting of one text to another. Robert Hampson has amply and admirably demonstrated the presence in Conrad of the *Thousand and One Nights*; Wit Tarnawski and Andrzej Busza have shown the significance of the *gawęda*.[8] One might easily do the same for *Don Quixote, La Vida es sueño,* and *Gil Blas* – inspirations, all of them, to Potocki as well as Conrad.

Why speculate, therefore, about a connection between Conrad and Potocki? The latter's initial fame among romantic writers soon faded away. Until Roger Caillois, a perennial connoisseur of bizarrerie, rescued him during the 1950s, Potocki's work had undergone a veritable hundred years of solitude. His ability to be at home in many cultures found him a home in none. Culturally – ethnically, if you will – he has been hard to classify, even an object of suspicion. Here is a Pole who wrote in French and, in the case of *The Saragossa Manuscript,* published in Saint Petersburg. What would Eliza Orzeszkowa have made of that?

Arguably it is the very complexity of Potocki's relation to Poland that might have captured the attention of the mature Conrad. The action of *The Saragossa Manuscript* takes place in Spain, Mexico, Malta, France, the Low Countries, Tunisia, Palestine – anywhere but Poland, the absent center. "Prince Roman" (that fine example of the *gawęda*) aside, the same goes for Conrad's work.

There is a reasonable chance that Conrad might at least have heard of Potocki long before he himself became a writer. To take one example of overlapping circles of friendship and kinship in Podolia, Prince Roman Sanguszko's tragic bride was a Potocka, and her daughter Maria Klementyna married Jan Potocki's grandson Alfred.[9] More significantly, Izydor Kopernicki, Conrad's mentor in his Cracow days, a comparative anthroplogist and collector of Slavic and Gypsy folk-poems and tales, might well be described as Potocki's intellectual heir.[10]

Towards the end of 1912, Conrad made the acquaintance of

Józef Retinger. Although Retinger does not mention Potocki in *Le Conte Fantastique dans la romantisme français*,[11] the published version of his doctoral dissertation at the Sorbonne, it is hard to imagine that a scholar working on the milieu of Charles Nodier and his ilk would not have come across Potocki and – especially if that scholar were a cosmopolitan Pole – one would expect him to have been intrigued. Furthermore, the Zamoyski family, Retinger's patrons, had in their possession until 1945 a draft of the "Fifth Decameron" in Potocki's own hand.[12]

In any case, it was in the early days of his friendship with Retinger that Conrad wrote what could, at least on a superficial level, be termed his most Potockian story. Despite some memorably eerie passages, "The Inn of the Two Witches" has never attracted an enthusiastic following: no one has ventured to call it major Conrad; moreover, as the "Author's Note" to *Within the Tides* attests, it soon fell under the suspicion of plagiarism. The story bears some resemblance to Wilkie Collins's "A Terribly Strange Bed."[13] Both stories have the murderous four-poster, and both stories have a frame narrator. In Collins, a resourceful wife married to a temporarily blinded painter writes down the tales told him by his sitters, one of whom has narrowly escaped being murdered for his winnings in a Parisian gambling hell. The bed istelf belongs with Sweeney Todd's, deadly barber's chairin the repertoire of nineteenth- -century urban (not to mention rural) folklore. In other respects Conrad's story has more in common with Potocki than it does with Collins. Among other features we have a setting during the Napoleonic Wars and in the Spanish mountains; the locale is in the north, but the landscape Conrad describes looks much more like the Sierra Morena or the Sierra Nevada than it does the Cantabrians or the Pyrenees. At least figuratively speaking, there is a strong father: the murdered boatswain, who continues to guide the young naval officer even from beyond the grave. The inn to which the title refers yields an unexpected corpse and is inhabited by two eldritch women and a Gypsy straight from Potocki's accursed mountains. Conrad's guerrillas lead an

outlaw existence in the wild much as Potocki's fearsome but
sometimes good-hearted robbers do. All these characters, set-
tings, and events appear in an autobiographical narrative taken
by the story's outer narrator from an old manuscript.

Now I am not trying to save Conrad from one charge of
literary light-fingeredness in order to accuse him of another.
Minor story though it is, "The Inn of the Two Witches" has
more in it of Conrad than of Collins or Potocki. Whether the
slave scenes from *Salammbô*, Masterman's *Seven Eventful Years*
or, hypothetically, *The Saragossa Manuscript,* Conrad transmuted what he touched. My main interest in proposing Potocki
as a Conradian author does not lie in the quest for sources or
influences at all.

Nor does it lie in cramming Potocki into one of Conrad's
elegant suits. When placing authors side by side, it helps to think
of that valuable philosopher's tool, the Venn Diagram. There is
much in Potocki's fiction that overlaps with Conrad; there is
much that does not. Potocki's text concerns itself far more with
the magical, the mythical, and the mystical; his absurdities are
more blatant; his cryptic references to Freemasonry[14] put him
– in this respect alone – closer to Kipling than to Conrad.

Whether or not Conrad knew Potocki and his works, the
parallels between them lead in suggestive directions. The evidence of direct knowledge remains circumstantial; it may well
persuade some people while leaving others doubtful. Nevertheless, sceptics and believers may still find common ground on
the question of resemblances. In the realm of biology, species
may resemble each other in some way (in the method of
disseminating spores, for instance) whether or not a close genetic
connection exists. The absence of such connections torments the
phylogenist – the biological equivalent of a genealogist – but is of
much less concern to the ecologist. For the latter, likeness occurs
when organisms, closely related or not, respond to similar
environmental challenges. Let me suggest that for the moment
we become literary ecologists. From a biographical standpoint,
it would be fascinating to know that Conrad found in Potocki
a kindred spirit – an inspiration or, if you prefer Harold Bloom's

agonistic vision of literary history, yet another influence to be anxious about – but to a biographer bloodlines need not be the only fascination.

To sketch in the environment, here is Velasquez the "geometer" speaking on the Thirty-ninth Day:

> A man who has seen the whole world through the eyes of a traveller and has absorbed all the important events of history, carries in his head a multitude of pictures that a peasant does not have. If, in addition, the traveller arranges, compares and combines his ideas then we say he has intelligence and knowledge.[15]

Here, as the theorists of the 1970s and 1980s would have said, the discourse of the Enlightenment speaks itself with all its spurious claims to universality and its willful blindness to the privileges of gender, race, and class. It just happens to do the speaking, however, through a character who mingles the rational with the absurd and might not have felt out of place on the flying island of Laputa. The discourse, in other words, has not escaped the creative powers of an ironic intelligence. Yet although the context is ironic, Velasquez does map out the author's position, and it is one that Conrad shares. Both he and Potocki were humane and sceptical travellers who had seen too much, done too much, known too much to settle on any fixed and limited intellectual territory. That is not to deny, of course, that their understanding had its limits. Neither Potocki nor Conrad was immune to the prejudices of his day, any more than we are to ours. Nor did either lack involvement in the work of subjugation: Potocki with Russian imperialism,[16] Conrad with British, French, and Belgian. Nevertheless, both of them wrote as if they were far less content with those prejudices, privileges, and affiliations than the bulk of their contemporaries. Both of them had a will to complicate.

That will expresses itself in narrative disruptions and delayed decodings, in abrupt shifts of perspective and vertiginous jumps back and forth through time and space. One critic has written of *"l'élément décisif de la rupture"* in Potocki;[17] others have written of the effects of synchronicity, whereby temporal order and progress are replaced by a paradoxical alliance of surprise and repetition.[18] With these conditions in mind, one might say that Conrad's most Potockian work was not "The Inn of the Two Witches" but *Nostromo*.

One might also say that in such manifestations of ideology as Fussy Joe's bland belief in progress, Carlos Gould's unrelenting pursuit of material interests, or Don José Avellanos's self--satisfied liberalism, *Nostromo* displays Enlightenment values at the end of their tether. Here Conrad goes – not *beyond* benevolence, for that would restore the very rhetoric that Conrad is challeging – but *around* benevolence, as if to scrutinize it from outside. Something similar happens in Potocki. In *Orientalism*, Edward Said identifies a moment when

> Imbued with the populist and pluralist sense of history advocated by Herder and others, an eighteenth-century mind could breach the doctrinal walls erected between the West and Islam and see hidden elements of kinship between himself and the Orient.[19]

Having cited Mozart's *Magic Flute* and *Abduction from the Seraglio*, he continues:

> It is very difficult nonetheless to separate such intuitions of the Orient as Mozart's from the entire range of pre-Romantic and Romantic representations of the Orient as exotic locale.

Potocki belongs to that moment; in fact *The Saragossa Manuscript* resounds with echoes of *The Magic Flute*. On the other hand, his primary locale though undeniably exotic is not at first encounter "Oriental." The Oriental motif appears when the Moorish sisters arrive on the scene. They emerge, however, at a Spanish inn, not only to seduce a Walloon who is a devout Catholic and a loyal subject of the Spanish king, but to tell the Walloon that he is their cousin. His own mother was a Moor, a Gomelez. Meanwhile, right under the invisible but ever alert noses of the Spanish Inquisition, the Gomelez family, Shi'ite Muslims, mine their gold, carry on their intrigues and work their illusions. Most appropriately, the inn straddles a frontier: on one side lies Castille, heartland of rigorous Catholicism and *limpieza de sangre* ("purity of blood"), on the other, Andalusia, the lost world of el Andalous where once upon a time, before the Christian reconquest, Muslims, Jews, and Christians prospered alike. The uncanniness of *The Saragossa Manuscript* emanates from the return of what has been repressed on racial or religious grounds. Potocki avoids the temptations of *de haut en bas* benevolence by making his Orient and his Occident one territory instead of two and subjecting its inhabitants to the impartial rule of irony. Admittedly in a more somber fashion, Conrad makes a like maneuver when he brings the dark places of the earth together: when the Thames leads to the Great River, when Africa and its ghosts come crowding into the Sepulchral City.

An emphasis on the international qualities of these two authors does not in the least negate their national origins. For all his cosmopolitanism, Potocki was not simply a traveller and a sceptic, but a Polish traveller and a Polish sceptic – and so all the more likely to attract Conrad's interest and our own. Their sense of the vagaries and complexities of history and of the tensions and complexities of negotiations among the creeds, sacred and secular, originates in the cultural and historical experience of a particular and highly distinctive nation. The resemblance between them is piquant, and the mutual il-lumination bright. To associate Conrad with Potocki is, more than ever, to think of them both as writers of and about many cultures.

NOTES

1. For a chronology of Potocki's life, see Dominique Triaire, *Potocki: essai* (Arles: Actes Sud, 1991), 257-61; Edouard Krakowski, *Le Comte Jean Potocki* (Paris: Gallimard, 1963), *passim*; and *Polski słownik biograficzny,* vol. 4 (Kraków: Polska Akademia Umiejętności, 1938) *s.v.* Potocki, Jan. Another helpful biographical source is the "Preface" by Roger Caillois to his edition of *Manuscrit trouvé à Saragosse* (Revised edition: Paris: Gallimard, 1958).

2. See, for example, Jerzy Skowronek, "Jean Potocki: politicien éclairé et conservateur," in *Jean Potocki et le Manuscrit trouvé à Saragosse. Actes*

du Colloque organisé par le Centre de Civilisation Française de l'Université de Varsovie (Avril 1972), Cahiers de Varsovie, 3 (Warszawa: 1981), 39-55.

3. *Manuscrit trouvé à Saragosse,* ed. René Radrizzani (Paris: José Corti, 1989). For Daniel Beauvois's hostile critique of this edition and replies by Radrizzani and his publisher, see "Jean Potocki méritait mieux," *Dix--huitième siècle,* 22 (1990), 441-9.

4. In his "Introduction" to *Tales from The Saragossa Manuscript,* trans. Christine Donougher (New York: Hippocrene, 1990), Brian Stableford argues that the search for an integral primary text is misguided and the ascription to Potocki of this perhaps mythical whole, deluded.

5. See "Preface" in R. Caillois, 1958, 20-8, for the intricate history of publication.

6. Trans. C. Donougher, 57-8. In French the passage reads:

Lorsqu'ils furent seuls, mon père dit à l'autre voyageur: "Seigneur Cavalier, votre chaise a devancé mon carrosse pour arriver à la poste avant moi. Ce procédé, qui en lui-même n'est point une insulte, a cependant quelque chose de désobligeant, dont je crois devoir vous demander raison."

Le colonel, très surpris, rejeta toute la faute sur les postillons et assura qu'il n'y en avait aucune de sa part.

"Seigneur Cavalier, reprit mon père, je ne pretends pas non plus faire de ceci une affaire sérieuse, et je me contenterai du premier sang." En disant cela, il tira son épée.

"[Attendez encore un instant, dit le Français. Il me semble] que ce ne sont point mes postillons qui ont devancé les vôtres, mais que ce sont les vôtres qui, allant plus lentement, sont restés en arrière."

Mon père, après avoir un peu réfléchi, dit au colonel: "Seigneur Cavalier, je crois que vous avez raison, et si vous m'eussiez fait cette observation plus tôt et avant que j'eusse tiré l'épée, je pense que nous ne nous serions pas battus; mais vous sentez bien qu'au point où en sont les choses, il faut un peu de sang." (R. Radrizzani, "Troisième Journée," 36-7; quoted after Caillois, 84),

7. D. Triaire, 153-7.

8. Robert Hampson in *"The Arabian Nights" in English Literature,* ed. Peter L. Caracciolo, (Basingstoke: Macmillan, 1988), 218-43; Andrzej Busza, "Conrad's Polish Literary Background and Some Illustrations of the Influence of Polish Literature on His Work," *Antemurale,* 10 (1966), Rome-London: Institutum Historicum Polonicum – Societas Polonica Scientiarum et Litterarum in Exteris, 208, 237.

9. Count Alfred Potocki, *Master of Łańcut: The Memoirs of Count Alfred Potocki* (London: W. H. Allen, 1959), 12, 16, 20; *Conrad under Familial Eyes,* ed. Zdzisław Najder, trans. Halina Carroll-Najder (Cambridge: Cambridge U.P., 1983), 8-10.

10. Busza, 142-3, gives an account of Kopernicki's work.

11. *Le Conte Fantastique dans le romantisme français* (Paris: Grasset, 1909).

12. Marie-Eveline Żółtowska, "La genèse du *Manuscrit trouvé à Saragosse*," *Cahiers de Varsovie*, 3 (1981), 97.

13. First published in *Household Words*, then in *After Dark and Other Stories* (New York: Harper & Brothers, 1875).

14. See Claire Nicolas, "Du bon usage de la Franc-maçonnerie dans le *Manuscrit trouvé à Saragosse*," *Cahiers de Varsovie*, 3 (1981), 271-89.

15. *The New Decameron: Further Tales from The Saragossa Manuscript*, trans. Elisabeth Abbott (New York: Orion, 1966), 269. Radrizzani has: *"L'homme qui a vu toute la terre par les yeux de voyageurs, qui a vu tous les événements dans l'histoire, a réellement une infinité d'images dans la tête que n'a point le paysan: et s'il combine ses idées, les rapproche, les compare, cet homme a du savoir et d'esprit"* (426).

16. Daniel Beauvois has an acute discussion of this issue: "Jean Potocki's *Voyages*: From Mythic Orient to Conquered Orient," in *L'Hénaurme Siècle: A Miscellany of Essays on Nineteenth-Century French Literature*, ed. Will L. McLendon (Heidelberg: Carl Winter, 1984), 13-26.

17. Jean Decottignies, "A propos du *Manuscrit trouvé à Saragosse*. Décameron et texte 'polyphonique'," *Cahiers de Varsovie*, 3 (1981), 195.

18. Julian Krzyżanowski, cited by Maciej Żurowski, "Le *Manuscrit trouvé à Saragosse* e la technique romanesque du XVIIIe siècle," *Cahiers de Varsovie*, 3 (1981), 107. Triaire, 197-9, finds this phenomenon even in Potocki's historical works.

19. Edward Said, *Orientalism* (New York: Vintage, 1979), 118.

I am very happy to acknowledge the help of my undergraduate research assistant, Ms. Elizabeth Rybicki.

WORKS CITED

Beauvois Daniel. "Jean Potocki meritait mieux," in *Dix-huitième siècle*, 22 (1990), 441-9.

Busza Andrzej. "Conrad's Polish Literary Background and Some Illustrations of the Influence of Polish Literature on His Work," *Antemurale* 10, (1966), 109-247, Rome-London: Institutum Historicum Polonicum – Societas Polonica Scientiarum et Litterarum in Exteris.

Caillois Roger, ed. and "Introduction," *Manuscript trouvé à Saragosse*, Revised edition. Paris: Gallimard, 1958.

Caracciolo Peter L., ed. *"The Arabian Nights" in English Literature* (especially Robert Hampson article). Basingstoke: Macmillan, 1988.

Decottignies Jean. "A propos du *Manuscrit trouvé à Saragosse*. Décameron et texte 'polyphonique'," in *Jean Potocki et le Manuscrit trouvé à Saragosse. Actes du Colloque organisé par le Centre de Civilisation Française de l'Université de Varsovie (Avril 1972), Cahiers de Varsovie*, 3 (1981).

Krakowski Edouard. *Le Comte Jean Potocki*. Paris: Gallimard, 1963.

McLendon Will L., ed. *Hénaurme Siècle: A Miscellany of Essays on Nineteenth-Century French Literature.* Heidelberg: Carl Winter, 1984.

Najder Zdzisław ed. *Conrad under Familial Eyes,* trans. Halina Carroll--Najder. London: Cambridge U.P., 1983.

Nicolas Claire. "Du bon usage de la Franc-maçonnerie dans le *Manuscrit trouvé à Saragosse,*" in *Jean Potocki et le Manuscrit trouvé à Saragosse. Actes du Colloque organisé par le Centre de Civilisation Française de l'Université de Varsovie (Avril 1972), Cahiers de Varsovie,* 3 (1981).

Polski słownik biograficzny, vol. 4. Kraków: Polska Akademia Umiejętności, 1938.

Potocki Count Alfred. *Master of Łańcut: The Memoirs of Count Alfred Potocki.* London: W. H. Allen, 1959.

Potocki Jan. *The New Decameron: Further Tales from The Saragossa Manuscript,* trans. Elisabeth Abbott. New York: Orion, 1966.

Radrizzani Rene, ed. *Manuscrit trouvé à Saragosse.* Paris: Jose Corti, 1989.

Retinger Józef. *Le Conte fantastique dans le romantisme français.* Paris: Grasset, 1909.

Said Edward. *Orientalism.* New York: Vintage, 1979.

Skowronek Jerzy. "Jean Potocki: Politicien éclairé et conservateur," in *Jean Potocki et le Manuscrit trouvé à Saragosse. Actes du Colloque organisé par le Centre de Civilisation Française de l'Université de Varsovie (Avril 1972), Cahiers de Varsovie,* 3 (1981).

Stableford Brian. "Introduction," in *Tales from The Saragossa Manuscript,* trans. Christine Donougher. New York: Hippocrene, 1990.

Triaire Dominique. *Potocki: essai.* Arles: Actes Sud, 1991.

Żółtowska Marie-Eveline. "La genèse du *Manuscrit trouvé à Saragosse,*" in *Jean Potocki et le Manuscrit trouvé à Saragosse. Actes du Colloque organisé par le Centre de Civilisation Française de l'Université de Varsovie (Avril 1972), Cahiers de Varsovie,* 3 (1981).

Żurowski Maciej. "*Le Manuscrit trouvé à Saragosse* et la technique romanesque du XVIIIe siècle," in *Jean Potocki et le Manuscrit trouvé à Saragosse. Actes du Colloque organisé par le Centre de Civilisation Française de l'Université de Varsovie (Avril 1972), Cahiers de Varsovie,* 3 (1981).

Wiesław Krajka,
Maria Curie-Skłodowska University Lublin/University of Wrocław,
Lublin/Wrocław, Poland

The Alien in Joseph Conrad's "Amy Foster" and Jerzy Kosiński's *The Painted Bird*

Joseph Conrad's personality and works seem to play a significant role in the creative imagination of Jerzy Kosiński, a Jewish-Polish-born American writer who died in 1991. In his last, intensely intertextual novel, *The Hermit of 69th Street,* one finds numerous quotations (or quasi-quotations) and references to Conrad's texts.[1] The most conspicuous and meaningful parallel between the works of these two authors concerns "Amy Foster" and *The Painted Bird.*

The topography of action in *The Painted Bird* applies Conradian patterns of geographical isolation[2] – those of *Lord Jim, Almayer's Folly, An Outcast of the Islands, The Rescue,* "Because of the Dollars," "The End of the Tether," "The Lagoon," "Heart of Darkness," and "An Outpost of Progress:"

> *Vast marshlands and bogs cut into the region,* [which was the location of the protagonist's wanderings and ordeal] *while dense forests traditionally sheltered bands of rebels and outlaws.* (J. Kosiński, *The Painted Bird,* 2)

Kosiński's protagonist frequently has to travel far to reach the successive place of his temporary stay. But principally, the spatial separaton of this area means its complete isolation from civilization:

> *The villages in that region* [were]...[*i*]*naccessible and distant from any urban centers, they were in the most backward parts of Eastern Europe. There were no schools or hospitals, few paved roads or bridges, no electricity. Poeple lived in small settlements in the manner of their great-grandfathers.* (2)

Such depiction of this realm enhances the protagonist's ethno-cultural isolation, the predominant opposition between the primitive rural world of superstition (in which he is forced to wander and undergo humiliation and sufferings), and the domain of the industrial civilization of his native town (where he stayed before and after his adventures). Thus, *The Painted Bird* resembles Conrad's "Amy Foster," in which Yanko Goorall's native realm is separated spatially from the rural Kent where he escapes from his sinking ship (he remembers his land and sea journey as taking a number of days). In "Amy Foster," too, spatial distance is symbolically charged: it denotes an unbridgeable gap between two totally different cultures and ethnicities. The plight of the protagonists in "Amy Foster" and *The Painted Bird* illustrates some typical kinds of isolation used in the literary works of Joseph Conrad and Jerzy Kosiński,[3] as well as certain universal patterns of behavior of the sociology of the alien.[4]

Both Yanko Goorall and the boy in *The Painted Bird* become separated from their domestic milieu. The boy in Kosiński's novel is sent by his parents to the countryside to secure his survival during the Holocaust. After some time he loses contact with them; the possibility of their reunion becomes very uncertain. In the course of his ordeal he remembers his father's smile, his mother's piano-playing and singing, his toys, his nanny's story-telling (Kosiński, *The Painted Bird,* 8-9); he misses his parents in times of danger (3, 12-13). His is principally a separation from the world of civilization, culture, and educated people. Forced to live in an ethno-culturally alien and primitive enivronment, he feels united with the realm of his parents and childhood only by his reminiscences and hopes for alleviation from his predicament.

Whereas in Kosiński's novel the boy's transfer takes place from the open world of urban civilization and the culture of the intelligentsia to a closed, rural, pagan realm of superstition and witchcraft, the analogous transfer in Conrad's short story comes from one isolated community (Yanko Goorall's "homeland" in the Carpathian mountains) to another (rural Kent). The narrow--mindedness of Yanko's worldview becomes manifest in his interpretation of his recruitment for emigration: he thinks the men enlisting him for overseas travel are negotiating the matter with the "Emperor of America" by telegraph and is extremely happy to be accepted by them. In the course of his railway and sea journey, Goorall compares the new reality surrounding him to phenomena from his familiar native world. This tendency is evident, for example, in his ignorance of a general notion of ship and sea, as well as in his perception of the railway station in Berlin and the port in Hamburg ("Amy Foster," *TS,* 114-16). He notices cultural differences between his fellow Carpathian highlanders and the Englishmen inhabiting the country of his miraculous rescue:

> The land he looked upon seemed to him kept neatly, like the grounds round a landowner's house; the size of the cart-horses struck him with astonishment; the roads resembled garden walks, and the aspect of the people, especially on Sundays, spoke of opulence. He wondered what made them so hardhearted and their children so bold. (128)

Yanko's perception of the alien reality testifies to the distinct and closed nature of his ethos and ethnicity. The reception he receives at the hands of the indigenous people in Kent shows them to be similarly narrow-minded, unable to understand and appreciate lifestyles different from their own, viewing others exclusively in terms of their own provincial outlook, treating them as a source of danger.[5]

In both *The Painted Bird* and "Amy Foster," the narrator and the narratee belong to the same community, they share its culture and value system. The alien/familiar antagonism (the group vs. the individual who is perceived as foreign) takes place within the fictional world resulting from the relationship in among characters. Whereas in *The Painted Bird* a member of "our" society (comprising the narrator, the narratee, the implied author, and the implied reader) is placed in an unfamiliar environment, in "Amy Foster" the alien individual is located in "our" community.[6] In both texts the familiar/alien antithesis – as a binary opposition of universal categories ordering all human experience – leads to the presentation of an intercultural conflict and to the depiction of general patterns of human interrelationships, social bonds, or mechanisms of culture.[7] The group regards the foreign individual as an exact antinomy, a negative copy of its own self-image (which is constituted by a combination of features and attitudes considered natural, normal, proper, and right).[8] A stranger does not share the social group's ethnic, territorial, class, religious, and professional identity,[9] and lacks any bonds with it[10] – as is the case of "Amy Foster" and *The Painted Bird*. Simultaneously, he is disinherited from his native culture.[11] And primarily, he belongs to a category different from the average members of this group – in terms of anthropology, ethnicity, culture, and lifestyle.[12]

Both Yanko in "Amy Foster" and the protagonist in *The Painted Bird* are clearly distinct from their alien environments. In Kosiński's novel this principal difference concerns language, education, and outward appearance. This is well described in the author's prologue to the novel:

> *The villages in which he was to spend the next four years differed ethnically from the region of his birth. The local peasants, isolated and inbred, were fair-skinned with blond hair and blue or gray eyes. The boy was olive-skinned, dark-haired, and black-eyed. He spoke a language of the educated class, a language barely intelligible to the peasants of the east.*
> *He was considered a Gypsy or Jewish stray....*(Kosiński, *The Painted Bird*, 2)

These eastern European villages are backward; distant from urban centers; without schools, hospitals, or electricity; they do not have many paved roads or bridges. People live there *"in the manner of their great-grandfathers"* (2), they abide by the law of the stronger and wealthier, *"Divided between the Roman Catholic and the Orthodox faiths, the people were united only by their extreme superstition and the innumerable diseases plaguing men and animals alike"* (2). The protagonist's dark hair and black eyes are constantly emphasized as sharply distinguishing him from the peasants in successive stages of his wanderings; almost all of the indigenous people he meets perceive him as a Gypsy or a Jewish orphan. "Compared to the soft, drawling local speech, [his] city talk, full of hard consonants which rattled like machine-gun fire, sounded [to the indigenous people] like a caricature" (85). And Yanko's ethno-cultural difference from the Kentish villagers is even more articulated. He views them as people with sad, mute, incomprehensible faces, as if dead ("Amy Foster," *TS,* 128-9). Kennedy the narrator sharply contrasts him with the inhabitants of the Brenzett-Colebrook area – phlegmatic, hard-working farmers, exhausted by their toil (10-11), as well as with his fiancée, Amy (135). In his new environment Goorall is distinguished by his "highly sensitive nature" (118), excitability (132), outward appearance, dress, vitality, and ways of moving and speaking, but principally by his features of character, axiology, religious habits, and courting and marriage customs (111, 120, 126-7, 132).[13]

The different nature of strangers, as well as the multifarious negative features attributed to them,[14] leads to a lack of interest and scorn for them and their culture, to ostracism and pejorative evaluation of their actions and ways of being.[15] A community's antagonistic attitude towards an alien takes on varying shades and degrees of intensity: from mere dislike to aggression and cruel persecution.[16]

In *The Painted Bird* and "Amy Foster," the protagonists' ethno-cultural isolation culminates with the primitive communities' negative and hostile reactions to these transplants from other cultures. The Eastern villagers in *The Painted Bird* view the black-eyed, dark-haired boy as possessed by evil spirits, in league with the devil and casting evil spells (in folk symbolism blackness is viewed as belonging to the realm of the Prince of Darkness). Motivated by superstition, they constantly treat him with fear and ostracism:

> Other people also feared me. Whenever I attempted to walk through the village alone, people would turn their heads and make the sign of the cross. What is more, pregnant women would run away from me in panic. The bolder peasants unleashed dogs on me, and had I not learned to flee quickly and always keep close to Olga's hut, I would not have returned alive from many of these excursions. (Kosiński, *The Painted Bird,* 19; see also 85, 100, 125)

                                          Wiesław Krajka

The villagers frequently beat or even torture the alien foundling:
after Marta's death he is maltreated and locked in a closet
(14-15); the carpenter drives him outside the village to a distant
field and chains him to a harness (58); children and adults strike
him when transported by cart to the Germans (116-17); Garbos
permanently mistreats him and inflicts suffering on him (cf.
especially chapter 11); he is often attacked and beaten by peasant
children, and handed over to Germans for certain death. His
ordeal in this land makes up an endless cycle of violent, hostile,
and cruel rejections.

Yanko's different nature, too, exposes him to constant
humiliations and rejections by the community in which he is
placed.[17] This castaway, entreating for help, food, and shelter, is
met with unfavorable, aggressive reactions at the hands of the
local people who consider him a dangerous beggar, tramp and
maniac: the fishermen of West Colebrook, disturbed by his
shouts, chased him away with "their rough, angry tones" ("Amy
Foster," *TS,* 118); the Brenzett carrier drew back intimidated by
the sight of him sleeping on roadside grass in the rain (118); the
schoolmistress "spoke indignantly to a 'horrid-looking man'"
for frightening the schoolchildren (118); "[t]he driver of Mr.
Bradley's milk-cart...lashed with his whip at a hairy sort of gipsy
fellow [who made desperate endeavours to get help]...that made
him drop down in the mud" (118-19); three boys were "throwing
stones at a funny tramp, knocking about all wet and muddy,
and, it seemed, very drunk, in the narrow deep lane by the
limekilns" (119); Mrs. Finn "called out to him to go away, and as
he persisted in coming nearer, she hit him courageously with her
umbrella over the head" and escaped to the village (119); Mrs.
Smith grew alarmed and hysterical at the sight of him, which
made her husband indignant at this dirty tramp scaring women,
whereas he in fact, "was being addressed as 'gracious lord,' and
adjured in God's name to afford food and shelter," (120) – he
finally "bundle[d] [the stranger] headlong into the wood-lodge
...[thinking] [h]e had done his duty to the community by shutting
up a wandering and probably dangerous maniac" (120-1).
According to Kennedy, imprisoned Goorall's sufferings must
have been immense:

> And I daresay the man inside had been very near to insanity on that night. Before his excitement collapsed and he became unconscious he was throwing himself violently about in the dark, rolling on some dirty sacks, and biting his fists with rage, cold, hunger, amazement, and despair. (121)

Later, taken by Swaffer in a deplorable state, he undergoes a long convalescence.

All the newcomer's attempts at making contact with the Kentish villagers are futile, since he uses codes totally misunderstood by them. He reacts to all his painful experiences with wonder and indignation:

> He had approached them as a beggar, it is true, he said; but in his country, even if they gave nothing, they spoke gently to beggars. The children in his country were not taught to throw stones at those who asked for compassion. (124)

He finds the locals' attitudes impermissible in view of his native ethos.

Disapproval of Yanko's personality and conduct – of his ways of living, dressing, speaking, moving, and his customs and manners – continues, in spite of his partial integration into the new environment (131-2). He is ill-treated twice at the inn when he tries to dance in the manner of the Carpathian mountaineers:

> One evening, in the tap-room of the "Coach and Horses," (having drunk some whisky), he upset them all by singing a love-song of his country. They hooted him down, and he was pained; but Preble, the lame wheelwright, and Vincent, the fat blacksmith, and the other notables, too, wanted to drink their evening beer in peace. On another occasion he tried to show them how to dance...when suddenly he sprang upon a table and continued to dance among the glasses, the landlord interfered. He didn't want any "acrobat tricks in the tap-room." They laid their hands on him. Having had a glass or two, Mr. Swaffer's foreigner tried to expostulate: was ejected forcibly: got a black eye. (132-3)
> When the boy was born, he got elevated at the "Coach and Horses," essayed again a song and a dance, and was again ejected. (136-7)

Every spontaneous, natural expression of his ethnicity is met with negation and aggression by the environment. The villagers' enmity intensifies with his declaration to marry Amy Foster: to this news, old women react with indignation, and Smith – with hostility; his fiancée's father cherishes "genuine aversion to that match" and considers Yanko "not fit for any girl to marry" (135); according to Miss Swaffer, "He certainly won't get any other girl to marry him" (136); the villagers express "their commiseration for a woman married to that Jack-in-the-box" (137). Later, nobody is of help to him in illness, and after his death everybody calls their child "Amy Foster's boy" (153). Most painful and tragic of all, however, is Amy's final repudiation: terrified by the look of her sick husband, murmuring in delirium in his native dialect, she refuses to give him a drink of water, takes the child, and escapes.

The psycho-social foundations of these instances of ostracism of the alien are apparently the same in *The Painted Bird* and "Amy Foster." The Eastern villagers in Kosiński's novel and the Kentish farmers in Conrad's short story personify the primitive, closed, and narrow-minded cultures of their communities. They treat the aliens with an irrational fear, disapproval, and hostility, as a danger to the internal order of their communities. The indigenous people in *The Painted Bird* are motivated by superstitious terror of the protagonist. And the provincially--minded autochthones in "Amy Foster" do not associate Yanko's appearance in the area with the bodies of victims of the sea catastrophe driven ashore: "for days, nay, for weeks – it didn't enter our heads that we had amongst us the only living soul that had escaped from that disaster" (123; see also 121). In both these cases, the narrator blames the locals for the strangers' tragedies and sufferings.

From a sociological point of view, and individual's estrangement can be explained by his representing a system of values different from the society's. An alien does not approve of its values, traditions, culture, ideas, and mentality; he does not partake of an emotional-conceptual bond rooted in its language. He interferes in a closed set of axiological patterns of the group which he enters. The more the social hierarchy is violated by this confrontation, the greater is the conflict between the alien individual and the community. Their coexistence consists in an antagonism or a violent clash; the stranger's culture, ethos and ethnicity are condemned and rejected by the society.[18] This type of relationship is clearly exemplified by *The Painted Bird* and "Amy Foster." In both these texts, the conflict is based on totally disparate, polarized sets of axiological patterns represented by the group and the foreigner. An authentic dialogue between cultures is nonexistent: each partner exclusively articulates and affirms his own values, and rejects and despises those represented by the other side. This excludes coexistence and intercommunication of ideas and patterns of conduct, real partnership, and sincere cooperation.[19] In both works, the strangers enter isolated village communities cemented by a culture that was created in the long-term interaction of its participants and strengthened in long-lasting contacts, common traditions, ideology, values, recollections and interests. These ties determine the mutual familiarity of the community's members. The aliens' estrangement is manifest in each instance of contact with these groups.[20]

To the primitive, closed communities of both *The Painted Bird* and "Amy Foster," the alien individual's interference brings the threat of disintegration and destruction of its internal structure and entire conception of the world. Such groups always perceive of the alien's intrusion into its cultural space as an offense made by one who dares to question everything that seems unquestionable to its members, all attributes of the universe itself.[21] He "becomes willy-nilly the epicentre of a total earthquake, since he tends to challenge not just one but all the distinctions which make up the intelligible world".[22] Such an inimical act of profane violation of the group's sacred realm, endangering its independence, provokes its defensive reaction. Motivated by a collective instinct of self-preservation, the community unanimously and strongly defends itself by condemning foreign structures, evaluating them pejoratively, eliminating them from its social life; it sternly opposes such a radical questioning of the mental and spiritual foundations of its existence.[23]

The isolation of both Goorall and the boy in *The Painted Bird* is alleviated by those characters who do not yield to the pressure of their community, but extend a helping hand to the stranger. In sociological terms, they function almost as traitors, as they do not repel the alien, but dare to appreciate his axiology, condemned by their group.[24] In "Amy Foster," old Swaffer gives Yanko food, shelter, and work; moreover, later, in token of gratitude for the foreigner's saving his granddaughter's life, he pays him regular wages and presents him with a cottage and a piece of land, which contributes substantially to making his marriage possible. And Amy, acting out of pity and the goodness of her heart, shares a loaf of bread with the starving castaway, thus helping him at a critical moment: "Through this act of impulsive pity he was brought back again within the pale of human relations with his new surroundings" (*TS*, 125). Later, his gratitude and her compassion develop into mutual fascination, love, and marriage.

Neither Swaffer nor Amy, however, are typical representatives of their milieu, they are estranged from it. Swaffer is distinguished by his intelligence, broad-mindedness, and his fondness of reading and of curiosities (especially of foreign origin). Although viewed as an eccentric, he is greatly respected by the village community. And Amy is known for her tenderness and infinite kind-heartedness. She lives with the Smiths in their isolated farmhouse; she is a daughter of Isaac Foster, whose runaway marriage with the cook of his widowed father was treated as a scandalous affair. Yet the villagers do not appreciate Amy's good heart: they regard her as a dull person.

Eventually, Goorall becomes isolated from these two protectors, too. Swaffer neither comes to understand his distinct ethnicity and culture, nor engages in a sincere interchange of ideas and values. And when the initial attraction is gone, Amy feels growing alienation from her husband. She does not accept their son's exposure to Yanko's speech, songs, and prayers in his native Carpathian dialect. She comes to react to her husband's ethos and ethnicity with disapproval, hostility and aggression (like her community). Yanko's strangeness starts to evoke fright and disgust in her dull nature – cf. Kennedy's following rhetorical question:

> I wondered whether his difference, his strangeness, were not penetrating with repulsion that dull nature they had begun by irresistibly attracting. ("Amy Foster," *TS,* 137-8)

Overpowered by fright, Amy is not humanitarian to her dying husband: she does not tend him at night; she places him, in spite of his pneumonia, in a draughty room; she suspects him of pretending sickness; with a thoughtless, horrified gaze she observes his movements and raving; she refuses to grant the suffering man's request for a drink of water made in his native dialect; and finally, in reaction to his desperation, she snatches the child and escapes, leaving her husband alone to die of a heart attack soon afterwards:

> She had left him. She had left him – sick – helpless – thirsty. The spear of the hunter had entered his very soul. "Why?" he cried, in the penetrating and indignant voice of a man calling to a responsible Maker. (141)

An analogous pattern applies in *The Painted Bird,* where many humane characters help the protagonist: they lessen his painful estrangement by offering him food and shelter. And they are also isolated in their peasant communities. In the inital phase of the novel, the protagonist is successively protected by two witches – Marta and Olga. They are separated from locals both spatially (their cottages are some distance from the village) and by their magic practices and superstitious way of life. Like Swaffer in "Amy Foster," Olga the Wise is held in great esteem by the villagers; she terminates their persecutions of the boy by buying him and taking him to her hut.

In the course of the novel, some other characters – also lonely deviants – take a similar attitude vis-à-vis him. Lekh lives by catching and selling birds, he either stays with them in his forest cottage, or leads a truant life. His lover, lascivious Stupid Ludmila, is said:

> to belong to that pagan, primitive kingdom of birds and forests where everything was infinitely abundant, wild, blooming, and royal in its perpetual decay, death and rebirth; illicit and clashing with the human world. (Kosiński, *The Painted Bird,* 48)

This connection enhances his estrangement: "In the villages people laughed at Lekh. They said that Stupid Ludmila had cast a spell over him and put fire in his loins, a fire that would drive him insane" (51). Similarly, Garbos lives "at the far end of the village at a rather isolated farmhouse" (121); no one ever visits him. The priest, who takes the boy from Germans and places him with Garbos, is different by his vocation and life style. "Makar lived with his son and daughter on a farmstead set apart from the rest of the settlement....He had arrived only a few years before and was treated as a stranger" (149). His daughter Ewka never comes there; she is not liked by the peasants who think "she had a ram in her eyes" (150; i.e. a devil – cf. mythical, aitiological etymology of "she-goat"); the old witch Anulka is her only friend. Makar, his son, and daughter are suspected of perverse sexual relationships with one another; many people mutter "that Makar's strange family should be turned out of the village and his house burned down" (150). Labina is distinguished by her violent protests against handing the boy over to Germans.

In Kosiński's novel, as in Conrad's short story, separation of the protagonist and his protectors from the environment coexists with their mutual estrangement. The boy finds the superstitious outlook and witchcraft practices of Marta and Olga impossible to understand. He views Marta's outward appearance, mentality, ideas, ways of living, and actions appropriate for a witch (3-4). He considers Olga a little less wild but equally superstitious in her treatment of various illnesses. The women also feel isolated from him. Marta regards him as a Gypsy bastard, kin to the Devil; she blames him for casting spells and forbids him to look directly into her and her animals' eyes, for fear of bringing "crippling illness, plague, or death" (7). Olga the Wise views the boy as attracting phantoms and vampires, as possessed by an evil spirit, and as putting spells on people with his bewitched black eyes; she even suspects him of being a vampire himself. He is also far from sharing the strange lifestyle of Lekh, who once "shouted that [his] presence scared his woman [Stupid Ludmila] off because she was afraid of his [the protagonist's] Gypsy eyes" (51). The carpenter and his wife are afraid that the boy's black eyes will attract lightning to their farm and drive him outside the village to a distant field in rainstorm. He feels alien in church: he does not understand the Christian religion and the meaning of liturgical objects; he views Mass and church observances as a magic "more splendid and elaborate than Olga's witchcraft, but just as difficult to fathom" (126). He hates Garbos, who permanently maltreats him and turns his dog loose on him (Garbos thinks the boy throws Gypsy charms on him). During the protagonist's stay in Makar's hut, only his erotic actions and fantasies with Ewka diminish his isolation. He later views them with repulsion, after having seen her copulation with a he-goat, as well as the perverse sexual practices of her father and brother. All these negative, rejecting attitudes result from the indigenous people's superstition – they are convinced that the boy's presence among them can only bring misfortune.

In both texts, the protagonists' ethno-cultural estrangement is represented metaphorically as well. In "Amy Foster," Kennedy compares Yanko to "a wild bird caught in a snare" ("Amy Foster," *TS*, 126, 142), "a wild creature under the net" (141). In *The Painted Bird* this kind of presentation is introduced first and foremost by the title metaphor of the bird painted by Lekh, which is treated by birds of its kind as a stranger, rejected by them, and pecked to death. Lekh, Stupid Ludmila, and especially Handsome Laba impersonate this metaphor. Laba returns to his village in a rich and elegant dress (such as the townsmen wear), which becomes an object of admiration by all. He is distinguished from other peasants by his style of life, too: he neither works in field nor in farm, but only loiters, bathes, and participates in receptions. His treasures and dresses are everything to him: upon their theft, "Laba's reason for living had disappeared with the contents of his chest" (Kosiński, *The Painted Bird,* 179). This is an end to his proud self-display at weddings and burials and to the admiration of women. Unable to put up with this loss, he commits suicide.[25]

The boy's plight is also represented by means of animal metaphors. In Marta's household he notices a lonely pigeon trying to join a flock of hens and chickens, but rejected by them.

On one such attempt, the pigeon is attacked by a hawk and carried off in its beak (4-5). The protagonist also observes a squirrel chased by boys, who finally hit it with a piece of rock, catch it, and burn it alive (6). All these episodes foreshadow allegorically certain aspects of his own ethno-cultural isolation and ordeal. In the final part of the novel, the narrator tells a story of a hare caught in Makar's trap: locked in a cage it raged for a time; finally it gave up and became tame, but when it left the cage it became insensitive to the value of its newly-gained freedom and returned by its own free will to confinement (241-2). The hare is very much like the protagonist, who is unwilling to reunite with his parents and considers the possibility of living according to the principles of communist ideology, at the same time despairing for his lost freedom (243).[26]

The experiences of the protagonist in *The Painted Bird* are extremely painful, and the persecutions he meets – exceptionally cruel (they are only partly caused by the primitive and uncivilized nature of the hostile communities).[27] In "Amy Foster," on the other hand, the emphasis is much more on the tragic character of Goorall's estrangement: he is entangled in the contradiction of two cultures, ethnicities, and kinds of ethos; doomed to a split personality, his death expresses a protest against the conflicting relationship of his two worlds. In the commentary by Kennedy the narrator, his predicament is regarded as resulting from "irreconcilable differences" and "fear of the [i]ncomprehensible" ("Amy Foster," *TS,* 107-8), and his sufferings – as more tragic than those of any other outcast (113, 142).

Kennedy's utterances appear within a broad frame of generalization: he views Yanko's plight as typifying the loneliness of a castaway, as well as of a human being. A similar sweeping statement occurs in the conclusion of *The Painted Bird*:

> Every one of us stood alone,...people did not understand one another anyway. They collided with or charmed one another, hugged or trampled one another, but everyone knew only himself. His emotions, memory, and senses divided him from others as effectively as thick reeds screen the mainstream from the muddy bank. Like the moutain

> peaks around us, we looked at one another, separated by valleys, too high to stay unnoticed, too low to touch the heavens. (Kosiński, *The Painted Bird*, 249-50)

In Kosiński's novel, however, generalization is conveyed mainly through a metafictional commentary at the beginning: the protagonist is presented there as a typical Jewish child avoiding Germans, undergoing numerous humiliations and persecutions during World War II (1-3).[28]

In both *The Painted Bird* and "Amy Foster," the distance between the social group and the alien is magnified by the use of magic, in a way typical of primitive communities. The alien's incomprehensible, mysterious speech is regarded as verbal magic.[29] In traditional cultures, strangers were viewed as agents of dangerous, inimical forces, of evil, sin, and even crime; as being in league with demons, devils, and ghosts; as coming from the realm of night, chaos, and death. This status of foreigners engendered active opposition to them: a necessity to isolate them, to avoid any contact with them in order to prevent a transfer of evil power, or a contamination of familiar values.[30] In the final part of "Amy Foster," the title character treats her husband's songs, religious customs, and utterances directed at their child in his native dialect, as magic practices which may bring him harm (her reasoning is understandable, as in all cultures unkown, mysteriously sounding words were considered to be characteristic of incantations). Frightened to death, Amy takes the boy and leaves Yanko Goorall alone. In *The Painted Bird*, Marta, Olga, and other peasants ostracize the protagonist – they think he casts evil spells over people and is aligned with the Devil.

Repudiation of strangers is much stronger and longer-lasting on the part of a community of uneducated people than of educated ones.[31] A primitive group's culture is closed; it aims primarily at expressing itself. Such a society views the world in terms of clear oppositions of good and evil, right and wrong, normal and abnormal – the oppositions equivalent to that of the familiar vs. the alien, our wold vs. the outside world, *orbis interior* vs. *orbis exterior*. These people evaluate pejoratively all manifestations of unknown, external reality from which an alien individual emerges (*orbis exterior*), and positively – their own, closed, internal reality (*orbis interior*). This juxtaposition functions both in various manifestations of spiritual culture, beliefs, mentality, etc., and in attitudes in actual social life. The ostracism of foreigners arises from a group's cultural and mental isolation – as in the discussed works by Conrad and Kosiński. An uneducated community sharply demarcates a psychological barrier between its own world (the domain of the familiar, known, natural, useful, accepted), and the outside world (the domain of the unfamiliar, strange, unknown, uninteresting, abnormal, not useful, unacceptable). A closed social group deliberately avoids contact with other people and the rest of the world; it condemns and eliminates all external relationships. It treats its own *orbis interior* as the only existing one, as a realm of inhabited, organized space – opposed to the outside world (*orbis exterior*), constituting a sphere of the unknown, the mysterious; of shapeless infinity, demons, strangers, the ill and the dead, of night and chaos.[32] This mental isolation leads to a conservative outlook: the acceptance of the world as it is and a violent opposition to any attempts at changing it.[33] Such an ideology is represented by the communities in *The Painted Bird* and "Amy Foster" – they impersonate cultures which are self-expressive, psychologically and socially isolated, non-elitist (peasant or tribal), favoring the oral transmission of tradition.[34]

Biographical context provides another level of comparison of *The Painted Bird* and "Amy Foster," as the leading characters in both these works are to some extent modelled upon the authors themselves. Conrad was called by critics a homo duplex – an Englishman with a deeply hidden Polish self, which largely determined his mentality, writings, and actions. Kosiński, born and educated in Poland, strongly affirmed his ties with the Polish tradition, ethos and culture, and reacted against charges of anti-Semitism levelled against this nation. *The Painted Bird* should not be read as a censure of Poles, as the novel is not documentary, and its fictional world and characters' actions are shaped by the principles of hyperbole and fantasy. Both *The Painted Bird* and "Amy Foster" convey acute portrayals of relationships between the familiar and the alien – relationships comprising universal patterns of human social behavior. And it was Conrad and Kosiński's common experience of emigration and its attendant cultural dislocation which conditioned such artistically penetrating presentations of this theme.

NOTES

1. For a pejorative commentary on Kosiński's application of this method see Barry Popik, "Conrad in Kosiński's Last Novel," *Joseph Conrad Today,* 16: 3-4 (1991), 7-8.

2. On this type of Conradian isolation see Wiesław Krajka, *Isolation and Ethos: A Study of Joseph Conrad* (New York-Boulder, CO: Columbia U.P. – East European Mongraphs, 1992), 5-31.

3. See comments on Yanko Goorall's isolation in Osborn Andreas, *Joseph Conrad: A Study in Non-conformity* (London: Vision Press, 1962), 70-2; Jocelyn Baines, *Joseph Conrad: A Critical Biography* (London: Weidenfeld and Nicolson, 1960), 263-7; C. F. Burgess, "Conrad's Catholicism," *Conradiana,* 15: 2 (1983), 111-26; Adam Gillon, *The Eternal Solitary: A Study of Joseph Conrad* (New York: Bookman Associates, 1960), 123-4; Albert J. Guerard, *Conrad, the Novelist* (Cambridge, MA: Harvard U.P., 1958), 49-50; Krajka, *Isolation and Ethos:*...51-3, 59-60, 66; Juliet McLauchlan, "'Amy Foster' – Echoes from Conrad's Own Experience?," *The Polish Review,* 23: 3 (1978), 3-8; Krystyna Urbisz, "The Theme of Isolation in Joseph Conrad," *Zeszyty Naukowe Uniwersytetu Jagiellońskiego,* 362 (1974), 302-3.

4. This study disregards psychological and existential aspects of estrangement (discussed e.g. in Colin Wilson, *The Outsider* [London: Victor Gallancz, 1956]), as they are less essential in the case of the protagonists of "Amy Foster" and *The Painted Bird.*

5. See Wiesław Krajka, "The Dialogue of Cultures in Joseph Conrad's 'Amy Foster'," *New Comparison,* 9 (Spring 1990), 149-57.

6. This typology is used after Seweryna Wysłouch, "Powieściowe wyobcowanie (Próba typologii)," in *Literatura a wyobcowanie: Studia,* ed. Jerzy Święch (Lublin: Lubelskie Towarzystwo Naukowe, 1990), 224-6; Florian Znaniecki, "Studia nad antagonizmem do obcych," in Florian Znaniecki, *Współczesne narody* (Warszawa: Państwowe Wydawnictwo Naukowe, 1990), 331.

7. See Jerzy Święch, "Wstęp," in *Literatura a wyobcowanie:*...,7. On the significance of the opposition familiar/alien in contemporary humanities see Roch Sulima, *Słowo i etos: Szkice o kulturze* (Kraków: FA ZMW "Galicja," 1992), 198-202.

8. See Ludwik Stomma, *Antropologia kultury wsi polskiej XIX w.* (Warszawa: PAX, 1986), 23-5.

9. See Georg Simmel, "The Stranger," in Georg Simmel, *On Individuality and Social Forms,* ed. D. N. Levine (Chicago: U. of Chicago P., 1971), 143-9. On the criteria of foreignness see Stomma 48-9, 56-64.

10. See Simmel, 145; Znaniecki, 275, 302.

11. See Zygmunt Bauman, *Culture as Praxis* (London: Routledge and Kegan Paul, 1973), 131-2.

12. See Bauman, 271, 275, 284, 302, 308-9.

13. See Krajka, "Dialogue...."

14. See e.g., a catalogue of pejorative features attributed to aliens by Polish peasants: Stomma, chapters I ("Od 'czarnej legendy' do kategorii 'swój-obcy'") and II ("Wierzenia o obcych"). On the functioning of the familiar/alien opposition in Polish folk culture and mentality and in texts of Polish folklore see Stomma; Sulima, 144-8, 204-8.

15. See Święch, 7; Znaniecki, 321-2, 342, 350.

16. See Wysłoch, 223.

17. See Keith Carabine, "'Irreconcilable Differences:' England as 'an Undiscovered Country' in Conrad's 'Amy Foster'," in *The Ends of the Earth: English Literature and the Wider World,* ed. S. Gatrell, vol. 4 (London: The Ashfield Press, 1992), 187-204.

18. See Wilson, 10; Wysłoch, 223, 225, 228, 235; Znaniecki, 299-300, 303, 305-6, 308.

19. See comments on the lack of realization of a potential dialogue of cultures in "Amy Foster" in Krajka "Dialogue...." According to Simmel, 43-4, every true exchange or interaction involves reciprocity.

20. See theoretical comments in Znaniecki, 305-6.

21. See Bauman, 130-1.

22. Bauman, 130.

23. This self-defense is manifest, e.g., in strictly guarded borders against strangers; see Bauman, 133. See also general considerations about the alien as a source of danger: Stomma, 138, 206; Znaniecki, 270-1, 344, 349, 351.

24. See Znaniecki, 350.

25. On the meanings of the title metaphor of this novel see M. Skau, M. Carroll, D. Cassidy, "J. Kosiński *The Painted Bird*: a Modern Bestiary," *The Polish Review*, 27: 3/4 (1982), 45-54. The vanity of handsome Laba is reminiscent of that of Nostromo, for whom the meaning of life consisted entirely in the admiration of politicians, women, and the common people.

26. On functions of animal imagery as related to the characters' attitudes and actions (parallelism, hyperbole, explication, illustration, etc.)

in *The Painted Bird* see Skau et al. See also Jerzy Kosiński, *Notes of the Author on "The Painted Bird."* (New York: Scientia-Factum, 1967), 17-18.

27. This cruelty turned Kosiński into the target of attacks by the Polish and emigré press for accusing Polish peasants of barbarism, brutality, backwardness, and anti-Semitism. The attitude has recently reemerged in *Czarny ptasior* by Joanna Siedlecka (Gdańsk – Warszawa: "Marabut" – "Cis", 1994). In the preface to this book, the author declares her intention to reconstruct the war period in Jerzy Kosiński's life. She carries out this task mainly on the basis of interviews with the people who, as they claim, remember the writer from that time. The reliability of presented evidence, however, is questionable; the book merely creates the appearance of documentation. In fact the version of events it presents is rather reminiscent of a fictionalized one, a product of the author's imagination. Principally, *Czarny ptasior,* by emphasizing the autobiographical dimension of *The Painted Bird,* condemns the morality of Jerzy Kosiński and his father, and stresses the writer's black ingratitude to the Poles and their families, who hid and protected him during the war. Another group of emigré literary critics, as well as English, American, German, and French ones, emphasized the metaphorical-symbolic-universal as opposed to the historical-concrete aspect of the presented reality and characters in *The Painted Bird,* see Jadwiga Jurkszus-Tomaszewska, "Na szczęście nie best-seller," *Oficyna poetów* (London), 3: 2 (1968), 45-6; Leon Mitkiewicz, "Polskie recenzje o *Malowanym ptaku,*" *Horyzonty* (Paris), 12: 129 (1967), 74-6. Kosiński himself shared this attitude in numerous interviews and popular articles: he negated the novel's realism and protested against its interpretation in terms of autobiographical reductionism. He also stressed his ties with Polish culture · and the positive role which it has played for the development of the Jewish nation and civilization. In an auto-commentary to his novel Jerzy Kosiński, *Notes of the Author on "The Painted Bird,"* 9-31, he stresses the temporal, geographical, and historical indefiniteness of its place of action, and the metaphorical and visionary character of the story. In a symbolic-mythical interpretation of *The Painted Bird,* a crucial role is played by the child--protagonist which represents a preconscious phase of the human self, the Jungian collective unconscious phase. See Jerzy Kosiński, *Notes...,* 13; Maria Janion, "Sam w ciemni," in *Jerzy Kosiński: Twarz i maski,* ed. and photos Cz. Czapliński (Warszawa: Muzeum Sztuki, 1992): 50-3. His ordeal is echoed in *Passion Play,* where Fabian confesses that in his childhood, having left the town during the war, he was isolated as a stranger among peasants; for Stella, a Negro albino, there is no place among her black parents and relatives.

28. The motto taken from Mayakovsky, "and only God, / omnipotent inded, / knew they were mammals / of a different breed," constitutes another metafictional element in the narrative frame of this novel. This motto indicates clearly that ethno-cultural estrangement is to be the main theme of this novel.

29. On the magic nature of an alien's interference see Stomma, 6-7, 31-4, 48; Znaniecki, 342, 348-9, 354-5.

30. See Stomma, 6-7, 21, 30-1, 35, 48-9; Znaniecki, 342-4, 353.

31. See Znaniecki, 270, 305.

32. See Stomma, 35, 65, 132-5, 143-4; Znaniecki, 266-7, 282-3, 349.

33. See Stomma, 82.

34. See Stomma, 145-6.

WORKS CITED

Andreas Osborn. *Joseph Conrad: A Study in Non-conformity.* London: Vision Press, 1962.

Baines Jocelyn. *Joseph Conrad: A Critical Biography.* London: Weidenfeld and Nicolson, 1960.

Bauman Zygmunt. *Culture as Praxis.* London: Routledge and Kegan Paul, 1973.

Burgess C. F. "Conrad's Catholicism," *Conradiana,* 15: 2 (1983), 111-26.

Carabine Ketih. "'Irreconcilable Differences:' England as 'An Undiscovered Country' in Conrad's 'Amy Foster'," in *The Ends of the Earth: English Literature and the Wider World,* ed. S. Gatrell, vol. 4. London: The Ashfield Press, 1992.

Gillon Adam. *The Eternal Solitary: A Study of Joseph Conrad.* New York: Bookman Associates, 1960.

Guerard Albert J. *Conrad, the Novelist.* Cambridge, MA: Harvard U.P., 1958.

Janion Maria. "Sam w ciemni," in *Jerzy Kosiński: Twarz i maski,* ed. and photos Czesław Czapliński. Warszawa: Muzeum Sztuki, 1992.

Jurkszus-Tomaszewska Jadwiga. "Na szczęście nie best-seller," *Oficyna poetów* (London), 3: 2 (1968), 45-6.

Kosiński Jerzy. *Notes of the Author on "The Painted Bird."* New York: Scientia-Factum, 1967.

Kosiński Jerzy. *The Painted Bird.* New York: Bantam Books, 1981.

Krajka Wiesław. "The Dialogue of Cultures in Joseph Conrad's 'Amy Foster'," *New Comparison,* 9 (Spring 1990), 149-57.

Krajka Wiesław. *Isolation and Ethos: A Study of Joseph Conrad.* New York–Boulder, CO: Columbia U.P. – East European Monographs, 1992.

McLauchlan Juliet. "'Amy Foster' – Echoes from Conrad's Own Experience?," *The Polish Review,* 23: 3 (1978), 3-8.

Mitkiewicz Leon. "Polskie recenzje o *Malowanym ptaku,*" *Horyzonty* (Paris), 12: 129 (1967), 74-6.

Popik Barry. "Conrad in Kosiński's Last Novel," *Joseph Conrad Today,* 16: 3-4 (1991), 7-8.

Siedlecka Joanna. *Czarny ptasior*. Gdańsk – Warszawa: "Marbut" – "Cis", 1994.

Simmel Georg. "The Stranger," in Simmel Georg. *On Individuality and Social Forms*, ed. D. N. Levine. Chicago: U. of Chicago P., 1971.

Skau M., Carroll M. and Cassidy D. "J. Kosiński: *The Painted Bird*: a Modern Bestiary," *The Polish Review*, 27: 3-4 (1982), 45-54.

Stomma Ludwik. *Antropologia kultury wsi polskiej XIX w*. Warszawa: PAX, 1986.

Sulima Roch. *Słowo i etos: Szkice o kulturze*. Kraków: FA ZMW "Galicja," 1992.

Święch Jerzy. "Wstęp," in *Literatura a wyobcowanie: Studia*, ed. Jerzy Święch. Lublin: Lubelskie Towarzystwo Naukowe, 1990.

Urbisz Krystyna. "The Theme of Isolation in Joseph Conrad," *Zeszyty Naukowe Uniwersytetu Jagiellońskiego*, 362 (1974), 302-3.

Wilson Colin. *The Outsider*. London: Victor Gallancz, 1956.

Wysłoch Seweryna. "Powieściowe wyobcowanie (Próba typologii)," in *Literatura a wyobcowanie: Studia*, ed. Jerzy Święch. Lublin: Lubelskie Towarzystwo Naukowe, 1990.

Znaniecki Florian. "Studia nad antagonizmem do obcych," in Znaniecki Florian. *Współczesne narody*. Warszawa: Państwowe Wydawnictwo Naukowe, 1990.

Jakob Lothe,
University of Oslo,
Oslo, Norway

Andrzej Wajda's Adaptation of Conrad's
The Shadow-Line

The visual quality of Conrad's fiction is striking. The first part of
Nostromo, for instance, is distinguished by the wealth of
topographical detail which the third-person narrator incorporates into his extended introductory descriptions. Both the
substance of these details (as physical objects within the fictional
universe) and the narrative presentation of them suggest that
they are *seen,* visually registered by the narrator before he
presents them through fictional language.

Yet, although David Lodge's characterization of Thomas
Hardy as a "cinematic novelist" (Lodge, 95) could also be
applied to Conrad, the word "novelist" needs to be stressed. As
a writer of fiction, Conrad uses language to create literary
worlds; and his verbal art is very different from the medium of
film. As the Russian formalist Boris Eikhenbaum noted as early
as 1926:

> The cinema audience is placed in completely new conditions of
> perception, which are to an extent opposite to those of the reading
> process. Whereas the reader moves from the printed word to
> visualisation of the subject, the viewer goes in the opposite direction:
> he moves from the subject, from comparison of the moving frames to
> their comprehension, to naming them; in short, to the construction of
> internal speech. The success of film is partially connected to this new
> and heretofore undeveloped kind of intellectual exercise. (Eikhen-
> baum, 123)

Eikhenbaum's observation on the basic difference between
literature and film bears a twofold relevance to this essay. First,
it implicitly warns that the media of literature and film are
possibly too different to allow for a frutiful, and critically
persuasive, comparison. But Eikhenbaum also suggests that, for

all the differences between literature and film, the relationship of
the two media is interesting and artistically productive. For
instance, although film has its own methods, "It needs material.
It takes literature and translates it into filmic language" (126).

This is precisely what Andrzej Wajda does with Conrad's *The
Shadow-Line*. His film is an adaptation in that it is inspired by,
and actively uses, the literary material of Conrad's text; yet it is
also a film in its own right, exploring and interpreting thematic
aspects of *The Shadow-Line* through filmic language. As this
essay will discuss Wajda's film as an adaptation, the film needs to
be related to the novella on which it is based. There is a linkage
between our interpretation of the literary text and our reading of
the film, which generalizes and visually presents Wajda's reading
of the same text.

The most striking difference between Conrad's literary text
and Wajda's adaptation is that Wajda presents the protagonist,
the young captain who is also the text's first-person narrator, *as
Conrad*. Although the film credits the screenplay to Bolesław
Sulik and Andrzej Wajda and states that it is "from the novel *The
Shadow-Line* by Joseph Conrad," Wajda's adaptation is not
only a film version of a literary work; it also transforms
a fictional text into an autobiografical one. This twofold
difference between Wajda's film and Conrad's novella actualizes
some interesting critical issues which this essay will discuss,
concentrating on the beginning (of the novella as well as the film)
and on the relationship between fiction and autobiography.

The Shadow-Line is often regarded as the masterpiece of
Conrad's final creative period. In his "Author's Note" to the
novella, Conrad describes it as "in its brevity a fairly complex
piece of work," adding that "primarily the aim of this piece of
writing was the presentation of certain facts which certainly were
associated with the change from youth...to the more self-
-conscious and more poignant period of maturer life" (*SL,*
xxxviii). Obviously, this description cannot be accepted uncritically, but must be compared with the thematic implications of
the narrative as it is actually presented and developed. If we
proceed to do so, however, this characterization appears to be

one of the most suggestive ever given by Conrad on a piece of his fiction. Part of the reason for the aptness of his commentary is to be sought in the relative proximity in time between the publication of the novella and the writing of the "Author's Note." More importantly, a partial explanation is also suggested by the text's subtitle, "A Confession," which indicates an exceptionally close relationship between author and narrator-protagonist.

The prominence of the narrator is central to Conrad's narrative method in *The Shadow-Line*. The narration is consistently first-person throughout: the protagonist relates a particular succession of experiences – revolving around a sea voyage during which he exercises his first command – that constitutes his crucial transition from youth to adulthood. The tale is the story of its narrator, at a particularly challenging and difficult point in his life. And yet there are, as Ian Watt observes when reflecting on the change of title from "First Command" to "Shadow-Line" (Watt, 144), far-reaching thematic implications attached to the subjective, introverted account. The most important implications obviously result from a combination of the various constituent elements of the narrative, and thus cannot be fully appreciated until the text is finished, or preferably reread. Even so, there are characteristics of the narrator's discourse that are more immediately observable. The most noticeable instance of these "visible" narrative characteristics is probably the narrator's striking generalizations, one of which opens the story:

> Only the young have such moments. I don't mean the very young. No. The very young have, properly speaking, no moments. It is the privilege of early youth to live in advance of its days in all the beautiful continuity of hope which knows no pauses and no introspection.
>
> One closes behind one the little gate of mere boyishness – and enters an enchanted garden....One knows well enough that all mankind has streamed that way. It is the charm of universal experience from which one expects an uncommon or personal sensation – a bit of one's own. (*SL,* 3)

This beginning not only contains searching generalizations; it also tells us something important about their form and content. The opening or prologue, constituted by the first four paragraphs, adumbrates a central thematic concern of the tale as a whole: a troubled experience of existence in time, and of life as a process not only towards adulthood, but also towards death – a painfully self-conscious awareness of the aging process. A major narrative characteristic is observable in the way these introductory reflections are presented. For they presuppose experience and hindsight; they presuppose, in fact, successful handling of the challenge facing the narrator in the main action of *The Shadow-Line*. One aspect of the generalizations is that they are based, in a fairly straightforward manner, on the narrator's own experiences. This is, indeed, the main reason why they are so convincing: they are to a large extent verified by the incidents (and the narrator's response to them) later dramatized. Thus it is the distance – not only in time, but also in knowledge – which enables the narrator to focus his story on its essential aspects and to intensify the central experience.

How does Wajda's adaptation begin? It is indicative of the great difference between the two media that in order to consider this question properly, we first need to make some theoretical points about narration in narrative fiction and film. Clearly, film is also a form of narrative – and a very effective form at that. The main constituents of a verbal narrative (causality, time, and space) also serve to constitute film narration; and narrative concepts such as plot, repetition, and characterization are equally applicable to both media. Although verbal fiction and fiction film are both narratives, however, the forms and techniques of narrative presentation are strikingly dissimilar.

This point also applies to the narrator. In verbal fiction, the narrator is the author's primary means of shaping a text, which is constituted by the activites and functions the narrator is made to perform. In Conrad's fiction, these functions are crucial for presenting the fictional content. Generally, as well as in Conrad, it is essential to draw a distinction between third- and first--person narrators. Although this distinction is not unproblematic, much is to be gained by applying it to Conradian narrative. Moreover, there is – and this is relevant to the narrative of *The Shadow-Line* – a crucial point involved here concerning the narrator's ontological status. The contrast between an embodied (first-person) narrator and a (third--person) narrator without such bodily determination accounts for an essential difference in the narrator's motivation to narrate: "For an embodied narrator, this motivation is existential; it is directly connected with his practical experiences....For the third-person narrator, on the other hand, there is no existential compulsion to narrate" (Stanzel, 93).

That the narrative of *The Shadow-Line* is first person (contrasting with the wide-ranging third-person narrative of *Nostromo* or with the intricate interplay of third-person and first-person narrative in *Lord Jim*) is consistent with the protagonist's "compulsion to narrate." As indicated already, the narrative and thematic characteristics of the novella's beginning are closely associated with the kind of first-person narrative Conrad employs; later on in the narrative, the narrator's "existential" motivation to narrate is illustrated particularly well in the diary extracts. In Wajda's film, on the other hand, the narrator's identity is less clear; and consequently his ontological status is more uncertain. Wajda does, it is true, begin his film by focusing on the protagonist, whose first words are:

> This is not a marriage story. My action, such as it was, had more the quality of divorce, of desertion. For no good reason, I abandoned my ship. It was in an Eastern port, in Singapore.

Actually, the actor does not (as we watch him on the screen) speak these words aloud, but comments – retrospectively, the spectator infers – on his own situation in this particular place and at this point in time. These voice-over comments, which correspond quite well with the relevant textual segment early in the novella,[1] constitute only a small part of the film narration, however. For although narrative has long been the dominant mode of filmmaking, narrative communication through film is essentially visual, though it also exploits auditive communication channels. If the concept of narrator is to be applied to film, it needs to be sufficiently inclusive to accommodate the various communicative devices and techniques pertaining to narrative film. On the one hand, the film narrator is a heterogeneous, technical instrument in the service of the film director; on the other hand, he – or rather, it – guides and manipulates the spectator's reading of the film. If Conrad as author writes *The Shadow-Line* by making his first-person narrator speak, Wajda's film narrator is a heterogeneous, mechanical, and highly flexible instrument, constituted by a variety of techniques and performing diverse functions. The film narrator therefore needs to be distinguished from the voice-over Wajda uses at the beginning of the adaptation. Though important, such a technique is merely one component in a far more complex narrative communication.

Theoretically as well technically, the narrative system of film is too complex to be properly considered here. But when discussing Wajda's adaptation we need to be aware of one of the most distinctive qualites of film:

> that every object that is reproduced appears simultaneously in two entirely different frames of reference, namely the two-dimensional and the three-dimensional, and that as one identical object it fulfills two different functions in the two contexts. (Arnheim, 59)

The film spectator thus encounters two major frames of reference in film, "the space and time of a *screen* as well as (a sample of) the space and time of a *story world*" (Branigan, 33). In Wajda's *The Shadow-Line*, the protagonist's opening words (the voice-over commentary quoted above) initiate the space and time of the story world, whereas the filmic segments preceding them foreground the frame of reference associated with the screen. It does not follow that there is no connection between these two frames of reference. "Light and sound create two fundamental systems of space, time, and causal interaction: on screen and within a story world" (Branigan, 34). Watching the phenomenal appearances on the screen, the spectator attempts to relate them to possible functions in a story world. This is, as Edward Branigan notes, a complicated process during which major changes can occur; particularly at the beginning of a film it is often difficult to identify and interpret the key functions of the story world. The beginning of Wajda's *The Shadow-Line* further complicates this process as the opening shots of the film do not refer to the story world directly, but instead present a succession of pictoral frames which photographically reproduce historical reality: a picture of a sailing ship, another picture of officers and crew on the deck of such a ship, and further shots showing pictures of sailing ships at rest in what appears to be a major port of the nineteenth century. Thus while reading that this film by Andrzej Wajda is "from the novel *The Shadow-Line* by Joseph Conrad," the spectator also watches the photographs over which this information is projected, wondering about their significance and relevance for the story that follows.

This relevance is at least twofold. First, it suggests that a sailing ship will feature prominently in the film; the action of the film, we also infer, is spatially connected with some Eastern port and temporally related to the last phase of the era of sailing ships. Second, and more interestingly, the presentation of photographs warns us that although we initially expect to see a fiction film based on "a novel," the distinction between fiction and nonfiction may turn out to be blurred in this particular adaptation.

Now it could be countered that the word "relevance" distracts from, rather than illuminates, the frame of reference associated with the screen. Such criticism has some force: as narrative aims to reconcile screen presentation and story world, so the narrative bias of this discussion unavoidably entails a rather cursory treatment of screen-related issues. It needs to be remembered, though, that story is also related to, and influences, our reading of the screen. Actually, at this particular point there is a significant difference between viewing the film "as film" or as adaptation. For anyone who watches Wajda's *The Shadow-Line* after having read Conrad's novella, the introductory succession of photographic images will be charged with relevant, though potentially problematic, information, since both the pictures of sailing ships and those of the harbor (which the voice-over identifies as Singapore) make us think of the setting, action, and author of the novella. Still, aspects of the screen are discernible in the succession of the photographs (guiding, as it were, the spectator into the harbor), in the selection of them, and in the decision to make use of them in the first place. This decision, which we must attribute to Wajda as director, is artistically productive: highlighting the importance of the sailing ship as the central metaphor of both novella and film, it also suggests a parallel between the first presentation of the ship as something static (since the film here reproduces a photograph) and the later shots of the becalmed ship, which, motionless, also conveys a peculiarly static impression.

Having informed the spectator that he has abandoned his ship, the voice-over continues:

> I had been first mate on the *Vidar*, an excellent ship, and I had the highest regard for her master, Captain Kent, who must have wondered what ailed his first mate. But he was a sailor, and he too had been young – and perhaps understood what I found so difficult to express....And so I left Captain Kent's ship, as a bird leaves a comfortable branch. One day I was perfectly all right, and the next everything was gone: glamour, flavour, interest, contentment, everything. It was the moment, you know, when one senses ahead the shadow-line, warning one that the period of late youth must be left behind. The green sickness of late youth descended upon me.

In one sense, the perspective of this voice-over, as well as the content of the information it provides, correspond well with the relevant textual segment in Conrad's novella. Like Conrad's first-person narrator, the voice-over is introductory and retrospective. It indicates that the story we are to be shown has already happened and that the filmic presentation will be broadly analeptic, selectively focusing on the most significant constituent aspects of the narrator-protagonist's central experience. That the content of this experience is as yet unknown serves to increase suspense. Moreover, as Conrad invites the reader of his novella to relate suspense to the text's title, so Wajda asks the spectator to draw a connection between the title of the film and the narrator's mention of the word "shadow--line." The corresponding sentence in the novella occurs in the third paragraph: "time, too, goes on – till one perceives ahead a shadow-line warning one that the region of early youth, too, must be left behind" (*The Shadow-Line, SL,* 3).

If Wajda's adaptation begins by relating the first introductory shots to the narrator-protagonist's opening reflections, the semantic thrust of these shots is closely connected with the preceding photographs. By beginning his film in this somewhat unusual manner, and by incorporating the word "shadow-line" into his narrator's opening reflections, Wajda manages to retain several of the qualities of the novella's opening. This is all the more remarkable in view of the complexity and interpretative richness of the title pages of Conrad's novella:

> The mysteriously evocative title, which positively invites interpretation, is supplied with a subtitle: *A Confession*; with a motto: "Worthy of my undying regard;" with an epigraph: "*D'autres fois, calme plat, grand miroir | De mon désespoir*;"[2] and, most strikingly, with a dedication: "To Borys and all others who like himself have crossed in early youth the shadow-line of their generation, with love." (Berthoud, 7)

As Jacques Berthoud goes on to note in his thoughtful introduction to the novella, "the dedication explicitly associates something outside the narrative – the enlistment of Conrad's eldest son as a second-lieutenant – with something inside it – his own appointment to his first command twenty-seven years earlier" (7). Thus the dedication affirms, and strengthens, the autobiographical element which the subtitle indicates. It also relates the text to Conrad's experience of World War I. About a month before he finished the tale he now called *The Shadow-Line,* his son Borys had been transferred to France; and "Conrad must have frequently thought about his isolation from the terrible realities of the front" (Najder, 408). Yet although Conrad seems to have "regarded the *writing* of *The Shadow-Line* as an act of solidarity with the youthful combatants with whom he could no longer serve" (Berthoud, 9), it is no war novel. Nor is it (in contrast to a text such as *A Personal Record*) an autobiographical work, at least not in the ordinary sense of the word "autobiography." Rather, Conrad's novella is a meditative and peculiarly intense first-person narrative which incorporates into its fiction some highly significant (partially suppressed and critically very interesting) autobiographical elements provoked by, and indirectly responding to, the "Great War." With the possible exceptions of "Heart of Darkness" and *Under Western Eyes,* no fictional work by Conrad probes more deeply into the complicated, and frequently paradoxical, relationship between fiction and autobiography than does *The Shadow-Line.* Our critical focus on narrative strengthens, rather than qualifies, this observation. As John Sturrock observes in *The Languge of Autobiography*:

> A human life can be brought to display a meaning only on condition of being turned into a story; once subject to the public order of narrative, it acquires both the gravity of a settled and venerable literary form, and the orientation of hindsight which alone raises the past from an aimless sum of reminiscence into a personal history. If we crave significance for ourselves as historical beings, we can have it only by an intelligent and sequential ordering of what we retain or can recover from our past – in which the autobiographer is a model for us all. A life storied is a life made meaningful, and any life, however vapid, is at least storiable. (Sturrock, 20)

An autobiography, then, is a narrative; moreover, the strategy of deferment so noticeable in Conrad's writing of *The Shadow-Line* is also a characteristic feature of many autobiographies. Sturrock's main example is "the paradigm of all autobiographical stories" (20), Augustine's *Confessions*: Augustine was baptized as a Christian in Milan in 387; his *Confessions* were not published in North Africa until ten years later. As Augustine's chosen title indicates, the word "confession" is central to the genre of autobiography. At first sight; therefore, its appearance as the subtitle of *The Shadow-Line* might lead one to expect an autobiographical work. Yet Conrad carefully avoids identifying the narrator-protagonist with himself as author. Unlike Augustine, who consistently uses the personal pronoun "I" in order to refer to himself at an earlier (sinful) stage of his own life, Conrad employs an unidentified narrator who, narrating the story of his first command, also functions as a distancing device – paradoxically enabling Conrad to deal with an episode from his own past, while at the same time preserving a necessary distance from it.

This kind of double maneuver goes some way towards explaining the novella's strange blend of "intellectual concentration and expressiveness, as well as its synthesis of the typically Conradian moral and psychological problems" (Najder, 410; cf. 102-5). Conrad's reluctance to use geographical names (for instance, he prefers "Eastern port" [*The Shadow-Line, SL,* 4] to Singapore) is consistent with this distancing strategy, which bears some resemblance to that employed in the writing of "Heart of Darkness."[3] "Explicitness," wrote Conrad to Richard Curle in 1922, "is fatal to the glamour of all artistic work, robbing it of all suggestiveness, destroying all illusion" (Kimbrough, 232). Constantly aiming at a form of artistic suggestiveness which presupposes considerable narrative flexibility (Hawthorn, xxiv), Conrad suppresses explicitness and overtly autobiographical references in *The Shadow-Line*. Thus the novella is not, as Conrad himself claimed in a letter to Sidney Colvin, "exact biography" (*CL,* II, 182), though the autobiographical elements which the reminiscences bring into the fiction serve to give it a rare authenticity.

In his adaptation of Conrad's novella, however, Wajda crosses the borderline between fiction and autobiography. As his film identifies the narrator-protagonist as Conrad, the novella's anonymous first-person narrator in a sense disappears. In other ways too (compare the use of photographs and the identification of the ship as the *Vidar*[4]), the film purports to present a segment – a significant, test-like phase – of Joseph Conrad's life. Noticeable as they are from the start, these markers of autobiography become quite unambiguous somewhat later in the film. As in the novella, the narrator decides to stay at the Sailors' Home while waiting for the next "homeward mail boat." Wajda also follows the text closely in his presentation of Captain Giles, another guest at the home for whom the narrator has great respect, but who provokes him by asking: "Why did you give up your berth?" Irritated, the narrator retorts: "Why? Do you disapprove?" And Giles responds: "I? Oh, in a general sort of way." Let us compare this dialogue excerpt with the corresponding textual segment in Conrad's novella:

> "Why did you throw up your berth?"
> I became angry all of a sudden; for you can understand how exasperating such a question was to a man who didn't know. I said to myself that I ought to shut up that moralist; and to him aloud I said with challenging politeness:
> "Why...? Do you disapprove?" He was too disconcerted to do more than mutter confusedly: "I!...In a general way...." and then gave me up. (*The Shadow-Line, SL,* 14)

Given the general need for compression of dialogue in film, it is remarkable how accurately the extract reproduces the text from the novella. The key words are all there in the film: "give up" (virtually synonymous with "throw up"), "berth," "disapprove," and "general way." What is missing is the narrative commentary which, in Conrad's text, is colored by the insights gained from the subsequent, test-like experience. This kind of insight – showing a mental growth or *Bildung* on the part of the narrator – is particularly noticeable in the sentence "for you can understand how exasperating such a question was to a man who didn't know." This kind of narrative commentary, which effectively exposes the narrator's relative ignorance at the time of the conversation with Captain Giles, is difficult to present in film. But the dialogue itself is very similar to that of Conrad's text; and it provides a good basis for the following filmic segment, to which there is no corresponding textual one. When Captain Giles decides to take his siesta, the narrator-protagonist returns to his room. As we are watching him there, alone, the voice-over invites us to share his thoughts:

Having broken away from my home in Poland, removed by great distances from such natural affections as were still left me, I can safely say that the sea was to be all my world. The sole link with my homeland was the parcels that my uncle sent from Ukraine. The letters and photographs were a reminder of the world I had left thirteen years previously. From time to time he would enclose a copy of the Polish paper *Wędrowiec* for me to contribute some impressions of my travels abroad. By such means he encouraged me to keep my native tongue and to retain the customs I had learned in childhood...[reads aloud in Polish]. But the photographs that he sent of himself and his wife and the remaining members of our family looked out at me from a very

> different world from the one which now I occupied. My childhood in
> Ukraine and schooling in Cracow were now in memory only and my
> future lay with the path I had chosen. To show that a man from
> a country with no sea could be as good a sailor as anyone.

Identifying the narrator as Conrad, the voice-over also presents itself as Conrad's voice – addressing the spectator from a temporal vantage point thirteen years after the departure from Poland.[5] By making his narrator (or Conrad) read Polish fluently, Wajda elegantly justifies his decision to make the Polish actor Marek Kondrat play the part of the narrator, while the other parts are played by native speakers of English. Further, Wajda establishes an interesting connection between the photographs the narrator is looking at in this scene and the photographs he (as director) employs at the very beginning of the film. The thematic impact of these photographs will probably vary from spectator to spectator. For some, they are likely to enhance the film's reflective character, encouraging the spectators, perhaps, to compare (or contrast) the narrator's family photographs with their own, possibly also inducing them to think of their own childhood. "From the past," writes Roland Barthes, "it is my childhood which fascinates me most; these images alone, upon inspection, fail to make me regret the time which has vanished. For it is not the irreversible I discover in my childhood, it is the irreducible: everything which is still in me" (Barthes, 22). For Barthes as for the narrator (or Conrad, or the reader/spectator), thoughts about childhood tend to blend with reflections on time. Although the narrator's use of the word "childhood" is provoked by the photographs he is looking at, the combination of "childhood" and photograph implicitly invites the spectator to reflect both on the first paragraph of the novella and on the use of photographs at the very beginning of the film. There is a sense, then, in which this overtly autobiographical scene subtly responds to the novella's opening paragraph. Since this paragraph *precedes* the narrator's first words (cf. the quotation above), one thematic effect of this scene is autobiographically to adapt, in a thematically enriching manner, some of the first-person narrator's reflections at the beginning of Conrad's text.

At the same time, the narrator's (or Conrad's) family photographs relate Wajda's adaptation more directly to a specific historical period (the nineteenth century) and to one particular personal biography. Reinforcing the static impression of the film's beginning, they also strengthen the linkage between the prologue at the Sailors' Home and the narrator's subsequent test as a sea captain, with his ship becalmed and his crew laid low by fever.

The use of music is noteworthy in this later, and very central, part of the film. Throughout this prolonged scene, Wojciech Kilar's music plays the significant narrative function of auditively illustrating, and accentuating, the narrator-protagonist's mental strain, his loneliness as the only fit officer on board, his (and the crew's) vulnerability, and his growing existential anxiety and threatened self-possession. Thus the film music responds, in its own way, to the predominant mood of the narrator's diary extracts: "I remain on deck, of course, night and day....All sense of time is lost in the monotony of expectation, of hope, and of desire" (97).

The effect of music in this part of the film depends partially on its productive interplay with film photography and, more specifically, with the use of camera angle and spatial distance. In the novella, part of the narrator's ordeal as captain is that he cannot, and will not, leave his ship. Conrad's novella maintains the temporal distance between the narration of the story after the ordeal and the narrator-protagonist's actual experience of it (compare the diary extracts). Wajda attains a similar effect by combining shots of the captain and his crew with shots of the ship from a distance. Enhanced by Kilar's music, these shots of the becalmed ship – alone at sea and surrounded by water and sky only – invite the spectator to relate the filmic perspective to the narrator's perspective after the test-like experience. Thus camera angle, distance, and music here combine to constitute a form of narration which is just as effective as, for instance, the use of voice-over in other parts of the film.

If the first-person narrative of Conrad's *The Shadow-Line* is distinguished by its quality of self-conscious reflection arising from the incidents and sense impressions with which the voyage confronts the narrator-protagonist, Wajda's adaptation, partaking of the universal situation of film practice (Andrew, 106), intelligently responds to this literary text by presenting it as an autobiography which, through the medium of film, preserves many of the novella's qualities and characteristics. Although some literary characteristics necessarily disappear in the adaptation process, other, essentially filmic, qualities are added; and several of these are interesting and thought-provoking if related to Conrad's text. All in all, Wajda's adaptation is both a tribute to a great work of a literature and a valuable aesthetic product in its own right.

NOTES

1. Actually, the corresponding textual segment is the fifth paragraph of chapter one, not the first.

2. "At other times, flat calm, great mirror / Of my despair." From Baudelaire, "La Musique," *Les Fleurs du Mal,* 74. The quotation should end with an exclamation mark rather than a full stop.

3. Although, unlike *The Shadow-Line,* "Heart of Darkness" has no subtitle, there can be no doubt that this novella also incorporates autobiographical elements into its thematic structure. As Conrad's use of Marlow serves to constitute "Heart of Darkness" as a fictional text, so the avoidance of geographical names (e.g., "the sepulchral city" for Brussels) helps to make the narrative less explicit and more suggestive. Cf. my discussion of "Heart of Darkness" in *Fiksjon og film* [Fiction and Film], 184-8.

4. On 4 January 1888, "J. Korzeniowski" (according to the certificate of discharge) signed off the *Vidar* in Singapore (See Najder, 102 and Sherry, 212). Whereas Sherry finds this decision hard to explain, Najder argues that in reality Conrad "had quite rational reasons for resigning" and that he made his decision appear quite arbitrary because "he wanted to achieve a more marked contrast between impulsive youth and responsible maturity" (Najder, 102).

5. Interestingly, as these thoughts depart from the fictional text of *The Shadow-Line,* they approximate to the openly autobiographical *A Personal Record* with Conrad's "Familiar Preface." Compare the narrator's first sentence with the following extract:

Having broken away from my origins under a storm of blame from every quarter which had the merest shadow of right to voice an opinion, removed by great distances from such natural affections as were still left to me....I may safely say that through the blind force of circumstances the sea was to be all my world....(*PR,* xiv).

WORKS CITED

Andrew J. Dudley. *Concepts in Film Theory*. Oxford: Oxford U.P., 1984.

Arnheim Rudolf. *Film as Art* [1933]. Berkeley: U. of California P., 1957.

Barthes Roland. *Roland Barthes*. New York: Hill and Wang, 1977.

Baudelaire Charles. *Le Fleurs du Mal*. Paris: Garnier, 1961.

Berthoud Jacques. "Introduction: Autocracy and War," in Joseph Conrad, *The Shadow-Line,* ed. Jacques Berthoud. Harmondsworth: Penguin Books, 1987, 7-24.

Branigan Edward. *Narrative Comprehension and Film*. London: Routledge, 1992.

Eikhenbaum Boris. "Literature and Cinema," in *Russian Formalism: A Collection of Articles and Texts in Translation,* ed. Stephen Bann and John E. Bowlt. Edinburgh: Scottish Academic Press, 1973.

Hawthorn Jeremy. "Introduction," in Joseph Conrad, *The Shadow-Line,* ed. Jeremy Hawthorn. Oxford: Oxford U.P., 1985, vii-xxv.

Kimbrough Robert. *Joseph Conrad: Heart of Darkness,* 3rd. ed. New York: Norton, 1988. Conrad's letter to Curle (24 April 1922) is reprinted from Curle Richard. *Conrad to a Friend*. New York: Dobuleday, 1928, 112-14.

Lodge David. "Thomas Hardy as a Cinematic Novelist," in *Working with Structuralism: Essays and Reviews on Nineteenth- and Twentieth-Century Literature*. London: Routledge, 1981, 95-105.

Lothe Jakob. *Conrad's Narrative Method*. Oxford: Clarendon Press, 1989.

Lothe Jakob. *Fiksjon og film: Narrativ teori og analyse* [Fiction and Film: Narrative Theory and Analysis]. Oslo: Norwegian U. P., 1994.

Najder Zdzisław. *Joseph Conrad: A Chronicle*. Cambridge: Cambridge U. P., 1983.

Sherry Norman. *Conrad's Eastern World*. Cambridge: Cambridge U.P., 1966.

Stanzel Franz K. *A Theory of Narrative*. Cambridge: Cambridge U.P., 1984.

Sturrock John. *The Language of Autobiography: Studies in the First Person Singular*. Cambridge: Cambridge U.P., 1993.

Wajda Andrzej. Adaptation of Joseph Conrad. *The Shadow-Line* (1976). A co-production by Unit X of *Film Polski* and Thames Television. Adapted from the novel *The Shadow-Line* by Joseph Conrad. Starring Marek Kondrat, Graham Lines, Tom Wilkinson, and Martin Wyldeck; Music Wojciech Kilar; Photography Witold Sobociński; Screenplay Andrzej Wajda and Bolesław Sulik; Directed Andrzej Wajda.

Watt Ian. "Story and Idea in Conrad's *The Shadow-Line*," *Critical Quarterly*, 2 (1960), 133-48.

Alex S. Kurczaba,
University of Illinois at Chicago,
Chicago, USA

"Heart of Darkness" and the Poetry of Czesław Miłosz

Exiled in Italy in the aftermath of the November 1830 Rising, Juliusz Słowacki, whom Conrad memorably dubbed *"l'âme de toute la Pologne,"*[1] penned a stanza which serves as my point of departure:

> If Europe is a Nymph – Naples
> is the nymph's azure eye – Warsaw
> her heart – the brambles in her feet: Sevastopol,
> Azov, Mitau, Petersburg, Odessa –
> Paris her head – London her starched collar –
> and Rome...her scapular.
> (trans. A. K.)

> *Jeśli Europa jest nimfą – Neapol*
> *jest nimfy okiem błękitnem – Warszawa*
> *· Sercem – cierniami w nodze: Sewastopol,*
> *Azov, Odessa, Petersburg, Mitawa –*
> *Paryż jej głową – a Londyn kołnierzem*
> *Nakrochmalonym – a zaś Rzym...szkaplerzem*
> (Słowacki, I, 189)[2]

Building on this geographic metaphor the historian Norman Davies has canonized Poland as the "heart of Europe."[3] If this provocative label be apt – (and the Welshman weaves an elegant argument in its support) – then Conrad's now classic metaphor, "heart of darkness," presciently evokes the physical and moral wasteland that befell Conrad's first homeland during the years of Nazi occupation and the ensuing period of sovietization.

Historically, the genre of lyric poetry shines as the crown jewel of Polish letters. "I would like to think," the British critic John Bayley avers, "that the Polish language as written by Miłosz, or Herbert, has a peculiar clarity and power of transmission, a synthesizing and synergistic power which comes from Latin

233

and from its position in the heart of an always changing and self-transforming European culture" (Bayley, 96). Since his debut in 1930, Czesław Miłosz, the 1980 Nobel Laureate in Literature, has registered in prose and verse the horrors and follies of his century filtered through a distinctive East Central European consciousness. Miłosz has fashioned his poetic voice as a Central European insistently. Joseph Conrad – the person, the artist, the myth – has played a key, though muted, role in this process of self-construction.

Topical and formal allusions to Conrad's life and works constitute an abiding motif of Miłosz's poetry and prose. These allusions possess a critical mass which moves one critic to proclaim: "Czesław Miłosz, a poet soaked in Conrad" (Epstein, 231). My purpose in this essay is to trace Conrad's imprint on Miłosz's poetry. Conrad's presence in Miłosz's prose[4] – which includes three essays devoted to the author of *Under Western Eyes* – is a topic deserving separate attention.

Miłosz's debut as poet falls in the interwar period, "a true Renaissance" (Carpenter, 191) in the history of Polish poetry.[5] In the debate on the nature and function of poetry which then raged, the young Miłosz fell in on the side of those opposing the concept of pure poetry, a concept advanced by the Cracow Avantgarde. Miłosz anchored his position in poetry's primal role in the life of the *polis*. In a manifesto titled "The Lie of Today's Poetry" the young poet threw down the gauntlet to "formists:"

> So is this supposed to be poetry, these poems
> of yours written not to share with people a faith, not
> to praise or condemn, but only to create a combination
> of images and sounds? These poems about which it is
> impossible to say what concept of the world they serve,
> or what wisdom they express? Poems that do not come
> under any definition except that they are badly or
> cleverly made?
>
> (Miłosz quoted in Carpenter, 197)

As the leading voice of Wilno's *Żagary* circle, Miłosz expressed his generation's "desire to return to ethical values in art"

(Carpenter, 198).[6] The imperatives of a poetry charged with ethics required of the poet: a sense of moral responsibility, "inner discipline," and "truth to oneself" (198). These imperatives are consonant with Conrad's aesthetics as defined in his "Preface" to *The Nigger of the "Narcissus:"*

> the artist descends within himself, and in that lonely region of stress and strife, if he be deserving and fortunate, he finds the terms of his appeal....[The artist] speaks to our capacity for delight and wonder, to the sense of mystery surrounding our lives; to our sense of pity, and beauty, and pain; to the latent feeling of fellowship with all creation – to the subtle but invincible conviction of solidarity that knits together the loneliness of innumerable hearts, to the solidarity in dreams, in joy, in sorrow, in aspirations, in illusions, in hope, in fear, which binds men to each other, which binds together all humanity – the dead to the living and the living to the unborn. (*NN*, xii)

If Miłosz's aesthetics are born under the sign of the "Preface" to *The Nigger of the "Narcissus,"* the critique of European culture evident in Miłosz's verse and prose rests under the sign of "Heart of Darkness." The Conradian origins of Miłosz's aesthetics and ethics are especially apparent in his early poetry cast in the mold of catastrophism.

Miłosz's poems from the 1930s are marked by prescience. Early that decade the poet perceived the outlines of the darkness about to descend upon his native continent. The country that barely two decades earlier withstood the onslaught of the Red Army again rested at the eye of the storm. Faced with Nazism on one side and Communism on the other, Poland exercised her *liberum veto*: she opted for neither, resisted both, and paid the price for the next half century.

A *locus classicus* of Miłosz's catastrophist vision is his poem, "On the Book;" it is also the earliest Miłosz text bearing a clear Conradian imprint. Published in 1936 in *Three Winters* (*Trzy zimy*), Miłosz's second volume of poetry, the 36-line text is dated 1934 – a year distinguished by Hitler's accession to Reichsführer. For the Polish critic Kazimierz Wyka, "On the Book" epitomizes the catastrophist current of inter-war Polish poetry (Carpenter, 199).

To begin at the end, "On the Book" closes with the word "darkness" (*ciemność*); earlier in the poem Conrad's name is invoked in a way which leaves no doubt as to the genealogy of the poem's last word:

> Never again from your pages will a foggy evening
> glisten for us on the quiet waters as in Conrad's prose
>   (199)
>
> *Już nam z twoich kart nigdy nie zaświeci mglisty*
> *wieczór na cichych wodach jak w prozie Conrada*
>   (200)

The end of the second line here coincides with the end of the clause and, more to the point, unlike the English rendition, in the original, the proper name "Conrad" rests in final position; rendered literally the Polish reads: "the prose of Conrad." In other words, the original emphasizes "Conrad" by featuring it in the strategic final position. This line also plays an important structural role: it lends the poem an almost perfect symmetry. Thus, in terms of rhetoric as well as the graphics of the text, the "darkness" that closes Miłosz's poem summons the earlier invoked proper name "Conrad."

Given this, the final "darkness" of Miłosz's poem summons the final word of Conrad's tale of the Congo, thereby appropriating the thematics and ethos of "Heart of Darkness." Let us recall the clause closing Conrad's narrative:

> and the tranquil waterway leading to the uttermost ends of the earth
> flowed somber under an overcast sky – seemed to lead into the heart of
> an immense darkness. ("Heart of Darkness," *YS*, 162)

Miłosz's poem closes thus:

> Anxious, blind, and faithful to our epoch
> we go somewhere far away...
>
> Thus we were marked to create a fame – nameless,
> like a farewell shout of those departing – into
> darkness.
>   (Carpenter, 199)

My niespokojni, ślepi i epoce wierni,
gdzieś daleko idziemy,...

Więc sławę nam znaczono stworzyć – bezimienną,
jak okrzyk pożegnalny odchodzących – w ciemność.
(200)

In light of its Conradian provenance, can there be any doubt as to
the content of this communal "farewell shout?" Like Marlow
returning to the sepulchral city, Miłosz brings home from the
center of Africa to the European heartland the cry "The horror!
The horror!" ("Heart of Darkness," *YS,* 149) the last judgment of
the deranged "universal genius" to whose making "All Europe
contributed" (117). The poem's pluralized subject, the text's
"we," underscores the communal character of "the unspeakable
rites" unleashed on Kurtz's home continent in the 1930s.

The title of Miłosz's catastrophist poem alerts us to its pivotal
image: the book. The titular image is apostrophized by a question posed exactly midway through the text (verse 19):

Where is the place for you in this tumult,
wise, quiet book, alloy of the elements
reconciled for eternity by the sight of the artist?
(Carpenter, 199)

Gdzież jest miejsce dla ciebie w tym wieku zamętu
książko mądra, spokojna, stopie elementów
pogodzonych na wieki spojrzeniem artysty?
(200)

The eighteen lines of verse preceding this pivotal question
provide a catalogue of images concretizing "this age of tumult"
("*ten wiek zamętu*"):

We lived in strange, hostile, marvelous times,
bullets sang above our heads
and years no less threatening than tearing shrapnel
taught greatness to those who did not see
war. *In the fire of the dryly flaming weeks*
we worked hard and were hungry
for bread, for unearthly miracles appearing on earth

> and often, unable to sleep, suddenly saddened
> *we looked through the windows if over the blue night*
> *flocks of zeppelins were not flowing in again,*
> *if a new signal did not explode to the continents*
> and we looked in the mirror if a stigma did not grow
> on the forehead as *a sign we were already condemned.*
> In those times it was not enough to lament
> with pure words the eternal pathos of the world,
> *it was an epoch of storm, the day of the apocalypse,*
> *old nations were destroyed, capitals turning*
> *like a spindle, drunk, under the foaming sky.*
>
> (199, my emphases)

The insertion at this juncture and within this textual environment of an object as incongruous as a book produces an effect no less startling than Marlow's discovery of a book midway through his pilgrimage to the Inner Station. To my mind, the book in Miłosz's poem plays a function similar to that of the manual carried by "Conrad's pesky Russian" (Burgess, 189) on his African peregrinations. The wellworn tome titled Towson's *An Inquiry into Some Points of Seamanship* draws Marlow's rapt attention. The very incongruity of an object as innocuous and dispensable as a book in an environment of violent struggle endows it with special significance. It is this dry manual that provides a momentary oasis of peace for the weary adventurer, Marlow. "I handled this amazing antiquity with the greatest possible tenderness" ("Heart of Darkness," *YS*, 99) he remarks, describing its effect as

> Luminous with another than a professional light. The simple old sailor [the author] made me forget the jungle and the pilgrims in a delicious sensation of having come upon something unmistakably real. (99)

By exploiting the apparent non-instrumentality of a book in a setting as inhospitable as the banks of the Congo, Conrad achieves a telling reversal of expectations. Thus a book found on the jungle floor projects itself with a reality more concrete than, for instance, the pilgrims, the Accountant, the chain gang, the French steamboat firing into the coast, or finally Kurtz himself

– all bearing the qualities of phantoms in a dream. Ironically, the discovery of Towson's manual produces an effect upon Marlow more tangible than the subsequently discovered owner of the book, the Russian harlequin himself. My point is this: in both Conrad's and Miłosz's texts the book serves as an emblem of sanity; its appearance brings a moment of illumination, a touch of serenity in the hostile environment that envelops it. As a product of human culture, the book – in Conrad's hands and Miłosz's – comes to symbolize the precariousness of human culture or, in Ewa M. Thompson's words, "the experience of civilizational mortality" (Thompson, 21-2).

Miłosz's poetry yields two additional cases of textual gestures towards Conrad's "Heart of Darkness." These occur in his two poetic treatises: "Traktat moralny" [Treatise on Morals] and "Traktat poetycki" [Treatise on Poetry]. Both texts arose in the immediate postwar decade – a period in which convictions and postures undercut by the experiences of war and occupation were subjected to wholesale reexamination. It was a time of radical dislocations in the life of Miłosz's native culture, dislocations generated by the fundamental postwar transformation of East Central Europe. It was also a period of rupture in the poet's life – a prologue to his final split with the postwar Polish regime and his ensuing emigration.

"Traktat moralny" was written in 1947 during Miłosz's sojourn in Washington as cultural attaché in the embassy of the Polish People's Republic. The question animating this long poem is, as Madeline Levine frames it: "To what extent should the individual allow himself to be bound by history and society?" (Levine, 43). The poem opens with a stanza set off by quotation marks from the body of the text, in effect an opening frame; within this frame lie three questions:

> Where, o poet, lies salvation?
> What can save the earth?
> What did the so-called dawn of peace bring forth?
> To ruins it gave a touch of morning glory,
> To hearts deceit, to hopes acridity,
> But I doubt that it awakened pity.
> ([Treatise on Morals], trans. A. K.)

Gdzież jest, poeto, ocalenie?
Czy coś ocalić może ziemię?
Cóż dał tak zwany świt pokoju?
Ruinom trochę dał powojów,
Nadziejom gorycz, sercom skrytość,
A wątpię, czy obudził litość.
("Traktat moralny," *Dzieła zbiorowe*, I, 190)

Delivered in an oracular tone by a voice extraneous to the world
of the poem, these lines are imbued with the bitter skepticism
that marked the intellectual climate of East Central Europe in
the immediate postwar years. The rest of this poem of digressions offers responses to the opening questions. The lyric subject,
the poet purportedly addressed by the opening stanza, defines
his epoch as transitory, counsels embracing it with caution, and
judges it ambivalently:

> Our epoch or obituary
> A giant *Die Likwidation*
> How long it'll last, I can't say,
> Nor of which scoundrels we've yet to hear.
> Treasure it, for through it the world changes
> Rousing slight reservations.
> > ([Treatise on Morals], trans. A. K.)

> *Epoka nasza czyli zgon*
> *Ogromna **Die Likwidation***
> *Jak długo, rzec nie umiem, potrwa*
> *O jakich usłyszymy łotrach.*
> *Ceń ją, bo przez nią świat się zmienia*
> *Budzący lekkie zastrzeżenia.*
> > ("Traktat moralny," 192)

One preliminary response strikes this note of caution:

> > > Don't reach
> For theories humbly and politely.
> The finest sentence string shall change
> When you change your point of observation.
> > ([Treatise on Morals], trans. A. K.)

Po teorie

Nie sięgaj grzecznie i pokornie.
Zmieni się zespół zdań najrzadszy,
Gdy zmienisz punkt z którego patrzysz.

("Traktat moralny," 190)

The poet here indicts, as did Witold Gombrowicz[7] in his play *The Marriage* written the same year, the abundant post-Enlightenment dogmas to which so many European intellectuals – including Miłosz himself – fell prey. This posture reflects the rejection of the "new Marxist faith" injected into the body politic of the ancient states of East Central Europe in the late 1940s. The distinctiveness of perspective of poems like "Traktat moralny" and the closely related "Child of Europe" is rooted in Miłosz's persona as the last poet of the mythopoeic Grand Duchy of Lithuania, as well as the quintessential Central European.[8]

The segment of the poem most charged with meaning – its closure – is suffused with Conradian elements. Here the lyric subject, addressing at once his audience and himself, speaks with a voice purged of illusion about the nature of his epoch and its challenges, but also mindful of the necessity to confront them:

> For this day I offer you no hope,
> Don't wait in vain for *treuga Dei,*
> For you won't escape through a magic gate
> The life that you've been granted.
> Let us go in peace, simple people,
> Before us lies the
> > "Heart of Darkness."
> ([Treatise on Morals], trans. A. K.)

> *Na dziś nie daję ci nadziei,*
> *Nie czekaj darmo* **treuga Dei,**
> *Bo z życia, które tobie dano,*
> *Magiczną nie uciekniesz bramą.*
> *Idźmy w pokoju, ludzie prości.*
> *Przed nami jest*
> > *– "Jądro ciemności."*
> ("Traktat moralny," 201)

The closing metaphor serves as the poem's closing frame. Thus "Heart of Darkness" – capitalized, in quotation marks, and occupying a line of its own – marks the transit from the world of the poem to the world outside it, in effect, a motto above the gate leading to the world which generates it and upon which it comments. This is the split world of the Europe of 1946 – its heartland lifting one foot from the inferno of National Socialism while stepping with the other into Stalinist horror.

Miłosz warns that there is no escaping the darkness of our epoch through "a magic gate;" the Polish poet's caveat echoes Marlow's passage from Europe's "sepulchral city" to the Congo. In the most Kafka-esque episodes of the Englishman's adventure, this passage ushers him through a sequence of doors on the trail to the Company's inner sanctum. He first confronts *"immense double doors* standing ponderously ajar. I slipped," he relates,

> through one of these cracks, went up a swept and ungarnished staircase, as arid as a desert, and opened *the first door* I came to. Two women, one fat and the other slim, sat on straw-bottomed chairs, knitting black wool....*A door* opened, a white-haired secretarial head, but wearing a compassionate expression, appeared, and a skinny forefinger beckoned me into the sanctuary....Often far away there I thought of these two, quarding *the door* of Darkness.... (*YS*, 55-7, my emphases)

A seminal feature of the mental landscape of the world beyond "the door of Darkness" – in Marlow's narrative as well as in Miłosz's poem – is a disposition of mind Miłosz labels "schizophrenia:"

> For schizophrenia – dissociation
> Of being into flower and root,
> The sense that these my deeds
> commit not I, but some other.
> To wring someone's neck's but a trifle.
> Then to read the Divine Comedy
> Or applaud an old quartet,
> Or discuss the avant garde.
> On a smaller scale, this is daily fare
> Someone says: evil's anonymous,
> And we've been used like tools.
> He's right. And rushes to his ruin.
>   ([Treatise on Morals], trans. A. K.)

> *Bo schizofrenia – rozdwojenie*
> *Istoty na kwiat i korzenie,*
> *Poczucie, że te moje czyny*
> *Spełniam nie ja, ale ktoś inny.*
> *Kark skręcić komuś jest drobnostką.*
> *Potem Komedię czytać Boską,*
> *Czy stary oklaskiwać kwartet,*
> *Lub dyskutować awangardę.*
> *Na mniejszą skalę, to codzienne,*
> *Ktoś mówi: zło jest bezimienne,*
> *A nas użyto jak narzędzi.*
> *Ma rację. I ku zgubie pędzi.*
> ("Traktat moralny," *Dzieła zbiorowe*, I, 197)

Sketched here is an early variant of the condition which later forms the centerpiece of Miłosz's *The Captive Mind*: the state of "ketman."[9] What is important here is that this condition, characteristic of the twentieth-century European mind, has as its literary source none other than Conrad's Faustian "apostle of progress," the fallen idalist Kurtz who exhorts the readers of his report, "On the Suppression of Savage Customs" to "Exterminate the brutes!" In his "Traktat moralny" Miłosz brings home the point that what I propose to call "the Kurtzian mind" formed fertile ground for twentieth-century Europe's chosen nightmares: totalitarianism of the Right and of the Left. In his "Child of Europe" (New York, 1946) Miłosz suggests bitterly the salient qualities of the Kurtzian mind:

> Treasure your legacy of skills, child of Europe,
> Inheritor of Gothic cathedrals, of baroque churches,
> Of synagogues filled with the wailing of a wronged people.
> Successor of Descartes, Spinoza, inheritor of the word "honor,"
> Posthumous child of Leonidas,
> Treasure the skills acquired in the hour of terror.
>
> You have a clever mind which sees instantly
> the good and bad of any situation.
> You have an elegant, skeptical mind which enjoys pleasures
> Quite unknown to primitive races.
> ...
> Grow your tree of falsehood from a small grain of truth.
> Do not follow those who lie in contempt of reality.

Let your lie be even more logical than the truth itself,
So the weary travelers may find repose in the lie.

After the Day of the Lie gather in select circles,
Shaking with laughter when our real deeds are mentioned.
("Child of Europe," *The Collected Poems*, 85-6)

Szanuj nabyte umiejętności, o dziecię Europy.
Dziedzicu gotyckich katedr, barokowych kościołów
I synagog w których rozbrzmiewał płacz krzywdzonego ludu,
Dziedzicu Kartezjusza i Spinozy, spadkobierco słowa "honor,"
Pogrobowcze Leonidasów,
Szanuj umiejętności nabyte w godzinie grozy.

Umysł masz wyćwiczony, umiejący rozpoznać natychmiast
Złe i dobre strony każdej rzeczy.
Umysł masz sceptyczny a wytworny, dający uciechy
O jakich nic nie wiedzą prymitywne ludy.
...
Z małego nasienia prawdy wyprowadzaj roślinę kłamstwa,
Nie naśladuj tych co kłamią lekceważąc rzeczywistość.

Niech kłamstwo logiczniejsze będzie od wydarzeń,
Aby znużeni wędrówką znaleźli w nim ukojenie.

Po dniu kłamstwa gromadźmy się w dobranym kole
Bijąc się w uda ze śmiechu, gdy wspomni kto nasze czyny.
("Dziecię Europy," *Utwory poetyckie: Poems*, 122-3)

If in "Traktat moralny" Miłosz ponders the split character of
Europe's cultural legacy, in his "Traktat poetycki" the author of
Native Realm turns his attention to the character of his native
culture.

Written in France in 1956, "Traktat poetycki" (published
1957) has been described as a "scholarly disquisition in verse"
(Schenker, xxi). Its prosody mimics Romantic poems of digress-
ion like Mickiewicz's *Grażyna* and Słowacki's *Beniowski*. Part
autobiography, part literary history, part cultural criticism, this
summa poetica surveys in pithy fashion the trends and constants
of modern Polish literature and offers a biting critique of the
Polish mind. Some rank it among the finest specimens of Polish
poetry:

> The semantic density of the poem, its multiple layers of meaning, the complex literary allusions and historical references place it among the richest and most suggestive works in the language. (Schenker, xxii)

In Miłosz's "Traktat poetycki" Conrad's "Heart of Darkness" again plays a prominent role: as touchstone for its thematics and guidepost for its critique of culture.

Part One, titled "Beautiful Times," of this four-part poem, locates the roots of twentieth-century Polish sensibility in the ethereal atmosphere of the waning Habsburg Empire. Cracow, Poland's ancient capital, then revolved in an orbit around Vienna. It is in this setting that we find Conrad in "Traktat poetycki" [Treatise on Poetry]:

> There's a small street in small Cracow.
> Two lads once lived there side by side.
> If one was returning from St. Anne's High
> He saw the other playing in a sandlot.
> A different fate was given each and a different fame.
>
> Enormous Seas, lands unimagined,
> Islands on which beyond the coral reef
> Naked tribes blow into a horned shell –
> This the sailor got to know. Till now the moment lasts
> When in Brussels' unpeopled heat
> He slowly climbed the marble steps
> And pressed the bell beside the company's "S"
> Listening intently to the silence.
> He entered. Two women were knitting on needles.
> To him they seemed the Fates.
> Twisting her skein she nodded in the door's direction.
> The director offered his anonymous hand.
> Thus Joseph Conrad became captain
> Of a boat on the river Congo, for so it was written.
> He concealed in his yarn from the banks of that river,
> A voice of warning for those who listened:
> The civilizer Kurtz, gone mad,
> Possessed an ivory tusk with traces of blood,
> In his memo on the light of culture
> He wrote "the horror" and thus had a foot
> In the twentieth century.
>   Meanwhile ram-ta-ta

> heel's snap, ribbons and dancing till dawn
> To the boom of the bass in a village near Cracow,
> And the ancient staging of Nativity plays.
> ([Treatise on Poetry], "Traktat poetycki," trans. A. K. *Utwory poetyckie: Poems,* 168-9)

A striking feature of this passage[10] is its circumvention of the parochial debate over the question of Conrad's national loyalty. In Miłosz's text Conrad is no more, no less than a Cracovian who leaves his hometown as a youth to take measure of the world and goes on to pronounce one of the most durably authoritative judgments on it. In doing so, he lifts Cracow, an emblem of Polishness, into the twentieth century. From the vantage of the volatile year of 1956 Conrad takes his place, by way of Miłosz's text, in the panorama of Polish cultural history of the twentieth century while "Heart of Darkness" is appropriated as a canonical text in this history. The fact that Conrad composed in a language other than Polish becomes a point as moot in the debate on Conrad's "patrotism" as was the Latinity of the classic texts of Polish Renaissance and Baroque literature.

The three Miłosz poems I have discussed evince pervasive links to "Heart of Darkness." The Conradian imprint on these poems forms part of a pattern of immersion in the Conrad opus by the author of *The Issa Valley*. Miłosz's appropriation of Conrad's texts and the values inscribed in them constitutes a re-writing rooted in a specifically East Central European reading of the author of *Lord Jim*. Josef Škvorecký, the distinguished Czech emigre writer, provides a perspective representative of this Central European mode of interpretation. In considering the young Russian sailor's sycophantic relation to Kurtz, Škvorecký observes:

> On the one side we have a one-time progressive politician turned monster, and idealist reformer metamorphosed into a terrible killer-
> -despot – and on the other side we have a fanatic crowd crawling before him in an unspeakable ceremony of utter abandonment, led by a man intoxicated by *el lider's* charisma beyond any capability of judgement. (Škvorecký, 261-2)

The Czech novelist concludes:

> In "Heart of Darkness" not only the map of Congo and the dangerous river journey are based on personal experience: the central story, that of the autocratic Mr. Kurtz, of the incomprehensible Russian buffoon, and of the skeptical Captain Marlow, is also anchored in reality. In the reality of the tender years of Józef Korzeniowski and of his life-long obsession with the Eastern neighbors, to whom – in *Under Western Eyes*, but also in "Heart of Darkness" – he tried to "render the highest kind of justice," the justice of his art. (262)

For Miłosz and Europeans inhabiting the center of the continent and its eastern borderlands Conrad is not so much an explorer of interior landscapes, a disaffected existentialist, or a keeper in the "prisonhouse of language;" rather, readers from "the other Europe" discover in texts like "Heart of Darkness" Janus-like perspectives on the ambivalent legacy of cultures East and West. In constructing his persona on the foundation of Conrad's books, Miłosz affirms the abiding relevance of Conrad's vision. The polyphony characteristic of Conrad's prose and Miłosz's poems is rooted in the cultural heterogeneity of the part of Europe which shaped both writers in their youth. This shared polyphony resonates poignantly in an era bent on leveling signs of difference.[11]

NOTES

1. In his interview with Marian Dąbrowski, "Rozmowa z Conradem," *Tygodnik Ilustrowany*, 16 (1917). English translation, "An Interview with Joseph Conrad," in *Conrad under Familial Eyes*, ed. Zdzisław Najder, trans. Halina Carroll-Najder (London: Cambridge U.P., 1983), 196. Regarding Conrad's links to Słowacki, see Camille La Bossière, *Joseph Conrad and the Science of Unknowing* (Fredericton, NB: York Press, 1979), 11, 17-18.

2. "Podróż po Ziemi Świętej z Neapolu," *Utwory wybrane*, PIW, 1970, I, 189. The image of Europe as a nymph echoes Słowacki's earlier metaphor evoking Europe as a Gothic cathedral in his "Oda do Wolności," of which the third stanza opens: "All Europe once was a Gothic cathedral" (*"Niegdyś Europa cała była gotyckim kościołem"*), *Utwory wybrane*, I, 8.

3. See his *Heart of Europe: A Short History of Poland* (Oxford: Oxford U.P., 1986). Davies cities Słowacki in his "Preface to the Hardback

Edition," x-xi. See also his earlier *God's Playground: A History of Poland,* 2 vols. (New York: Columbia U.P., 1982).

4. "Joseph Conrad in Polish Eyes," *Atlantic Monthly* (November 1957), 219-28, reprinted in *The Art of Joseph Conrad: A Critical Symposium,* ed. Robert W. Stallman (East Lansing: Michigan State U.P., 1960); "Apollo Nałęcz Korzeniowski," *Kultura,* 2/100 (1956), 60-80, reprinted in Czesław Miłosz, *Prywatne obowiązki,* 1972, English translation: "Joseph Conrad's Father," *Mosaic* 6: 4 (summer 1973), 121-40, reprinted in Czesław Miłosz, *Emperor of the Earth: Modes of Eccentric Vision* (Berkeley: U. California P., 1977), 157-85; "Stereotyp u Conrada," in *Conrad żywy,* ed. Wit Tarnawski (London: B. Świderski, 1957), 92-9. See also extensive discussion and allusions to Conrad in Miłosz's *The History of Polish Literature* (New York: Macmillan, 1969) and *Conversations with Czesław Miłosz,* eds. Ewa Czarnecka, Aleksander Fiut (New York: Harcourt, Brace, Jovanovich, 1987).

5. For a pioneering study of Miłosz's poetry, see Aleksander Fiut, *The Eternal Moment: The Poetry of Czesław Miłosz* (Berkeley: U. California P., 1990). Stefan Zabierowski has published a comprehensive survey of Conrad's Polish reception: *Dziedzictwo Conrada w literaturze polskiej XX wieku* [Conrad's legacy in twentieth-century Polish Literature] (Kraków: Oficyna Literacka, 1992). Chapters 2 and 4 document the appeal of Conrad's works on Miłosz's generation and on Miłosz's poetic circle: the Skamander poets. On the present state of research on Conrad's Polish reception and the challenges ahead, see Chapter 6 of Wiesław Krajka's *Joseph Conrad: konteksty kulturowe* (Lublin: Wydawnictwo Uniwersytetu Marii Curie-Skłodowskiej, 1995).

6. A position embraced by Wayne C. Booth in his *A Company We Keep: An Ethics of Fiction* (Berkeley: U. of California P., 1988).

7. On Gombrowicz's reading of Conrad see my essays: "Gombrowicz and Conrad: The Question of Autobiography" in *Contexts for Conrad,* eds. Keith Carabine, Owen Knowles, Wiesław Krajka (New York–Boulder–Lublin: Columbia U.P. – East European Monographs – Maria Curie--Skłodowska University, 1993; *Conrad: Eastern and Western Perspectives,* ed. Wiesław Krajka, vol. II), 73-86; "Witold Gombrowicz's *Princess Ivona* and Joseph Conrad's 'Amy Foster'," *L'Epoque Conradienne,* 19 (1993), 85-106.

8. For a perceptive reading of Miłosz's poetry as a window on Eastern Europe, see Ewa M. Thompson's essay: "Czesław Miłosz: Poetry, or a Primer on Eastern Europe," *Modern Age,* 36: 1 (Fall 1993), 17-25.

9. See Chapter 3, "Ketman," of *The Captive Mind.*

10. The other of the "two lads" described in the opening of this passage is the playwright-poet-painter Stanisław Wyspiański (1869-1907). Like Conrad Wyspiański left Cracow for France as a youth where he studied painting and immersed himself in drama and theater. Unlike Conrad Wyspiański returned to Cracow where he created a brilliant body of work

in theater and the graphic arts. The poetics of modernism and symbolism link Conrad's fiction with Wyspiański's contributions to Polish drama and theater. For a fine critical study of "the Cracovian hermit" (Terlecki, 133) see Tymon Terlecki, *Stanisław Wyspiański* (Boston: Twayne, 1983).

11. As Thompson aptly observes, Miłosz "is aware that the multiculturalism of a pre-industrial age was innocent of forced integration sloganeering" like Conrad, "[Miłosz's] fascination with the vulnerability of civilization goes against the grain of modern thinking which glorifies change." (Thompson, 21)

WORKS CITED

Bayley John. "Czesław Miłosz 'Encounter'," in *The Mature Laurel: Essays on Modern Polish Poetry,* ed. Adam Czerniawski. Chester Springs, PA: Dufour, 1991, 95-7.

Burgess C. F. "Conrad's Pesky Russian," *Nineteenth-Century Fiction,* 18 (September 1963), 189-93.

Carpenter Bogdana. *The Poetic Avant-Garde in Poland: 1918-1939.* Seattle: U. Washington P., 1983.

Dąbrowski Marian. "An Interview with Joseph Conrad," in Najder Zdzisław, ed. *Conrad under Familial Eyes,* trans. Halina Carroll-Najder, London: Cambridge U.P. 1983, 196-201.

Davies Norman. *Heart of Europe: A Short History of Poland.* Oxford: Oxford U.P., 1986.

Epstein Hugh. "'Where He Is Not Wanted:' Impression and Articulation in 'The Idiots' and 'Amy Foster'," *Conradiana,* 23: 3 (Autumn 1991), 217-32.

Levine Madeline G. *Contemporary Polish Poetry: 1925-1975.* Boston: Twayne, 1981.

Miłosz Czesław. *The Captive Mind,* trans. Jane Zielonko. London: Secker and Warburg, 1953.

Miłosz Czesław. *The Collected Poems: 1931-1987.* New York: The Ecco Press, 1988.

Miłosz Czesław. *Dzieła zbiorowe,* vol. 1. Paris: Instytut Literacki, 1981.

Miłosz Czesław. *The Issa Valley,* trans. Louis Iribarne. New York: Farrar, Straus & Giroux, 1984.

Miłosz Czesław. *Native Realm: A Search for Self-Definition,* trans. Catherine S. Leach. Garden City, NY: Doubleday, 1968.

Miłosz Czesław. "O książce," in Miłosz Czesław *Utwory poetyckie: Poems.* Ann Arbor: Michigan Slavic Publications, 1976, 17; English translation: "On the Book" by John and Bogdana Carpenter in Bogdana Carpenter, *The Poetic Avant-Garde in Poland: 1918-1939.* Seattle: U. of Washington P., 1983, 199.

Miłosz Czesław. "Traktat moralny," in Miłosz Czesław. *Utwory poetyckie: Poems*. Ann Arbor: Michigan Slavic Publications, 1976, 143-6.
Miłosz Czesław. "Traktat poetycki," in Miłosz Czesław. *Utwory poetyckie: Poems*. Ann Arbor: Michigan Slavic Pubications, 1976, 163-204.
Schenker Alexander M. "Introduction," in Miłosz Czesław, *Utwory poetyckie: Poems*. Ann Arbor: Michigan Slavic Publications, 1976, xv-xxvii.
Škvorecký Josef. "Why the Harlequin?," *Cross Currents: A Yearbook of Central European Cultre*, 3 (1984), 259-64.
Słowacki Juliusz. "Podróż po Ziemi Świętej z Neapolu," in Słowacki Juliusz, *Utwory wybrane*, 2 vols. Warszawa: Państwowy Instytut Wydawniczy, 1970.
Thompson Ewa M. "Czesław Miłosz: Poetry, or a Primer on Eastern Europe," *Modern Age*, 36: 1 (Fall 1993), 17-25.

INDEX OF NAMES

INDEX OF CONRAD'S WORKS